Just The facts101
Textbook Key Facts

Dominica Economic and Development Strategy Handbook

by Cram101
Textbook NOT Included

Table of Contents

Title Page

Copyright

Foundations of Business

Management

Business law

Finance

Human resource management

Information systems

Marketing

Manufacturing

Commerce

Business ethics

Accounting

Index: Answers

Just The Facts101

Exam Prep for

Dominica Economic and Development Strategy Handbook

Just The Facts101 Exam Prep is your link from
the textbook and lecture to your exams.

**Just The Facts101 Exam Preps are unauthorized and comprehensive reviews
of your textbooks.**

All material provided by CTI Publications (c) 2019

Textbook publishers and textbook authors do not participate in or contribute to these reviews.

Just The Facts101 Exam Prep

Copyright © 2019 by CTI Publications. All rights reserved.

eAIN 460066

Foundations of Business

A business, also known as an enterprise, agency or a firm, is an entity involved in the provision of goods and/or services to consumers. Businesses are prevalent in capitalist economies, where most of them are privately owned and provide goods and services to customers in exchange for other goods, services, or money.

:: Project management ::

Contemporary business and science treat as a _____ any undertaking, carried out individually or collaboratively and possibly involving research or design, that is carefully planned to achieve a particular aim.

Exam Probability: **High**

1. *Answer choices:*

(see index for correct answer)

- a. Project
- b. Project portfolio management
- c. ISO 21500
- d. Cost-benefit

Guidance: level 1

:: Statistical terminology ::

_____ es can be learned implicitly within cultural contexts. People may develop _____ es toward or against an individual, an ethnic group, a sexual or gender identity, a nation, a religion, a social class, a political party, theoretical paradigms and ideologies within academic domains, or a species. _____ ed means one-sided, lacking a neutral viewpoint, or not having an open mind. _____ can come in many forms and is related to prejudice and intuition.

Exam Probability: **High**

2. Answer choices:

(see index for correct answer)

- a. Floor effect
- b. Natural process variation
- c. Bias
- d. Likelihood

Guidance: level 1

:: Insolvency ::

_____ is a legal process through which people or other entities who cannot repay debts to creditors may seek relief from some or all of their debts. In most jurisdictions, _____ is imposed by a court order, often initiated by the debtor.

Exam Probability: **Low**

3. Answer choices:

(see index for correct answer)

- a. George Samuel Ford
- b. Insolvency law of Russia
- c. Liquidator
- d. Bankruptcy

Guidance: level 1

:: Supply chain management ::

_____ is the process of finding and agreeing to terms, and acquiring goods, services, or works from an external source, often via a tendering or competitive bidding process. _____ is used to ensure the buyer receives goods, services, or works at the best possible price when aspects such as quality, quantity, time, and location are compared. Corporations and public bodies often define processes intended to promote fair and open competition for their business while minimizing risks such as exposure to fraud and collusion.

Exam Probability: **Medium**

4. *Answer choices:*

(see index for correct answer)

- a. Procurement
- b. Scan-based trading
- c. Entry visibility
- d. Vendor-managed inventory

Guidance: level 1

:: Packaging ::

In work place, _____ or job _____ means good ranking with the hypothesized conception of requirements of a role. There are two types of job _____ s: contextual and task. Task _____ is related to cognitive ability while contextual _____ is dependent upon personality. Task _____ are behavioral roles that are recognized in job descriptions and by remuneration systems, they are directly related to organizational _____, whereas, contextual _____ are value based and additional behavioral roles that are not recognized in job descriptions and covered by compensation; they are extra roles that are indirectly related to organizational _____. Citizenship _____ like contextual _____ means a set of individual activity/contribution that supports the organizational culture.

Exam Probability: **High**

5. *Answer choices:*

(see index for correct answer)

- a. Cyperus tegetiformis
- b. Performance
- c. Oxygen transmission rate
- d. Oxygen scavenger

Guidance: level 1

:: Analysis ::

_____ is the process of breaking a complex topic or substance into smaller parts in order to gain a better understanding of it. The technique has been applied in the study of mathematics and logic since before Aristotle, though _____ as a formal concept is a relatively recent development.

Exam Probability: **Low**

6. *Answer choices:*

(see index for correct answer)

- a. Analysis
- b. Pinch analysis
- c. Hydrogen pinch
- d. EATPUT

Guidance: level 1

:: Critical thinking ::

An _____ is a set of statements usually constructed to describe a set of facts which clarifies the causes, context, and consequences of those facts. This description of the facts et cetera may establish rules or laws, and may clarify the existing rules or laws in relation to any objects, or phenomena examined. The components of an _____ can be implicit, and interwoven with one another.

Exam Probability: **Medium**

7. *Answer choices:*

(see index for correct answer)

- a. Fallacy
- b. Attacking Faulty Reasoning
- c. Seven Types of Ambiguity
- d. decision-making

Guidance: level 1

:: Alchemical processes ::

In chemistry, a _____ is a special type of homogeneous mixture composed of two or more substances. In such a mixture, a solute is a substance dissolved in another substance, known as a solvent. The mixing process of a _____ happens at a scale where the effects of chemical polarity are involved, resulting in interactions that are specific to solvation. The _____ assumes the phase of the solvent when the solvent is the larger fraction of the mixture, as is commonly the case. The concentration of a solute in a _____ is the mass of that solute expressed as a percentage of the mass of the whole _____ . The term aqueous _____ is when one of the solvents is water.

Exam Probability: **Medium**

8. *Answer choices:*

(see index for correct answer)

- a. Unity of opposites
- b. Solution

- c. Corporification
- d. Fermentation

Guidance: level 1

:: Stock market ::

A shareholder is an individual or institution that legally owns one or more shares of stock in a public or private corporation. _____ may be referred to as members of a corporation. Legally, a person is not a shareholder in a corporation until their name and other details are entered in the corporation's register of _____ or members.

Exam Probability: **Medium**

9. *Answer choices:*

(see index for correct answer)

- a. Shareholders
- b. CNBC Ticker
- c. Stock market data systems
- d. Block premium

Guidance: level 1

:: ::

_____ is the means to see, hear, or become aware of something or someone through our fundamental senses. The term _____ derives from the Latin word perceptio, and is the organization, identification, and interpretation of sensory information in order to represent and understand the presented information, or the environment.

Exam Probability: **Low**

10. *Answer choices:*

(see index for correct answer)

- a. empathy
- b. hierarchical perspective
- c. corporate values
- d. Perception

Guidance: level 1

:: ::

_____ is the collection of mechanisms, processes and relations by which corporations are controlled and operated. Governance structures and principles identify the distribution of rights and responsibilities among different participants in the corporation and include the rules and procedures for making decisions in corporate affairs. _____ is necessary because of the possibility of conflicts of interests between stakeholders, primarily between shareholders and upper management or among shareholders.

Exam Probability: **Medium**

11. *Answer choices:*

(see index for correct answer)

- a. process perspective
- b. similarity-attraction theory
- c. corporate values
- d. information systems assessment

Guidance: level 1

:: Unemployment ::

In economics, a _____ is a business cycle contraction when there is a general decline in economic activity. Macroeconomic indicators such as GDP, investment spending, capacity utilization, household income, business profits, and inflation fall, while bankruptcies and the unemployment rate rise. In the United Kingdom, it is defined as a negative economic growth for two consecutive quarters.

Exam Probability: **High**

12. *Answer choices:*

(see index for correct answer)

- a. Employment-to-population ratio
- b. Recession

- c. Mount Street Club
- d. Unemployment Provision Convention, 1934

Guidance: level 1

:: Business law ::

A _____ is an arrangement where parties, known as partners, agree to cooperate to advance their mutual interests. The partners in a _____ may be individuals, businesses, interest-based organizations, schools, governments or combinations. Organizations may partner to increase the likelihood of each achieving their mission and to amplify their reach. A _____ may result in issuing and holding equity or may be only governed by a contract.

Exam Probability: **Medium**

13. *Answer choices:*

(see index for correct answer)

- a. Registered agent
- b. Partnership
- c. Facilitating payment
- d. Financial Security Law of France

Guidance: level 1

:: Free trade agreements ::

A _____ is a wide-ranging taxes, tariff and trade treaty that often includes investment guarantees. It exists when two or more countries agree on terms that helps them trade with each other. The most common _____ s are of the preferential and free trade types are concluded in order to reduce tariffs, quotas and other trade restrictions on items traded between the signatories.

Exam Probability: **Low**

14. *Answer choices:*

(see index for correct answer)

- a. Ouchy Convention
- b. Trade agreement
- c. New West Partnership
- d. Regional Comprehensive Economic Partnership

Guidance: level 1

:: Meetings ::

A _____ is a body of one or more persons that is subordinate to a deliberative assembly. Usually, the assembly sends matters into a _____ as a way to explore them more fully than would be possible if the assembly itself were considering them. _____ s may have different functions and their type of work differ depending on the type of the organization and its needs.

Exam Probability: **High**

15. *Answer choices:*

(see index for correct answer)

- a. Assembly hall
- b. Committee
- c. Meeting point
- d. Mighty Men Conference

Guidance: level 1

:: Management ::

A _____ is a formal written document containing business goals, the methods on how these goals can be attained, and the time frame within which these goals need to be achieved. It also describes the nature of the business, background information on the organization, the organization's financial projections, and the strategies it intends to implement to achieve the stated targets. In its entirety, this document serves as a road map that provides direction to the business.

Exam Probability: **High**

16. *Answer choices:*

(see index for correct answer)

- a. Business plan

- b. Swarm Development Group
- c. Corporate recovery
- d. Matrix management

Guidance: level 1

:: Majority–minority relations ::

_____, also known as reservation in India and Nepal, positive discrimination / action in the United Kingdom, and employment equity in Canada and South Africa, is the policy of promoting the education and employment of members of groups that are known to have previously suffered from discrimination. Historically and internationally, support for _____ has sought to achieve goals such as bridging inequalities in employment and pay, increasing access to education, promoting diversity, and redressing apparent past wrongs, harms, or hindrances.

Exam Probability: **High**

17. *Answer choices:*

(see index for correct answer)

- a. cultural dissonance
- b. Affirmative action
- c. cultural Relativism

Guidance: level 1

:: Consumer theory ::

A _____ is a technical term in psychology, economics and philosophy usually used in relation to choosing between alternatives. For example, someone prefers A over B if they would rather choose A than B.

Exam Probability: **Medium**

18. *Answer choices:*

(see index for correct answer)

- a. Consumption
- b. Business contract hire
- c. Consumer sovereignty
- d. Permanent income hypothesis

Guidance: level 1

:: Classification systems ::

_____ is the practice of comparing business processes and performance metrics to industry bests and best practices from other companies. Dimensions typically measured are quality, time and cost.

Exam Probability: **Low**

19. *Answer choices:*

(see index for correct answer)

- a. Systematized Nomenclature of Medicine
- b. Class
- c. Transporter Classification Database
- d. Celestial Emporium of Benevolent Knowledge

Guidance: level 1

:: Globalization-related theories ::

_____ is an economic system based on the private ownership of the means of production and their operation for profit. Characteristics central to _____ include private property, capital accumulation, wage labor, voluntary exchange, a price system, and competitive markets. In a capitalist market economy, decision-making and investment are determined by every owner of wealth, property or production ability in financial and capital markets, whereas prices and the distribution of goods and services are mainly determined by competition in goods and services markets.

Exam Probability: **Low**

20. *Answer choices:*

(see index for correct answer)

- a. post-industrial
- b. Economic Development

- c. Capitalism

Guidance: level 1

:: Problem solving ::

In other words, _____ is a situation where a group of people meet to generate new ideas and solutions around a specific domain of interest by removing inhibitions. People are able to think more freely and they suggest as many spontaneous new ideas as possible. All the ideas are noted down and those ideas are not criticized and after _____ session the ideas are evaluated. The term was popularized by Alex Faickney Osborn in the 1953 book Applied Imagination.

Exam Probability: **High**

21. *Answer choices:*

(see index for correct answer)

- a. Brainstorming
- b. Einstellung effect
- c. Rogerian argument
- d. Project Euler

Guidance: level 1

:: Product management ::

A _____, trade mark, or trade-mark is a recognizable sign, design, or expression which identifies products or services of a particular source from those of others, although _____ s used to identify services are usually called service marks. The _____ owner can be an individual, business organization, or any legal entity. A _____ may be located on a package, a label, a voucher, or on the product itself. For the sake of corporate identity, _____ s are often displayed on company buildings. It is legally recognized as a type of intellectual property.

Exam Probability: **Low**

22. *Answer choices:*

(see index for correct answer)

- a. Product information management
- b. Swing tag
- c. Trademark
- d. Electronic registration mark

Guidance: level 1

:: Industrial design ::

In physics and mathematics, the _____ of a mathematical space is informally defined as the minimum number of coordinates needed to specify any point within it. Thus a line has a _____ of one because only one coordinate is needed to specify a point on it for example, the point at 5 on a number line. A surface such as a plane or the surface of a cylinder or sphere has a _____ of two because two coordinates are needed to specify a point on it for example, both a latitude and longitude are required to locate a point on the surface of a sphere. The inside of a cube, a cylinder or a sphere is three- _____ al because three coordinates are needed to locate a point within these spaces.

Exam Probability: **High**

23. *Answer choices:*

(see index for correct answer)

- a. Sustainable furniture design
- b. Dimension
- c. Sky-Sailor
- d. Japanese design law

Guidance: level 1

:: ::

In regulatory jurisdictions that provide for it, _____ is a group of laws and organizations designed to ensure the rights of consumers as well as fair trade, competition and accurate information in the marketplace. The laws are designed to prevent the businesses that engage in fraud or specified unfair practices from gaining an advantage over competitors. They may also provides additional protection for those most vulnerable in society. _____ laws are a form of government regulation that aim to protect the rights of consumers. For example, a government may require businesses to disclose detailed information about products—particularly in areas where safety or public health is an issue, such as food.

Exam Probability: **High**

24. *Answer choices:*

(see index for correct answer)

- a. hierarchical perspective
- b. Consumer Protection
- c. levels of analysis
- d. cultural

Guidance: level 1

:: Strategic management ::

_____ is a strategic planning technique used to help a person or organization identify strengths, weaknesses, opportunities, and threats related to business competition or project planning. It is intended to specify the objectives of the business venture or project and identify the internal and external factors that are favorable and unfavorable to achieving those objectives. Users of a _____ often ask and answer questions to generate meaningful information for each category to make the tool useful and identify their competitive advantage. SWOT has been described as the tried-and-true tool of strategic analysis.

Exam Probability: **Low**

25. *Answer choices:*

(see index for correct answer)

- a. business unit
- b. Talent portfolio management
- c. SWOT analysis
- d. PEST analysis

Guidance: level 1

:: Bribery ::

_____ is the act of giving or receiving something of value in exchange for some kind of influence or action in return, that the recipient would otherwise not offer. _____ is defined by Black's Law Dictionary as the offering, giving, receiving, or soliciting of any item of value to influence the actions of an official or other person in charge of a public or legal duty. Essentially, _____ is offering to do something for someone for the expressed purpose of receiving something in exchange. Gifts of money or other items of value which are otherwise available to everyone on an equivalent basis, and not for dishonest purposes, is not _____. Offering a discount or a refund to all purchasers is a legal rebate and is not _____. For example, it is legal for an employee of a Public Utilities Commission involved in electric rate regulation to accept a rebate on electric service that reduces their cost for electricity, when the rebate is available to other residential electric customers. Giving the rebate to influence them to look favorably on the electric utility's rate increase applications, however, would be considered _____.

Exam Probability: **High**

26. *Answer choices:*

(see index for correct answer)

- a. Global Corruption Barometer
- b. Cockerham bribery case
- c. Katta Subramanya Naidu
- d. Caribbean Football Union corruption scandal

Guidance: level 1

:: Stochastic processes ::

_____ is a system of rules that are created and enforced through social or governmental institutions to regulate behavior. It has been defined both as "the Science of Justice" and "the Art of Justice". _____ is a system that regulates and ensures that individuals or a community adhere to the will of the state. State-enforced _____ s can be made by a collective legislature or by a single legislator, resulting in statutes, by the executive through decrees and regulations, or established by judges through precedent, normally in common _____ jurisdictions. Private individuals can create legally binding contracts, including arbitration agreements that may elect to accept alternative arbitration to the normal court process. The formation of _____ s themselves may be influenced by a constitution, written or tacit, and the rights encoded therein. The _____ shapes politics, economics, history and society in various ways and serves as a mediator of relations between people.

Exam Probability: **Medium**

27. *Answer choices:*

(see index for correct answer)

- a. M/D/c queue
- b. Narrow escape problem
- c. Law
- d. Affine term structure model

Guidance: level 1

:: Marketing ::

_____ comes from the Latin neg and otsia referring to businessmen who, unlike the patricians, had no leisure time in their industriousness; it held the meaning of business until the 17th century when it took on the diplomatic connotation as a dialogue between two or more people or parties intended to reach a beneficial outcome over one or more issues where a conflict exists with respect to at least one of these issues. Thus, _____ is a process of combining divergent positions into a joint agreement under a decision rule of unanimity.

Exam Probability: **High**

28. *Answer choices:*

(see index for correct answer)

- a. Contact centre
- b. Price point
- c. Licensing International Expo
- d. Negotiation

Guidance: level 1

:: Loans ::

In finance, a _____ is the lending of money by one or more individuals, organizations, or other entities to other individuals, organizations etc. The recipient incurs a debt, and is usually liable to pay interest on that debt until it is repaid, and also to repay the principal amount borrowed.

Exam Probability: **Medium**

29. *Answer choices:*

(see index for correct answer)

- a. Construction loan
- b. Community Advantage Loan
- c. Installment loan
- d. Loan

Guidance: level 1

:: Telecommunication theory ::

In reliability theory and reliability engineering, the term _____ has the following meanings.

Exam Probability: **Low**

30. *Answer choices:*

(see index for correct answer)

- a. Call-second
- b. Noisy-channel coding theorem
- c. Turbo equalizer
- d. Availability

Guidance: level 1

:: Organizational theory ::

_____ is the process of groups of organisms working or acting together for common, mutual, or some underlying benefit, as opposed to working in competition for selfish benefit. Many animal and plant species cooperate both with other members of their own species and with members of other species.

Exam Probability: **Low**

31. *Answer choices:*

(see index for correct answer)

- a. Proactivity
- b. Cooperation
- c. Bureaucratic inertia
- d. Resource dependence theory

Guidance: level 1

:: Property ::

The right to property or right to own property is often classified as a human right for natural persons regarding their possessions. A general recognition of a right to private property is found more rarely and is typically heavily constrained insofar as property is owned by legal persons and where it is used for production rather than consumption.

Exam Probability: **Medium**

32. *Answer choices:*

(see index for correct answer)

- a. MagicBricks
- b. Housing tenure
- c. Intermediate rent
- d. Property rights

Guidance: level 1

:: Management accounting ::

In economics, _____ s, indirect costs or overheads are business expenses that are not dependent on the level of goods or services produced by the business. They tend to be time-related, such as interest or rents being paid per month, and are often referred to as overhead costs. This is in contrast to variable costs, which are volume-related and unknown at the beginning of the accounting year. For a simple example, such as a bakery, the monthly rent for the baking facilities, and the monthly payments for the security system and basic phone line are _____ s, as they do not change according to how much bread the bakery produces and sells. On the other hand, the wage costs of the bakery are variable, as the bakery will have to hire more workers if the production of bread increases. Economists reckon _____ as a entry barrier for new entrepreneurs.

Exam Probability: **Medium**

33. *Answer choices:*

(see index for correct answer)

- a. Fixed cost
- b. Dual overhead rate
- c. Invested capital
- d. Contribution margin

Guidance: level 1

:: Business terms ::

A _____ is a short statement of why an organization exists, what its overall goal is, identifying the goal of its operations: what kind of product or service it provides, its primary customers or market, and its geographical region of operation. It may include a short statement of such fundamental matters as the organization's values or philosophies, a business's main competitive advantages, or a desired future state—the "vision".

Exam Probability: **Low**

34. *Answer choices:*

(see index for correct answer)

- a. granular
- b. organizational capital
- c. Mission statement
- d. churn rate

Guidance: level 1

:: Business models ::

A _____, _____ company or daughter company is a company that is owned or controlled by another company, which is called the parent company, parent, or holding company. The _____ can be a company, corporation, or limited liability company. In some cases it is a government or state-owned enterprise. In some cases, particularly in the music and book publishing industries, subsidiaries are referred to as imprints.

Exam Probability: **Low**

35. *Answer choices:*

(see index for correct answer)

- a. Parent company
- b. Subsidiary
- c. Brainsworking
- d. Freemium

Guidance: level 1

:: Business models ::

_____ es are privately owned corporations, partnerships, or sole proprietorships that have fewer employees and/or less annual revenue than a regular-sized business or corporation. Businesses are defined as "small" in terms of being able to apply for government support and qualify for preferential tax policy varies depending on the country and industry. _____ es range from fifteen employees under the Australian Fair Work Act 2009, fifty employees according to the definition used by the European Union, and fewer than five hundred employees to qualify for many U.S. _____ Administration programs. While _____ es can also be classified according to other methods, such as annual revenues, shipments, sales, assets, or by annual gross or net revenue or net profits, the number of employees is one of the most widely used measures.

Exam Probability: **Low**

36. *Answer choices:*

(see index for correct answer)

- a. Copy to China
- b. Praenumeration
- c. Utility computing
- d. European Cooperative Society

Guidance: level 1

:: Training ::

_____ is teaching, or developing in oneself or others, any skills and knowledge that relate to specific useful competencies. _____ has specific goals of improving one's capability, capacity, productivity and performance. It forms the core of apprenticeships and provides the backbone of content at institutes of technology. In addition to the basic _____ required for a trade, occupation or profession, observers of the labor-market recognize as of 2008 the need to continue _____ beyond initial qualifications: to maintain, upgrade and update skills throughout working life. People within many professions and occupations may refer to this sort of _____ as professional development.

Exam Probability: **High**

37. *Answer choices:*

(see index for correct answer)

- a. Training

- b. Enforcement
- c. Adobe Captivate
- d. Practicum

Guidance: level 1

:: Survey methodology ::

An _____ is a conversation where questions are asked and answers are given. In common parlance, the word " _____ " refers to a one-on-one conversation between an _____ er and an _____ ee. The _____ er asks questions to which the _____ ee responds, usually so information may be transferred from _____ ee to _____ er. Sometimes, information can be transferred in both directions. It is a communication, unlike a speech, which produces a one-way flow of information.

Exam Probability: **Medium**

38. *Answer choices:*
(see index for correct answer)

- a. Interview
- b. Coverage error
- c. Inverse probability weighting
- d. Survey sampling

Guidance: level 1

:: Marketing ::

The _____ is a foundation model for businesses. The _____ has been defined as the "set of marketing tools that the firm uses to pursue its marketing objectives in the target market". Thus the _____ refers to four broad levels of marketing decision, namely: product, price, place, and promotion. Marketing practice has been occurring for millennia, but marketing theory emerged in the early twentieth century. The contemporary _____, or the 4 Ps, which has become the dominant framework for marketing management decisions, was first published in 1960. In services marketing, an extended _____ is used, typically comprising 7 Ps, made up of the original 4 Ps extended by process, people, and physical evidence. Occasionally service marketers will refer to 8 Ps, comprising these 7 Ps plus performance.

Exam Probability: **High**

39. *Answer choices:*

(see index for correct answer)

- a. Matomy Media
- b. Adobe Target
- c. Marketing mix
- d. Object Value

Guidance: level 1

:: Credit cards ::

A _____ is a payment card issued to users to enable the cardholder to pay a merchant for goods and services based on the cardholder's promise to the card issuer to pay them for the amounts plus the other agreed charges. The card issuer creates a revolving account and grants a line of credit to the cardholder, from which the cardholder can borrow money for payment to a merchant or as a cash advance.

Exam Probability: **High**

40. *Answer choices:*

(see index for correct answer)

- a. CardIt
- b. Revolution Money
- c. Credit card
- d. Credit card debt

Guidance: level 1

:: Health promotion ::

_____ , as defined by the World _____ Organization , is "a state of complete physical, mental and social well-being and not merely the absence of disease or infirmity." This definition has been subject to controversy, as it may have limited value for implementation. _____ may be defined as the ability to adapt and manage physical, mental and social challenges throughout life.

Exam Probability: **Low**

41. *Answer choices:*

(see index for correct answer)

- a. Eberhard Wenzel
- b. Jack Schwarz
- c. Health
- d. Health promotion

Guidance: level 1

:: Derivatives (finance) ::

_____ is any bodily activity that enhances or maintains physical fitness and overall health and wellness. It is performed for various reasons, to aid growth and improve strength, preventing aging, developing muscles and the cardiovascular system, honing athletic skills, weight loss or maintenance, improving health and also for enjoyment. Many individuals choose to _____ outdoors where they can congregate in groups, socialize, and enhance well-being.

Exam Probability: **High**

42. *Answer choices:*

(see index for correct answer)

- a. Currency swap

- b. Callable bullbear contract
- c. Exercise
- d. Commodity price index

Guidance: level 1

:: Human resource management ::

> _____ are the people who make up the workforce of an organization, business sector, or economy. "Human capital" is sometimes used synonymously with " _____ ", although human capital typically refers to a narrower effect. Likewise, other terms sometimes used include manpower, talent, labor, personnel, or simply people.

Exam Probability: **Medium**

43. *Answer choices:*
(see index for correct answer)

- a. Human resource accounting
- b. At-will employment
- c. ROWE
- d. Human resources

Guidance: level 1

:: Management ::

_____ is the practice of initiating, planning, executing, controlling, and closing the work of a team to achieve specific goals and meet specific success criteria at the specified time.

Exam Probability: **Medium**

44. *Answer choices:*
(see index for correct answer)

- a. Real property administrator
- b. Purchasing management
- c. Semiconductor consolidation
- d. Certified Energy Manager

Guidance: level 1

:: Auditing ::

_____, as defined by accounting and auditing, is a process for assuring of an organization's objectives in operational effectiveness and efficiency, reliable financial reporting, and compliance with laws, regulations and policies. A broad concept, _____ involves everything that controls risks to an organization.

Exam Probability: **Low**

45. *Answer choices:*

(see index for correct answer)

- a. Internal audit
- b. Auditor independence
- c. Clinical audit
- d. Internal control

Guidance: level 1

:: Logistics ::

_____ is generally the detailed organization and implementation of a complex operation. In a general business sense, _____ is the management of the flow of things between the point of origin and the point of consumption in order to meet requirements of customers or corporations. The resources managed in _____ may include tangible goods such as materials, equipment, and supplies, as well as food and other consumable items. The _____ of physical items usually involves the integration of information flow, materials handling, production, packaging, inventory, transportation, warehousing, and often security.

Exam Probability: **Medium**

46. *Answer choices:*

(see index for correct answer)

- a. Terminal Operating System
- b. Space logistics

- c. Logistics
- d. E2e Supply Chain Management

Guidance: level 1

:: Asset ::

In financial accounting, an _____ is any resource owned by the business. Anything tangible or intangible that can be owned or controlled to produce value and that is held by a company to produce positive economic value is an _____ . Simply stated, _____ s represent value of ownership that can be converted into cash . The balance sheet of a firm records the monetary value of the _____ s owned by that firm. It covers money and other valuables belonging to an individual or to a business.

Exam Probability: **Medium**

47. *Answer choices:*
(see index for correct answer)

- a. Asset
- b. Fixed asset

Guidance: level 1

:: International trade ::

An _____ is a good brought into a jurisdiction, especially across a national border, from an external source. The party bringing in the good is called an _____ er. An _____ in the receiving country is an export from the sending country. _____ ation and exportation are the defining financial transactions of international trade.

Exam Probability: **Medium**

48. *Answer choices:*

(see index for correct answer)

- a. Import
- b. Intervention stocks
- c. Ocean freight differential
- d. Endaka

Guidance: level 1

:: ::

A _____ is any person who contracts to acquire an asset in return for some form of consideration.

Exam Probability: **Low**

49. *Answer choices:*

(see index for correct answer)

- a. similarity-attraction theory
- b. open system
- c. corporate values
- d. Buyer

Guidance: level 1

:: Credit cards ::

The _____ Company, also known as Amex, is an American multinational financial services corporation headquartered in Three World Financial Center in New York City. The company was founded in 1850 and is one of the 30 components of the Dow Jones Industrial Average. The company is best known for its charge card, credit card, and traveler's cheque businesses.

Exam Probability: **Medium**

50. *Answer choices:*

(see index for correct answer)

- a. Access
- b. Black Card
- c. Visa Black Card
- d. American Express

Guidance: level 1

:: Evaluation ::

_____ is the practice of being honest and showing a consistent and uncompromising adherence to strong moral and ethical principles and values. In ethics, _____ is regarded as the honesty and truthfulness or accuracy of one's actions. _____ can stand in opposition to hypocrisy, in that judging with the standards of _____ involves regarding internal consistency as a virtue, and suggests that parties holding within themselves apparently conflicting values should account for the discrepancy or alter their beliefs. The word _____ evolved from the Latin adjective integer, meaning whole or complete. In this context, _____ is the inner sense of "wholeness" deriving from qualities such as honesty and consistency of character. As such, one may judge that others "have _____ " to the extent that they act according to the values, beliefs and principles they claim to hold.

Exam Probability: **Medium**

51. *Answer choices:*

(see index for correct answer)

- a. Defence Evaluation and Research Agency
- b. Integrity
- c. Quality assurance
- d. Common Criteria Testing Laboratory

Guidance: level 1

:: Statistical terminology ::

_____ is the magnitude or dimensions of a thing. _____ can be measured as length, width, height, diameter, perimeter, area, volume, or mass.

Exam Probability: **Medium**

52. *Answer choices:*
(see index for correct answer)

- a. Size
- b. Ridge regression
- c. Percentage point
- d. Treatment group

Guidance: level 1

:: Stock market ::

_____ is a form of corporate equity ownership, a type of security. The terms voting share and ordinary share are also used frequently in other parts of the world; " _____ " being primarily used in the United States. They are known as Equity shares or Ordinary shares in the UK and other Commonwealth realms. This type of share gives the stockholder the right to share in the profits of the company, and to vote on matters of corporate policy and the composition of the members of the board of directors.

Exam Probability: **Medium**

53. *Answer choices:*

(see index for correct answer)

- a. Common stock
- b. General Standard
- c. American depositary receipt
- d. Microexchanges

Guidance: level 1

:: Business law ::

_____ is where a person's financial liability is limited to a fixed sum, most commonly the value of a person's investment in a company or partnership. If a company with _____ is sued, then the claimants are suing the company, not its owners or investors. A shareholder in a limited company is not personally liable for any of the debts of the company, other than for the amount already invested in the company and for any unpaid amount on the shares in the company, if any. The same is true for the members of a _____ partnership and the limited partners in a limited partnership. By contrast, sole proprietors and partners in general partnerships are each liable for all the debts of the business.

Exam Probability: **Medium**

54. *Answer choices:*

(see index for correct answer)

- a. Limited liability

- b. Tacit relocation
- c. Lex mercatoria
- d. Personal Property Security Act

Guidance: level 1

:: Materials ::

A _____, also known as a feedstock, unprocessed material, or primary commodity, is a basic material that is used to produce goods, finished products, energy, or intermediate materials which are feedstock for future finished products. As feedstock, the term connotes these materials are bottleneck assets and are highly important with regard to producing other products. An example of this is crude oil, which is a _____ and a feedstock used in the production of industrial chemicals, fuels, plastics, and pharmaceutical goods; lumber is a _____ used to produce a variety of products including all types of furniture. The term "_____" denotes materials in minimally processed or unprocessed in states; e.g., raw latex, crude oil, cotton, coal, raw biomass, iron ore, air, logs, or water i.e. "...any product of agriculture, forestry, fishing and any other mineral that is in its natural form or which has undergone the transformation required to prepare it for internationally marketing in substantial volumes."

Exam Probability: **High**

55. *Answer choices:*
(see index for correct answer)

- a. Nanophase material
- b. Raw material

- c. Lute
- d. Ion Gel

Guidance: level 1

:: International trade ::

_____ or globalisation is the process of interaction and integration among people, companies, and governments worldwide. As a complex and multifaceted phenomenon, _____ is considered by some as a form of capitalist expansion which entails the integration of local and national economies into a global, unregulated market economy. _____ has grown due to advances in transportation and communication technology. With the increased global interactions comes the growth of international trade, ideas, and culture. _____ is primarily an economic process of interaction and integration that's associated with social and cultural aspects. However, conflicts and diplomacy are also large parts of the history of _____, and modern _____.

Exam Probability: **Medium**

56. *Answer choices:*
(see index for correct answer)

- a. Trade Act
- b. Globalization
- c. Bilateral trade
- d. End-use certificate

Guidance: level 1

:: Financial regulatory authorities of the United States ::

The _____ is the revenue service of the United States federal government. The government agency is a bureau of the Department of the Treasury, and is under the immediate direction of the Commissioner of Internal Revenue, who is appointed to a five-year term by the President of the United States. The IRS is responsible for collecting taxes and administering the Internal Revenue Code, the main body of federal statutory tax law of the United States. The duties of the IRS include providing tax assistance to taxpayers and pursuing and resolving instances of erroneous or fraudulent tax filings. The IRS has also overseen various benefits programs, and enforces portions of the Affordable Care Act.

Exam Probability: **Low**

57. *Answer choices:*

(see index for correct answer)

- a. Securities Investor Protection Corporation
- b. Office of Thrift Supervision
- c. Operation Choke Point
- d. National Credit Union Administration

Guidance: level 1

:: Information science ::

_____ is the resolution of uncertainty; it is that which answers the question of "what an entity is" and thus defines both its essence and nature of its characteristics. _____ relates to both data and knowledge, as data is meaningful _____ representing values attributed to parameters, and knowledge signifies understanding of a concept. _____ is uncoupled from an observer, which is an entity that can access _____ and thus discern what it specifies; _____ exists beyond an event horizon for example. In the case of knowledge, the _____ itself requires a cognitive observer to be obtained.

Exam Probability: **High**

58. *Answer choices:*

(see index for correct answer)

- a. American Documentation Institute
- b. Information
- c. Archetype
- d. Neuroheuristics

Guidance: level 1

:: Stochastic processes ::

_____ in its modern meaning is a "new idea, creative thoughts, new imaginations in form of device or method". _____ is often also viewed as the application of better solutions that meet new requirements, unarticulated needs, or existing market needs. Such _____ takes place through the provision of more-effective products, processes, services, technologies, or business models that are made available to markets, governments and society. An _____ is something original and more effective and, as a consequence, new, that "breaks into" the market or society. _____ is related to, but not the same as, invention, as _____ is more apt to involve the practical implementation of an invention to make a meaningful impact in the market or society, and not all _____ s require an invention. _____ often manifests itself via the engineering process, when the problem being solved is of a technical or scientific nature. The opposite of _____ is exnovation.

Exam Probability: **High**

59. *Answer choices:*

(see index for correct answer)

- a. Interacting particle system
- b. Mean value analysis
- c. G/M/1 queue
- d. Innovation

Guidance: level 1

Management

Management is the administration of an organization, whether it is a business, a not-for-profit organization, or government body. Management includes the activities of setting the strategy of an organization and coordinating the efforts of its employees (or of volunteers) to accomplish its objectives through the application of available resources, such as financial, natural, technological, and human resources.

A _____ is the ability to carry out a task with determined results often within a given amount of time, energy, or both. _____ s can often be divided into domain-general and domain-specific _____ s. For example, in the domain of work, some general _____ s would include time management, teamwork and leadership, self-motivation and others, whereas domain-specific _____ s would be used only for a certain job. _____ usually requires certain environmental stimuli and situations to assess the level of _____ being shown and used.

Exam Probability: **High**

1. *Answer choices:*

(see index for correct answer)

- a. corporate values
- b. Skill
- c. similarity-attraction theory
- d. imperative

Guidance: level 1

:: Decision theory ::

A _____ is a decision support tool that uses a tree-like model of decisions and their possible consequences, including chance event outcomes, resource costs, and utility. It is one way to display an algorithm that only contains conditional control statements.

Exam Probability: **High**

2. *Answer choices:*

(see index for correct answer)

- a. Decision tree
- b. Ambiguity aversion
- c. Optimal stopping
- d. TOPSIS

Guidance: level 1

:: ::

_____ or accountancy is the measurement, processing, and communication of financial information about economic entities such as businesses and corporations. The modern field was established by the Italian mathematician Luca Pacioli in 1494. _____ , which has been called the "language of business", measures the results of an organization's economic activities and conveys this information to a variety of users, including investors, creditors, management, and regulators. Practitioners of _____ are known as accountants. The terms " _____ " and "financial reporting" are often used as synonyms.

Exam Probability: **Low**

3. *Answer choices:*

(see index for correct answer)

- a. levels of analysis
- b. similarity-attraction theory
- c. interpersonal communication
- d. cultural

Guidance: level 1

:: Human resource management ::

_____ is the corporate management term for the act of reorganizing the legal, ownership, operational, or other structures of a company for the purpose of making it more profitable, or better organized for its present needs. Other reasons for _____ include a change of ownership or ownership structure, demerger, or a response to a crisis or major change in the business such as bankruptcy, repositioning, or buyout. _____ may also be described as corporate _____ , debt _____ and financial _____ .

Exam Probability: **Low**

4. *Answer choices:*

(see index for correct answer)

- a. Joint Personnel Administration
- b. Restructuring
- c. Adecco Group North America
- d. Occupational burnout

Guidance: level 1

:: Television commercials ::

_____ is a phenomenon whereby something new and somehow valuable is formed. The created item may be intangible or a physical object.

Exam Probability: **Medium**

5. *Answer choices:*
(see index for correct answer)

- a. World History. Bank Imperial
- b. Grrr
- c. Terry Tate: Office Linebacker
- d. Creativity

Guidance: level 1

:: Quality management ::

A _____ or quality control circle is a group of workers who do the same or similar work, who meet regularly to identify, analyze and solve work-related problems. Normally small in size, the group is usually led by a supervisor or manager and presents its solutions to management; where possible, workers implement the solutions themselves in order to improve the performance of the organization and motivate employees. _____ s were at their most popular during the 1980s, but continue to exist in the form of Kaizen groups and similar worker participation schemes.

Exam Probability: **Medium**

6. *Answer choices:*

(see index for correct answer)

- a. Quality management
- b. Product quality risk in supply chain
- c. Informal Methods
- d. Quality circle

Guidance: level 1

:: Economic globalization ::

_____ is an agreement in which one company hires another company to be responsible for a planned or existing activity that is or could be done internally, and sometimes involves transferring employees and assets from one firm to another.

Exam Probability: **Medium**

7. *Answer choices:*

(see index for correct answer)

- a. reshoring
- b. Outsourcing

Guidance: level 1

:: ::

In sales, commerce and economics, a _____ is the recipient of a good, service, product or an idea - obtained from a seller, vendor, or supplier via a financial transaction or exchange for money or some other valuable consideration.

Exam Probability: **Low**

8. *Answer choices:*

(see index for correct answer)

- a. personal values
- b. hierarchical perspective
- c. Customer
- d. functional perspective

Guidance: level 1

:: Systems thinking ::

In business management, a _____ is a company that facilitates the learning of its members and continuously transforms itself. The concept was coined through the work and research of Peter Senge and his colleagues.

Exam Probability: **Low**

9. *Answer choices:*

(see index for correct answer)

- a. Learning organization
- b. Thought leader
- c. IBZL
- d. Club of Budapest

Guidance: level 1

:: Industrial design ::

In physics and mathematics, the _____ of a mathematical space is informally defined as the minimum number of coordinates needed to specify any point within it. Thus a line has a _____ of one because only one coordinate is needed to specify a point on it for example, the point at 5 on a number line. A surface such as a plane or the surface of a cylinder or sphere has a _____ of two because two coordinates are needed to specify a point on it for example, both a latitude and longitude are required to locate a point on the surface of a sphere. The inside of a cube, a cylinder or a sphere is three-_____ al because three coordinates are needed to locate a point within these spaces.

Exam Probability: **High**

10. *Answer choices:*

(see index for correct answer)

- a. Dimension
- b. Prototype
- c. International Archive of Women in Architecture
- d. Cutaway

Guidance: level 1

:: Information technology management ::

_____ is a collective term for all approaches to prepare, support and help individuals, teams, and organizations in making organizational change. The most common change drivers include: technological evolution, process reviews, crisis, and consumer habit changes; pressure from new business entrants, acquisitions, mergers, and organizational restructuring. It includes methods that redirect or redefine the use of resources, business process, budget allocations, or other modes of operation that significantly change a company or organization. Organizational _____ considers the full organization and what needs to change, while _____ may be used solely to refer to how people and teams are affected by such organizational transition. It deals with many different disciplines, from behavioral and social sciences to information technology and business solutions.

Exam Probability: **High**

11. *Answer choices:*

(see index for correct answer)

- a. Acceptable use policy
- b. Enterprise output management
- c. Cumulus
- d. Computer-aided facility management

Guidance: level 1

:: Packaging ::

In work place, _____ or job _____ means good ranking with the hypothesized conception of requirements of a role. There are two types of job _____ s: contextual and task. Task _____ is related to cognitive ability while contextual _____ is dependent upon personality. Task _____ are behavioral roles that are recognized in job descriptions and by remuneration systems, they are directly related to organizational _____, whereas, contextual _____ are value based and additional behavioral roles that are not recognized in job descriptions and covered by compensation; they are extra roles that are indirectly related to organizational _____. Citizenship _____ like contextual _____ means a set of individual activity/contribution that supports the organizational culture.

Exam Probability: **High**

12. *Answer choices:*

(see index for correct answer)

- a. Bottle variation
- b. Grammy Award for Best Recording Package
- c. Thermal bag
- d. Punnet

Guidance: level 1

:: Power (social and political) ::

In a notable study of power conducted by social psychologists John R. P. French and Bertram Raven in 1959, power is divided into five separate and distinct forms. In 1965 Raven revised this model to include a sixth form by separating the informational power base as distinct from the _____ base.

Exam Probability: **Medium**

13. *Answer choices:*

(see index for correct answer)

- a. need for power
- b. Hard power
- c. Expert power

Guidance: level 1

:: Production and manufacturing ::

_____ consists of organization-wide efforts to "install and make permanent climate where employees continuously improve their ability to provide on demand products and services that customers will find of particular value." "Total" emphasizes that departments in addition to production are obligated to improve their operations; "management" emphasizes that executives are obligated to actively manage quality through funding, training, staffing, and goal setting. While there is no widely agreed-upon approach, TQM efforts typically draw heavily on the previously developed tools and techniques of quality control. TQM enjoyed widespread attention during the late 1980s and early 1990s before being overshadowed by ISO 9000, Lean manufacturing, and Six Sigma.

Exam Probability: **Medium**

14. *Answer choices:*

(see index for correct answer)

- a. Feeder line
- b. Shifting bottleneck heuristic
- c. Miniaturization
- d. Total quality management

Guidance: level 1

:: ::

_____ refers to a business or organization attempting to acquire goods or services to accomplish its goals. Although there are several organizations that attempt to set standards in the _____ process, processes can vary greatly between organizations. Typically the word "_____" is not used interchangeably with the word "procurement", since procurement typically includes expediting, supplier quality, and transportation and logistics in addition to _____ .

Exam Probability: **Low**

15. *Answer choices:*

(see index for correct answer)

- a. deep-level diversity

- b. Purchasing
- c. personal values
- d. functional perspective

Guidance: level 1

:: ::

A _____ is a leader's method of providing direction, implementing plans, and motivating people. Various authors have proposed identifying many different _____ s as exhibited by leaders in the political, business or other fields. Studies on _____ are conducted in the military field, expressing an approach that stresses a holistic view of leadership, including how a leader's physical presence determines how others perceive that leader. The factors of physical presence in this context include military bearing, physical fitness, confidence, and resilience. The leader's intellectual capacity helps to conceptualize solutions and to acquire knowledge to do the job. A leader's conceptual abilities apply agility, judgment, innovation, interpersonal tact, and domain knowledge. Domain knowledge encompasses tactical and technical knowledge as well as cultural and geopolitical awareness. Daniel Goleman in his article "Leadership that Gets Results" talks about six styles of leadership.

Exam Probability: **Low**

16. *Answer choices:*
(see index for correct answer)

- a. hierarchical perspective
- b. co-culture

- c. levels of analysis
- d. Leadership style

Guidance: level 1

:: Systems thinking ::

Systems theory is the interdisciplinary study of systems. A system is a cohesive conglomeration of interrelated and interdependent parts that is either natural or man-made. Every system is delineated by its spatial and temporal boundaries, surrounded and influenced by its environment, described by its structure and purpose or nature and expressed in its functioning. In terms of its effects, a system can be more than the sum of its parts if it expresses synergy or emergent behavior. Changing one part of the system usually affects other parts and the whole system, with predictable patterns of behavior. For systems that are self-learning and self-adapting, the positive growth and adaptation depend upon how well the system is adjusted with its environment. Some systems function mainly to support other systems by aiding in the maintenance of the other system to prevent failure. The goal of systems theory is systematically discovering a system's dynamics, constraints, conditions and elucidating principles that can be discerned and applied to systems at every level of nesting, and in every field for achieving optimized equifinality.

Exam Probability: **Low**

17. *Answer choices:*

(see index for correct answer)

- a. Involution
- b. Interdependence

- c. Scenario analysis
- d. Futuribles International

Guidance: level 1

:: Human resource management ::

_____ involves improving the effectiveness of organizations and the individuals and teams within them. Training may be viewed as related to immediate changes in organizational effectiveness via organized instruction, while development is related to the progress of longer-term organizational and employee goals. While _____ technically have differing definitions, the two are oftentimes used interchangeably and/or together. _____ has historically been a topic within applied psychology but has within the last two decades become closely associated with human resources management, talent management, human resources development, instructional design, human factors, and knowledge management.

Exam Probability: **Low**

18. *Answer choices:*

(see index for correct answer)

- a. Training and development
- b. Corporate Equality Index
- c. Four-day week
- d. Multiculturalism

Guidance: level 1

:: Organizational theory ::

_____ comprises the actual output or results of an organization as measured against its intended outputs .

Exam Probability: **Medium**

19. *Answer choices:*
(see index for correct answer)

- a. Organization theory
- b. Organigraph
- c. resource dependence
- d. Organizational performance

Guidance: level 1

:: Organizational behavior ::

In organizational behavior and industrial and organizational psychology, _____ is an individual's psychological attachment to the organization. The basis behind many of these studies was to find ways to improve how workers feel about their jobs so that these workers would become more committed to their organizations. _____ predicts work variables such as turnover, organizational citizenship behavior, and job performance. Some of the factors such as role stress, empowerment, job insecurity and employability, and distribution of leadership have been shown to be connected to a worker's sense of _____ .

Exam Probability: **Low**

20. *Answer choices:*

(see index for correct answer)

- a. Informal organization
- b. Organizational commitment
- c. Micro-initiative
- d. Organizational retaliatory behavior

Guidance: level 1

:: Employment compensation ::

_____ refers to various incentive plans introduced by businesses that provide direct or indirect payments to employees that depend on company's profitability in addition to employees' regular salary and bonuses. In publicly traded companies these plans typically amount to allocation of shares to employees. One of the earliest pioneers of _____ was Englishman Theodore Cooke Taylor, who is known to have introduced the practice in his woollen mills during the late 1800s.

Exam Probability: **Medium**

21. *Answer choices:*

(see index for correct answer)

- a. Salary cap
- b. Personal income
- c. Crowell v. Benson
- d. State Compensation Insurance Fund

Guidance: level 1

:: Outsourcing ::

_____ is the relocation of a business process from one country to another—typically an operational process, such as manufacturing, or supporting processes, such as accounting. Typically this refers to a company business, although state governments may also employ _____. More recently, technical and administrative services have been offshored.

Exam Probability: **High**

22. *Answer choices:*

(see index for correct answer)

- a. Offshoring
- b. Talentica Software
- c. Strategic sourcing
- d. NetRom Software BV

Guidance: level 1

:: Workplace ::

A _____ , also referred to as a performance review, performance evaluation, development discussion, or employee appraisal is a method by which the job performance of an employee is documented and evaluated. _____ s are a part of career development and consist of regular reviews of employee performance within organizations.

Exam Probability: **Medium**

23. *Answer choices:*

(see index for correct answer)

- a. Work etiquette
- b. Performance appraisal

- c. Workplace health surveillance
- d. Queen bee syndrome

Guidance: level 1

:: Materials ::

A _____, also known as a feedstock, unprocessed material, or primary commodity, is a basic material that is used to produce goods, finished products, energy, or intermediate materials which are feedstock for future finished products. As feedstock, the term connotes these materials are bottleneck assets and are highly important with regard to producing other products. An example of this is crude oil, which is a _____ and a feedstock used in the production of industrial chemicals, fuels, plastics, and pharmaceutical goods; lumber is a _____ used to produce a variety of products including all types of furniture. The term " _____ " denotes materials in minimally processed or unprocessed in states; e.g., raw latex, crude oil, cotton, coal, raw biomass, iron ore, air, logs, or water i.e. "...any product of agriculture, forestry, fishing and any other mineral that is in its natural form or which has undergone the transformation required to prepare it for internationally marketing in substantial volumes."

Exam Probability: **Medium**

24. *Answer choices:*
(see index for correct answer)

- a. Agricultural lime
- b. LRPu
- c. Layered double hydroxides

- d. Glass microsphere

Guidance: level 1

:: ::

_____ is the consumption and saving opportunity gained by an entity within a specified timeframe, which is generally expressed in monetary terms. For households and individuals, "_____ is the sum of all the wages, salaries, profits, interest payments, rents, and other forms of earnings received in a given period of time."

Exam Probability: **Medium**

25. *Answer choices:*

(see index for correct answer)

- a. surface-level diversity
- b. imperative
- c. information systems assessment
- d. Income

Guidance: level 1

:: Decision theory ::

Within economics the concept of _____ is used to model worth or value, but its usage has evolved significantly over time. The term was introduced initially as a measure of pleasure or satisfaction within the theory of utilitarianism by moral philosophers such as Jeremy Bentham and John Stuart Mill. But the term has been adapted and reapplied within neoclassical economics, which dominates modern economic theory, as a _____ function that represents a consumer's preference ordering over a choice set. As such, it is devoid of its original interpretation as a measurement of the pleasure or satisfaction obtained by the consumer from that choice.

Exam Probability: **Medium**

26. *Answer choices:*

(see index for correct answer)

- a. Normative model of decision-making
- b. Utility
- c. Applied information economics
- d. Inference engine

Guidance: level 1

:: Management ::

_____ is a method of quality control which employs statistical methods to monitor and control a process. This helps to ensure that the process operates efficiently, producing more specification-conforming products with less waste. SPC can be applied to any process where the "conforming product" output can be measured. Key tools used in SPC include run charts, control charts, a focus on continuous improvement, and the design of experiments. An example of a process where SPC is applied is manufacturing lines.

Exam Probability: **Medium**

27. *Answer choices:*

(see index for correct answer)

- a. Statistical process control
- b. Executive development
- c. Pomodoro Technique
- d. Quality

Guidance: level 1

:: Management ::

In organizational studies, _____ is the efficient and effective development of an organization's resources when they are needed. Such resources may include financial resources, inventory, human skills, production resources, or information technology and natural resources.

Exam Probability: **High**

28. *Answer choices:*

(see index for correct answer)

- a. Systems analysis
- b. Resource management
- c. Balanced scorecard
- d. Crisis management

Guidance: level 1

:: ::

An _____ is a person temporarily or permanently residing in a country other than their native country. In common usage, the term often refers to professionals, skilled workers, or artists taking positions outside their home country, either independently or sent abroad by their employers, who can be companies, universities, governments, or non-governmental organisations. Effectively migrant workers, they usually earn more than they would at home, and less than local employees. However, the term ` _____ ` is also used for retirees and others who have chosen to live outside their native country. Historically, it has also referred to exiles.

Exam Probability: **High**

29. *Answer choices:*

(see index for correct answer)

- a. hierarchical perspective
- b. Expatriate

- c. process perspective
- d. co-culture

Guidance: level 1

:: Management ::

A _____ is when two or more people come together to discuss one or more topics, often in a formal or business setting, but _____ s also occur in a variety of other environments. Many various types of _____ s exist.

Exam Probability: **Medium**

30. *Answer choices:*

(see index for correct answer)

- a. Crisis plan
- b. Meeting
- c. Remedial action
- d. Six phases of a big project

Guidance: level 1

:: Critical thinking ::

An _____ is a set of statements usually constructed to describe a set of facts which clarifies the causes, context, and consequences of those facts. This description of the facts et cetera may establish rules or laws, and may clarify the existing rules or laws in relation to any objects, or phenomena examined. The components of an _____ can be implicit, and interwoven with one another.

Exam Probability: **Low**

31. *Answer choices:*

(see index for correct answer)

- a. Merseyside Skeptics Society
- b. Explanation
- c. Inquiry
- d. Vagueness

Guidance: level 1

:: Management ::

A _____ is an idea of the future or desired result that a person or a group of people envisions, plans and commits to achieve. People endeavor to reach _____ s within a finite time by setting deadlines.

Exam Probability: **High**

32. Answer choices:

(see index for correct answer)

- a. Organizational space
- b. Logistics support analysis
- c. Executive compensation
- d. Goal

Guidance: level 1

:: Marketing ::

_____ , in marketing, manufacturing, call centres and management, is the use of flexible computer-aided manufacturing systems to produce custom output. Such systems combine the low unit costs of mass production processes with the flexibility of individual customization.

Exam Probability: **Medium**

33. Answer choices:

(see index for correct answer)

- a. Keyword research
- b. Mass customization
- c. Adobe Marketing Cloud
- d. Marketing decision support system

Guidance: level 1

:: Occupations ::

An _____ is a person who has a position of authority in a hierarchical organization. The term derives from the late Latin from officiarius, meaning "official".

Exam Probability: **Medium**

34. *Answer choices:*
(see index for correct answer)

- a. Direct support professional
- b. Gardener
- c. Archivist
- d. Special Advocate

Guidance: level 1

:: Offshoring ::

A _____ is the temporary suspension or permanent termination of employment of an employee or, more commonly, a group of employees for business reasons, such as personnel management or downsizing an organization. Originally, _____ referred exclusively to a temporary interruption in work, or employment but this has evolved to a permanent elimination of a position in both British and US English, requiring the addition of "temporary" to specify the original meaning of the word. A _____ is not to be confused with wrongful termination. Laid off workers or displaced workers are workers who have lost or left their jobs because their employer has closed or moved, there was insufficient work for them to do, or their position or shift was abolished. Downsizing in a company is defined to involve the reduction of employees in a workforce. Downsizing in companies became a popular practice in the 1980s and early 1990s as it was seen as a way to deliver better shareholder value as it helps to reduce the costs of employers. Indeed, recent research on downsizing in the U.S., UK, and Japan suggests that downsizing is being regarded by management as one of the preferred routes to help declining organizations, cutting unnecessary costs, and improve organizational performance. Usually a _____ occurs as a cost cutting measure.

Exam Probability: **Low**

35. *Answer choices:*

(see index for correct answer)

- a. Layoff
- b. Nearshoring
- c. TeleTech
- d. Programmers Guild

Guidance: level 1

:: Business law ::

A _____ is a business entity created by two or more parties, generally characterized by shared ownership, shared returns and risks, and shared governance. Companies typically pursue _____ s for one of four reasons: to access a new market, particularly emerging markets; to gain scale efficiencies by combining assets and operations; to share risk for major investments or projects; or to access skills and capabilities.

Exam Probability: **Low**

36. *Answer choices:*

(see index for correct answer)

- a. Business method patent
- b. Ease of doing business index
- c. Joint venture
- d. Arbitration award

Guidance: level 1

:: ::

A _____ is monetary compensation paid by an employer to an employee in exchange for work done. Payment may be calculated as a fixed amount for each task completed, or at an hourly or daily rate, or based on an easily measured quantity of work done.

Exam Probability: **High**

37. *Answer choices:*

(see index for correct answer)

- a. Wage
- b. Sarbanes-Oxley act of 2002
- c. hierarchical perspective
- d. co-culture

Guidance: level 1

:: ::

_____ or haggling is a type of negotiation in which the buyer and seller of a good or service debate the price and exact nature of a transaction. If the _____ produces agreement on terms, the transaction takes place. _____ is an alternative pricing strategy to fixed prices. Optimally, if it costs the retailer nothing to engage and allow _____ , s/he can divine the buyer's willingness to spend. It allows for capturing more consumer surplus as it allows price discrimination, a process whereby a seller can charge a higher price to one buyer who is more eager . Haggling has largely disappeared in parts of the world where the cost to haggle exceeds the gain to retailers for most common retail items. However, for expensive goods sold to uninformed buyers such as automobiles, _____ can remain commonplace.

Exam Probability: **Low**

38. *Answer choices:*

(see index for correct answer)

- a. information systems assessment
- b. co-culture
- c. Bargaining
- d. hierarchical

Guidance: level 1

:: Organizational behavior ::

_____ is the term now used more commonly in business management, particularly human resource management. _____ refers to the number of subordinates a supervisor has.

Exam Probability: **Low**

39. *Answer choices:*

(see index for correct answer)

- a. Group behaviour
- b. Organizational behavior management
- c. Conformity
- d. Counterproductive norms

Guidance: level 1

:: Goods ::

In most contexts, the concept of _____ denotes the conduct that should be preferred when posed with a choice between possible actions. _____ is generally considered to be the opposite of evil, and is of interest in the study of morality, ethics, religion and philosophy. The specific meaning and etymology of the term and its associated translations among ancient and contemporary languages show substantial variation in its inflection and meaning depending on circumstances of place, history, religious, or philosophical context.

Exam Probability: **Low**

40. *Answer choices:*

(see index for correct answer)

- a. Necessity good
- b. Free good
- c. Global commons
- d. Good

Guidance: level 1

:: Management occupations ::

_____ ship is the process of designing, launching and running a new business, which is often initially a small business. The people who create these businesses are called _____ s.

Exam Probability: **Medium**

41. *Answer choices:*

(see index for correct answer)

- a. General partner
- b. Geospatial information officer
- c. Entrepreneur
- d. Directeur sportif

Guidance: level 1

:: Product design ::

_____ as a verb is to create a new product to be sold by a business to its customers. A very broad coefficient and effective generation and development of ideas through a process that leads to new products. Thus, it is a major aspect of new product development.

Exam Probability: **Low**

42. *Answer choices:*

(see index for correct answer)

- a. Production drawing
- b. Andrea Fogli
- c. Peter Opsvik

- d. Product design

Guidance: level 1

:: Teams ::

A _____ usually refers to a group of individuals who work together from different geographic locations and rely on communication technology such as email, FAX, and video or voice conferencing services in order to collaborate. The term can also refer to groups or teams that work together asynchronously or across organizational levels. Powell, Piccoli and Ives define _____ s as "groups of geographically, organizationally and/or time dispersed workers brought together by information and telecommunication technologies to accomplish one or more organizational tasks." According to Ale Ebrahim et. al. , _____ s can also be defined as "small temporary groups of geographically, organizationally and/or time dispersed knowledge workers who coordinate their work predominantly with electronic information and communication technologies in order to accomplish one or more organization tasks."

Exam Probability: **Medium**

43. *Answer choices:*

(see index for correct answer)

- a. Team-building
- b. team composition

Guidance: level 1

:: ::

_____ is the capacity of consciously making sense of things, establishing and verifying facts, applying logic, and changing or justifying practices, institutions, and beliefs based on new or existing information. It is closely associated with such characteristically human activities as philosophy, science, language, mathematics and art, and is normally considered to be a distinguishing ability possessed by humans. _____ , or an aspect of it, is sometimes referred to as rationality.

Exam Probability: **Medium**

44. *Answer choices:*

(see index for correct answer)

- a. personal values
- b. Sarbanes-Oxley act of 2002
- c. imperative
- d. functional perspective

Guidance: level 1

:: Elementary mathematics ::

_____ is a numerical measurement of how far apart objects are. In physics or everyday usage, _____ may refer to a physical length or an estimation based on other criteria. In most cases, "_____ from A to B" is interchangeable with "_____ from B to A". In mathematics, a _____ function or metric is a generalization of the concept of physical _____. A metric is a function that behaves according to a specific set of rules, and is a way of describing what it means for elements of some space to be "close to" or "far away from" each other.

Exam Probability: **Low**

45. *Answer choices:*

(see index for correct answer)

- a. Distance
- b. Arg max
- c. Term
- d. Circular shift

Guidance: level 1

An _____ is the production of goods or related services within an economy. The major source of revenue of a group or company is the indicator of its relevant _____. When a large group has multiple sources of revenue generation, it is considered to be working in different industries. Manufacturing _____ became a key sector of production and labour in European and North American countries during the Industrial Revolution, upsetting previous mercantile and feudal economies. This came through many successive rapid advances in technology, such as the production of steel and coal.

Exam Probability: **High**

46. *Answer choices:*

(see index for correct answer)

- a. cultural
- b. similarity-attraction theory
- c. Industry
- d. interpersonal communication

Guidance: level 1

:: Management ::

A _____ is a method or technique that has been generally accepted as superior to any alternatives because it produces results that are superior to those achieved by other means or because it has become a standard way of doing things, e.g., a standard way of complying with legal or ethical requirements.

Exam Probability: **Medium**

47. *Answer choices:*

(see index for correct answer)

- a. Supply chain optimization
- b. Relational view
- c. Best practice
- d. Porter five forces analysis

Guidance: level 1

:: Organizational behavior ::

_____ is the state or fact of exclusive rights and control over property, which may be an object, land/real estate or intellectual property. _____ involves multiple rights, collectively referred to as title, which may be separated and held by different parties.

Exam Probability: **Medium**

48. *Answer choices:*

(see index for correct answer)

- a. Boreout
- b. Organizational justice
- c. Achievement Motivation Inventory

- d. Ownership

Guidance: level 1

:: Project management ::

_____ is a process of setting goals, planning and/or controlling the organizing and leading the execution of any type of activity, such as.

Exam Probability: **High**

49. *Answer choices:*

(see index for correct answer)

- a. American Society of Professional Estimators
- b. Management process
- c. Terms of reference
- d. Sequence step algorithm

Guidance: level 1

:: ::

An _____ is a contingent motivator. Traditional _____ s are extrinsic motivators which reward actions to yield a desired outcome. The effectiveness of traditional _____ s has changed as the needs of Western society have evolved. While the traditional _____ model is effective when there is a defined procedure and goal for a task, Western society started to require a higher volume of critical thinkers, so the traditional model became less effective. Institutions are now following a trend in implementing strategies that rely on intrinsic motivations rather than the extrinsic motivations that the traditional _____ s foster.

Exam Probability: **Medium**

50. *Answer choices:*

(see index for correct answer)

- a. empathy
- b. hierarchical perspective
- c. functional perspective
- d. Incentive

Guidance: level 1

:: Information systems ::

_____ is the process of creating, sharing, using and managing the knowledge and information of an organisation. It refers to a multidisciplinary approach to achieving organisational objectives by making the best use of knowledge.

Exam Probability: **High**

51. *Answer choices:*

(see index for correct answer)

- a. Intelligent decision support system
- b. Hybrid positioning system
- c. Knowledge management
- d. KarTrak

Guidance: level 1

:: Personality tests ::

The Myers–Briggs Type Indicator is an introspective self-report questionnaire with the purpose of indicating differing psychological preferences in how people perceive the world around them and make decisions. . Though the test superficially resembles some psychological theories it is commonly classified as pseudoscience, especially as pertains to its supposed predictive abilities.

Exam Probability: **Low**

52. *Answer choices:*

(see index for correct answer)

- a. Keirsey Temperament Sorter
- b. Johari window

- c. Myers-Briggs type
- d. personality quiz

Guidance: level 1

:: Decision theory ::

A _____ is a deliberate system of principles to guide decisions and achieve rational outcomes. A _____ is a statement of intent, and is implemented as a procedure or protocol. Policies are generally adopted by a governance body within an organization. Policies can assist in both subjective and objective decision making. Policies to assist in subjective decision making usually assist senior management with decisions that must be based on the relative merits of a number of factors, and as a result are often hard to test objectively, e.g. work-life balance _____ . In contrast policies to assist in objective decision making are usually operational in nature and can be objectively tested, e.g. password _____ .

Exam Probability: **Medium**

53. *Answer choices:*

(see index for correct answer)

- a. Mental accounting
- b. Secretary problem
- c. Rete algorithm
- d. Option grid

Guidance: level 1

_____ involves the development of an action plan designed to motivate and guide a person or group toward a goal. _____ can be guided by goal-setting criteria such as SMART criteria. _____ is a major component of personal-development and management literature.

Exam Probability: **Low**

54. *Answer choices:*

(see index for correct answer)

- a. interpersonal communication
- b. Goal setting
- c. hierarchical
- d. similarity-attraction theory

Guidance: level 1

In mathematics, a _____ is a relationship between two numbers indicating how many times the first number contains the second. For example, if a bowl of fruit contains eight oranges and six lemons, then the _____ of oranges to lemons is eight to six. Similarly, the _____ of lemons to oranges is 6:8 and the _____ of oranges to the total amount of fruit is 8:14.

Exam Probability: **High**

55. *Answer choices:*

(see index for correct answer)

- a. hierarchical perspective
- b. levels of analysis
- c. empathy
- d. Character

Guidance: level 1

:: Industrial Revolution ::

The _____, now also known as the First _____, was the transition to new manufacturing processes in Europe and the US, in the period from about 1760 to sometime between 1820 and 1840. This transition included going from hand production methods to machines, new chemical manufacturing and iron production processes, the increasing use of steam power and water power, the development of machine tools and the rise of the mechanized factory system. The _____ also led to an unprecedented rise in the rate of population growth.

Exam Probability: **High**

56. *Answer choices:*

(see index for correct answer)

- a. Industrial Revolution
- b. Haarlem Mill
- c. Peasant
- d. Masson Mill

Guidance: level 1

:: Human resource management ::

_____ are the people who make up the workforce of an organization, business sector, or economy. "Human capital" is sometimes used synonymously with "_____", although human capital typically refers to a narrower effect. Likewise, other terms sometimes used include manpower, talent, labor, personnel, or simply people.

Exam Probability: **Low**

57. *Answer choices:*

(see index for correct answer)

- a. Sham peer review
- b. Vendor management system

- c. At-will employment
- d. Human resources

Guidance: level 1

:: Management ::

_____ is an area of management concerned with designing and controlling the process of production and redesigning business operations in the production of goods or services. It involves the responsibility of ensuring that business operations are efficient in terms of using as few resources as needed and effective in terms of meeting customer requirements. _____ is primarily concerned with planning, organizing and supervising in the contexts of production, manufacturing or the provision of services.

Exam Probability: **High**

58. *Answer choices:*

(see index for correct answer)

- a. Management buyout
- b. Formula for change
- c. Modes of leadership
- d. Responsible autonomy

Guidance: level 1

:: Project management ::

In political science, an _____ is a means by which a petition signed by a certain minimum number of registered voters can force a government to choose to either enact a law or hold a public vote in parliament in what is called indirect _____, or under direct _____, the proposition is immediately put to a plebiscite or referendum, in what is called a Popular initiated Referendum or citizen-initiated referendum).

Exam Probability: **Medium**

59. *Answer choices:*

(see index for correct answer)

- a. Initiative
- b. Effort management
- c. Requirements traceability
- d. Cash flow diagram

Guidance: level 1

Business law

Corporate law (also known as business law) is the body of law governing the rights, relations, and conduct of persons, companies, organizations and businesses. It refers to the legal practice relating to, or the theory of corporations. Corporate law often describes the law relating to matters which derive directly from the life-cycle of a corporation. It thus encompasses the formation, funding, governance, and death of a corporation.

:: Patent law ::

A _____ is generally any statement intended to specify or delimit the scope of rights and obligations that may be exercised and enforced by parties in a legally recognized relationship. In contrast to other terms for legally operative language, the term _____ usually implies situations that involve some level of uncertainty, waiver, or risk.

Exam Probability: **Low**

1. *Answer choices:*

(see index for correct answer)

- a. Research tool patents
- b. Patent family
- c. Disclaimer
- d. Unity of invention

Guidance: level 1

:: Contract law ::

Offer and acceptance analysis is a traditional approach in contract law. The offer and acceptance formula, developed in the 19th century, identifies a moment of formation when the parties are of one mind. This classical approach to contract formation has been modified by developments in the law of estoppel, misleading conduct, misrepresentation and unjust enrichment.

Exam Probability: **Medium**

2. *Answer choices:*

(see index for correct answer)

- a. Unjust enrichment
- b. Offeree
- c. Proprietary estoppel
- d. Freedom of contract

Guidance: level 1

:: Shareholders ::

A _____ is a payment made by a corporation to its shareholders, usually as a distribution of profits. When a corporation earns a profit or surplus, the corporation is able to re-invest the profit in the business and pay a proportion of the profit as a _____ to shareholders. Distribution to shareholders may be in cash or, if the corporation has a _____ reinvestment plan, the amount can be paid by the issue of further shares or share repurchase. When _____ s are paid, shareholders typically must pay income taxes, and the corporation does not receive a corporate income tax deduction for the _____ payments.

Exam Probability: **Low**

3. *Answer choices:*

(see index for correct answer)

- a. Shareholder oppression
- b. Shareholder Rights Directive
- c. Dividend
- d. Proxy statement

Guidance: level 1

:: Real estate ::

_____ , real estate, realty, or immovable property In English common law refers to landed properties belonging to some person. It include all structures, crops, buildings, machinery, wells, dams, ponds, mines, canals, and roads, among other things. The term is historic, arising from the now-discontinued form of action, which distinguish between _____ disputes and personal property disputes. Personal property was, and continues to refer to all properties that are not real properties.

Exam Probability: **Low**

4. *Answer choices:*

(see index for correct answer)

- a. Transfer deed
- b. Owner-occupier
- c. Building
- d. Rent control in the United States

Guidance: level 1

:: Contract law ::

A _____ is a legally-binding agreement which recognises and governs the rights and duties of the parties to the agreement. A _____ is legally enforceable because it meets the requirements and approval of the law. An agreement typically involves the exchange of goods, services, money, or promises of any of those. In the event of breach of _____ , the law awards the injured party access to legal remedies such as damages and cancellation.

Exam Probability: **High**

5. *Answer choices:*

(see index for correct answer)

- a. Executory contract
- b. Good faith
- c. Contract
- d. Verbal contract

Guidance: level 1

:: Writs ::

In common law, a _____ is a formal _____ ten order issued by a body with administrative or judicial jurisdiction; in modern usage, this body is generally a court. Warrants, prerogative _____ s, and subpoenas are common types of _____ , but many forms exist and have existed.

Exam Probability: **High**

6. *Answer choices:*

(see index for correct answer)

- a. Writ of assistance
- b. Qui tam
- c. Writ

Guidance: level 1

:: White-collar criminals ::

_____ refers to financially motivated, nonviolent crime committed by businesses and government professionals. It was first defined by the sociologist Edwin Sutherland in 1939 as "a crime committed by a person of respectability and high social status in the course of their occupation". Typical _____ s could include wage theft, fraud, bribery, Ponzi schemes, insider trading, labor racketeering, embezzlement, cybercrime, copyright infringement, money laundering, identity theft, and forgery. Lawyers can specialize in _____ .

Exam Probability: **High**

7. Answer choices:

(see index for correct answer)

- a. Tongsun Park
- b. Du Jun

Guidance: level 1

:: Arbitration law ::

The United States Arbitration Act, more commonly referred to as the _____ or FAA, is an act of Congress that provides for judicial facilitation of private dispute resolution through arbitration. It applies in both state courts and federal courts, as was held constitutional in Southland Corp. v. Keating. It applies where the transaction contemplated by the parties "involves" interstate commerce and is predicated on an exercise of the Commerce Clause powers granted to Congress in the U.S. Constitution.

Exam Probability: **Low**

8. *Answer choices:*

(see index for correct answer)

- a. James A. Graham
- b. Federal Arbitration Act
- c. Title 9 of the United States Code
- d. Uniform Arbitration Act

Guidance: level 1

:: ::

A _____ is any person who contracts to acquire an asset in return for some form of consideration.

Exam Probability: **Medium**

9. *Answer choices:*

(see index for correct answer)

- a. Character
- b. Buyer
- c. similarity-attraction theory
- d. hierarchical

Guidance: level 1

:: Consumer theory ::

A _____ is a technical term in psychology, economics and philosophy usually used in relation to choosing between alternatives. For example, someone prefers A over B if they would rather choose A than B.

Exam Probability: **High**

10. *Answer choices:*

(see index for correct answer)

- a. Demand vacuum
- b. Revealed preference
- c. Preference
- d. Slutsky equation

Guidance: level 1

:: International trade ::

_____ involves the transfer of goods or services from one person or entity to another, often in exchange for money. A system or network that allows _____ is called a market.

Exam Probability: **Medium**

11. *Answer choices:*

(see index for correct answer)

- a. Import
- b. SinoLatin Capital
- c. Trade
- d. National Foreign Trade Council

Guidance: level 1

:: Contract law ::

An _____ —or acceleration covenant— in the law of contracts, is a term that fully matures the performance due from a party upon a breach of the contract. Such clauses are most prevalent in mortgages and similar contracts to purchase real estate in installments.

Exam Probability: **High**

12. *Answer choices:*

(see index for correct answer)

- a. Specific performance
- b. Convention on the Law Applicable to Contractual Obligations 1980
- c. Seal
- d. Intention to be legally bound

Guidance: level 1

:: Sexual harassment in the United States ::

In law, a _____, reasonable man, or the man on the Clapham omnibus is a hypothetical person of legal fiction crafted by the courts and communicated through case law and jury instructions.

Exam Probability: **Medium**

13. *Answer choices:*

(see index for correct answer)

- a. Reasonable person
- b. Alexander v. Yale
- c. Fitzgerald v. Barnstable School Committee
- d. Hostile Advances

Guidance: level 1

:: Contract law ::

_____ is a legal process for collecting a monetary judgment on behalf of a plaintiff from a defendant. _____ allows the plaintiff to take the money or property of the debtor from the person or institution that holds that property. A similar legal mechanism called execution allows the seizure of money or property held directly by the debtor.

Exam Probability: **Low**

14. *Answer choices:*

(see index for correct answer)

- a. Terms of service
- b. Third-party beneficiary
- c. enforceable
- d. Implied authority

Guidance: level 1

:: ::

A _____ is a law passed by a legislative body in a common law system to set the maximum time after an event within which legal proceedings may be initiated.

Exam Probability: **Low**

15. *Answer choices:*

(see index for correct answer)

- a. levels of analysis
- b. Statute of limitations
- c. corporate values
- d. functional perspective

Guidance: level 1

:: Marketing ::

_____ or stock is the goods and materials that a business holds for the ultimate goal of resale.

Exam Probability: **Medium**

16. *Answer choices:*

(see index for correct answer)

- a. Inventory
- b. Need
- c. Bayesian inference in marketing
- d. Ayelet Gneezy

Guidance: level 1

:: Contract law ::

A _____ is an event or state of affairs that is required before something else will occur. In contract law, a _____ is an event which must occur, unless its non-occurrence is excused, before performance under a contract becomes due, i.e., before any contractual duty exists.

Exam Probability: **High**

17. *Answer choices:*
(see index for correct answer)

- a. Morals clause
- b. Liquidated damages
- c. Severability
- d. Contractual term

Guidance: level 1

:: ::

The _____ to the United States Constitution prevents the government from making laws which respect an establishment of religion, prohibit the free exercise of religion, or abridge the freedom of speech, the freedom of the press, the right to peaceably assemble, or the right to petition the government for redress of grievances. It was adopted on December 15, 1791, as one of the ten amendments that constitute the Bill of Rights.

Exam Probability: **High**

18. *Answer choices:*

(see index for correct answer)

- a. First Amendment
- b. personal values
- c. functional perspective
- d. corporate values

Guidance: level 1

:: ::

According to the philosopher Piyush Mathur , "Tangibility is the property that a phenomenon exhibits if it has and/or transports mass and/or energy and/or momentum".

Exam Probability: **Medium**

19. *Answer choices:*

(see index for correct answer)

- a. deep-level diversity
- b. surface-level diversity
- c. Character
- d. Tangible

Guidance: level 1

:: Euthenics ::

_____ is an ethical framework and suggests that an entity, be it an organization or individual, has an obligation to act for the benefit of society at large. _____ is a duty every individual has to perform so as to maintain a balance between the economy and the ecosystems. A trade-off may exist between economic development, in the material sense, and the welfare of the society and environment, though this has been challenged by many reports over the past decade. _____ means sustaining the equilibrium between the two. It pertains not only to business organizations but also to everyone whose any action impacts the environment. This responsibility can be passive, by avoiding engaging in socially harmful acts, or active, by performing activities that directly advance social goals. _____ must be intergenerational since the actions of one generation have consequences on those following.

Exam Probability: **Medium**

20. *Answer choices:*

(see index for correct answer)

- a. Minnie Cumnock Blodgett
- b. Family and consumer science
- c. Social responsibility
- d. Euthenics

Guidance: level 1

:: Generally Accepted Accounting Principles ::

In accounting, _____ is the income that a business have from its normal business activities, usually from the sale of goods and services to customers. _____ is also referred to as sales or turnover. Some companies receive _____ from interest, royalties, or other fees. _____ may refer to business income in general, or it may refer to the amount, in a monetary unit, earned during a period of time, as in "Last year, Company X had _____ of $42 million". Profits or net income generally imply total _____ minus total expenses in a given period. In accounting, in the balance statement it is a subsection of the Equity section and _____ increases equity, it is often referred to as the "top line" due to its position on the income statement at the very top. This is to be contrasted with the "bottom line" which denotes net income .

Exam Probability: **Low**

21. *Answer choices:*

(see index for correct answer)

- a. deferred revenue
- b. Treasury stock
- c. Normal balance
- d. Revenue recognition

Guidance: level 1

:: Fraud ::

The _____ refers to the requirement that certain kinds of contracts be memorialized in writing, signed by the party to be charged, with sufficient content to evidence the contract.

Exam Probability: **High**

22. *Answer choices:*

(see index for correct answer)

- a. Statute of frauds
- b. Faked death
- c. Transcript fraud
- d. Mussolini diaries

Guidance: level 1

:: Negotiable instrument law ::

In the United States, The Preservation of Consumers' Claims and Defenses [_____ Rule], formally known as the "Trade Regulation Rule Concerning Preservation of Consumers' Claims and Defenses," protects consumers when merchants sell a consumer's credit contracts to other lenders. Specifically, it preserves consumers' right to assert the same legal claims and defenses against anyone who purchases the credit contract, as they would have against the seller who originally provided the credit. [16 Code of Federal Regulations Part 433]

Exam Probability: **High**

23. *Answer choices:*

(see index for correct answer)

- a. Real defense
- b. Swift v. Tyson
- c. Negotiable Instruments Act, 1881
- d. Blank endorsement

Guidance: level 1

:: ::

_____ is a marketing communication that employs an openly sponsored, non-personal message to promote or sell a product, service or idea. Sponsors of _____ are typically businesses wishing to promote their products or services. _____ is differentiated from public relations in that an advertiser pays for and has control over the message. It differs from personal selling in that the message is non-personal, i.e., not directed to a particular individual. _____ is communicated through various mass media, including traditional media such as newspapers, magazines, television, radio, outdoor _____ or direct mail; and new media such as search results, blogs, social media, websites or text messages. The actual presentation of the message in a medium is referred to as an advertisement, or "ad" or advert for short.

Exam Probability: **Medium**

24. *Answer choices:*

(see index for correct answer)

- a. Advertising
- b. hierarchical perspective
- c. empathy
- d. interpersonal communication

Guidance: level 1

:: ::

_____ is a process under which executive or legislative actions are subject to review by the judiciary. A court with authority for _____ may invalidate laws, acts and governmental actions that are incompatible with a higher authority: an executive decision may be invalidated for being unlawful or a statute may be invalidated for violating the terms of a constitution.
_____ is one of the checks and balances in the separation of powers: the power of the judiciary to supervise the legislative and executive branches when the latter exceed their authority. The doctrine varies between jurisdictions, so the procedure and scope of _____ may differ between and within countries.

Exam Probability: **Medium**

25. *Answer choices:*

(see index for correct answer)

- a. information systems assessment
- b. Judicial review
- c. hierarchical perspective
- d. empathy

Guidance: level 1

:: ::

The _____ is the central philosophical concept in the deontological moral philosophy of Immanuel Kant. Introduced in Kant's 1785 Groundwork of the Metaphysics of Morals, it may be defined as a way of evaluating motivations for action.

Exam Probability: **High**

26. *Answer choices:*

(see index for correct answer)

- a. Categorical imperative
- b. surface-level diversity
- c. hierarchical perspective
- d. Character

Guidance: level 1

:: Clauses of the United States Constitution ::

The _____ describes an enumerated power listed in the United States Constitution. The clause states that the United States Congress shall have power "To regulate Commerce with foreign Nations, and among the several States, and with the Indian Tribes." Courts and commentators have tended to discuss each of these three areas of commerce as a separate power granted to Congress. It is common to see the individual components of the _____ referred to under specific terms: the Foreign _____, the Interstate _____, and the Indian _____.

Exam Probability: **Medium**

27. *Answer choices:*

(see index for correct answer)

- a. Commerce Clause
- b. Full Faith and Credit Clause
- c. Full faith and credit

Guidance: level 1

:: Actuarial science ::

_____ is the possibility of losing something of value. Values can be gained or lost when taking _____ resulting from a given action or inaction, foreseen or unforeseen. _____ can also be defined as the intentional interaction with uncertainty. Uncertainty is a potential, unpredictable, and uncontrollable outcome; _____ is a consequence of action taken in spite of uncertainty.

Exam Probability: **High**

28. *Answer choices:*
(see index for correct answer)

- a. Maximum life span
- b. Actuarial science
- c. Extreme value theory
- d. Risk

Guidance: level 1

:: Commercial crimes ::

_____ is the act of withholding assets for the purpose of conversion of such assets, by one or more persons to whom the assets were entrusted, either to be held or to be used for specific purposes. _____ is a type of financial fraud. For example, a lawyer might embezzle funds from the trust accounts of their clients; a financial advisor might embezzle the funds of investors; and a husband or a wife might embezzle funds from a bank account jointly held with the spouse.

Exam Probability: **High**

29. *Answer choices:*

(see index for correct answer)

- a. Financial intelligence
- b. Price gouging
- c. Embezzlement
- d. The Informant

Guidance: level 1

:: ::

_____, in law, is a transaction or action that is valid but may be annulled by one of the parties to the transaction. _____ is usually used in distinction to void ab initio and unenforceable.

Exam Probability: **Low**

30. *Answer choices:*

(see index for correct answer)

- a. functional perspective
- b. co-culture
- c. Voidable
- d. corporate values

Guidance: level 1

:: Decision theory ::

Within economics the concept of _____ is used to model worth or value, but its usage has evolved significantly over time. The term was introduced initially as a measure of pleasure or satisfaction within the theory of utilitarianism by moral philosophers such as Jeremy Bentham and John Stuart Mill. But the term has been adapted and reapplied within neoclassical economics, which dominates modern economic theory, as a _____ function that represents a consumer's preference ordering over a choice set. As such, it is devoid of its original interpretation as a measurement of the pleasure or satisfaction obtained by the consumer from that choice.

Exam Probability: **Medium**

31. *Answer choices:*

(see index for correct answer)

- a. Fuzzy-trace theory
- b. Choice-supportive bias
- c. Emotional bias
- d. Health management system

Guidance: level 1

:: ::

_____, in United States trademark law, is a statutory cause of action that permits a party to petition the Trademark Trial and Appeal Board of the Patent and Trademark Office to cancel a trademark registration that "may disparage or falsely suggest a connection with persons, living or dead, institutions, beliefs, or national symbols, or bring them into contempt or disrepute." Unlike claims regarding the validity of the mark, a _____ claim can be brought "at any time," subject to equitable defenses such as laches.

Exam Probability: **Low**

32. *Answer choices:*
(see index for correct answer)

- a. process perspective
- b. levels of analysis
- c. Disparagement
- d. cultural

Guidance: level 1

:: Real property law ::

_____ is the judicial process whereby a will is "proved" in a court of law and accepted as a valid public document that is the true last testament of the deceased, or whereby the estate is settled according to the laws of intestacy in the state of residence [or real property] of the deceased at time of death in the absence of a legal will.

Exam Probability: **Medium**

33. *Answer choices:*

(see index for correct answer)

- a. Land contract
- b. Bargain and sale deed
- c. Catasto
- d. Ultimogeniture

Guidance: level 1

:: Debt ::

_____, in finance and economics, is payment from a borrower or deposit-taking financial institution to a lender or depositor of an amount above repayment of the principal sum, at a particular rate. It is distinct from a fee which the borrower may pay the lender or some third party. It is also distinct from dividend which is paid by a company to its shareholders from its profit or reserve, but not at a particular rate decided beforehand, rather on a pro rata basis as a share in the reward gained by risk taking entrepreneurs when the revenue earned exceeds the total costs.

Exam Probability: **High**

34. *Answer choices:*

(see index for correct answer)

- a. Compulsive buying disorder
- b. Christians Against Poverty
- c. Student debt
- d. Interest

Guidance: level 1

:: ::

A federation is a political entity characterized by a union of partially self-governing provinces, states, or other regions under a central _____. In a federation, the self-governing status of the component states, as well as the division of power between them and the central government, is typically constitutionally entrenched and may not be altered by a unilateral decision of either party, the states or the federal political body. Alternatively, federation is a form of government in which sovereign power is formally divided between a central authority and a number of constituent regions so that each region retains some degree of control over its internal affairs. It is often argued that federal states where the central government has the constitutional authority to suspend a constituent state's government by invoking gross mismanagement or civil unrest, or to adopt national legislation that overrides or infringe on the constituent states' powers by invoking the central government's constitutional authority to ensure "peace and good government" or to implement obligations contracted under an international treaty, are not truly federal states.

Exam Probability: **Low**

35. *Answer choices:*

(see index for correct answer)

- a. hierarchical
- b. process perspective
- c. deep-level diversity
- d. Federal government

Guidance: level 1

An _____ is a contingent motivator. Traditional _____ s are extrinsic motivators which reward actions to yield a desired outcome. The effectiveness of traditional _____ s has changed as the needs of Western society have evolved. While the traditional _____ model is effective when there is a defined procedure and goal for a task, Western society started to require a higher volume of critical thinkers, so the traditional model became less effective. Institutions are now following a trend in implementing strategies that rely on intrinsic motivations rather than the extrinsic motivations that the traditional _____ s foster.

Exam Probability: **High**

36. *Answer choices:*

(see index for correct answer)

- a. levels of analysis
- b. corporate values
- c. open system
- d. Incentive

Guidance: level 1

:: Real property law ::

_____ is an area of criminal law or tort law broadly divided into three groups: _____ to the person, _____ to chattels and _____ to land.

Exam Probability: **Low**

37. *Answer choices:*

(see index for correct answer)

- a. Tenancy deposit schemes
- b. Escheat
- c. Deed in lieu of foreclosure
- d. Land and Valuation Court of New South Wales

Guidance: level 1

:: United States federal public corruption crime ::

Mail fraud and _____ are federal crimes in the United States that involve mailing or electronically transmitting something associated with fraud. Jurisdiction is claimed by the federal government if the illegal activity crosses interstate or international borders.

Exam Probability: **Medium**

38. *Answer choices:*

(see index for correct answer)

- a. Wire fraud
- b. Racketeer Influenced and Corrupt Organizations Act

Guidance: level 1

:: Commercial crimes ::

_____ is the process of concealing the origins of money obtained illegally by passing it through a complex sequence of banking transfers or commercial transactions. The overall scheme of this process returns the money to the launderer in an obscure and indirect way.

Exam Probability: **Medium**

39. *Answer choices:*
(see index for correct answer)

- a. Financial intelligence
- b. Misappropriation
- c. Fraudulent conveyance
- d. Price fixing

Guidance: level 1

:: ::

In international relations, _____ is – from the perspective of governments – a voluntary transfer of resources from one country to another.

Exam Probability: **Medium**

40. *Answer choices:*

(see index for correct answer)

- a. levels of analysis
- b. Aid
- c. hierarchical perspective
- d. functional perspective

Guidance: level 1

:: Ethically disputed business practices ::

_____ is the trading of a public company's stock or other securities by individuals with access to nonpublic information about the company. In various countries, some kinds of trading based on insider information is illegal. This is because it is seen as unfair to other investors who do not have access to the information, as the investor with insider information could potentially make larger profits than a typical investor could make. The rules governing _____ are complex and vary significantly from country to country. The extent of enforcement also varies from one country to another. The definition of insider in one jurisdiction can be broad, and may cover not only insiders themselves but also any persons related to them, such as brokers, associates and even family members. A person who becomes aware of non-public information and trades on that basis may be guilty of a crime.

Exam Probability: **Low**

41. *Answer choices:*

(see index for correct answer)

- a. Insider trading
- b. Market abuse
- c. Gaming the system
- d. Unfair labor practice

Guidance: level 1

:: Business law ::

In the United States, the United Kingdom, Australia, Canada and South Africa, _____ relates to the doctrines of the law of agency. It is relevant particularly in corporate law and constitutional law. _____ refers to a situation where a reasonable third party would understand that an agent had authority to act. This means a principal is bound by the agent's actions, even if the agent had no actual authority, whether express or implied. It raises an estoppel because the third party is given an assurance, which he relies on and would be inequitable for the principal to deny the authority given. _____ can legally be found, even if actual authority has not been given.

Exam Probability: **High**

42. *Answer choices:*

(see index for correct answer)

- a. Refusal to deal
- b. Extraordinary resolution

- c. Jurisdictional strike
- d. Agency in English law

Guidance: level 1

:: Contract Clause case law ::

The _____ appears in the United States Constitution, Article I, section 10, clause 1. The clause prohibits a State from passing any law that "impairs the obligation of contracts" or "makes any thing but gold and silver coin a tender in payment of debts". It states.

Exam Probability: **High**

43. *Answer choices:*

(see index for correct answer)

- a. Fletcher v. Peck
- b. Smyth v. Ames
- c. Charles River Bridge v. Warren Bridge

Guidance: level 1

:: Forgery ::

____ is a white-collar crime that generally refers to the false making or material alteration of a legal instrument with the specific intent to defraud anyone. Tampering with a certain legal instrument may be forbidden by law in some jurisdictions but such an offense is not related to ____ unless the tampered legal instrument was actually used in the course of the crime to defraud another person or entity. Copies, studio replicas, and reproductions are not considered forgeries, though they may later become forgeries through knowing and willful misrepresentations.

Exam Probability: **Low**

44. *Answer choices:*

(see index for correct answer)

- a. Unapproved aircraft part
- b. Forgery of Foreign Bills Act 1803
- c. Archaeological forgery
- d. Signature forgery

Guidance: level 1

:: Stock market ::

____ is freedom from, or resilience against, potential harm caused by others. Beneficiaries of ____ may be of persons and social groups, objects and institutions, ecosystems or any other entity or phenomenon vulnerable to unwanted change by its environment.

Exam Probability: **Medium**

45. *Answer choices:*

(see index for correct answer)

- a. Security
- b. PLUS Markets Group
- c. French auction
- d. Central securities depository

Guidance: level 1

:: ::

Credit is the trust which allows one party to provide money or resources to another party wherein the second party does not reimburse the first party immediately, but promises either to repay or return those resources at a later date. In other words, credit is a method of making reciprocity formal, legally enforceable, and extensible to a large group of unrelated people.

Exam Probability: **High**

46. *Answer choices:*

(see index for correct answer)

- a. co-culture
- b. open system

- c. Sarbanes-Oxley act of 2002
- d. functional perspective

Guidance: level 1

:: Contract law ::

In contract law, _____ is an excuse for the nonperformance of duties under a contract, based on a change in circumstances, the nonoccurrence of which was an underlying assumption of the contract, that makes performance of the contract literally impossible.

Exam Probability: **High**

47. *Answer choices:*

(see index for correct answer)

- a. Severable contract
- b. Impossibility
- c. Acceleration clause
- d. Per minas

Guidance: level 1

:: Criminal procedure ::

In law, a verdict is the formal finding of fact made by a jury on matters or questions submitted to the jury by a judge. In a bench trial, the judge's decision near the end of the trial is simply referred to as a finding. In England and Wales, a coroner's findings are called verdicts .

Exam Probability: **Medium**

48. *Answer choices:*

(see index for correct answer)

- a. Directed verdict
- b. Exoneration

Guidance: level 1

:: Contract law ::

In jurisprudence, _____ is an equitable doctrine that involves one person taking advantage of a position of power over another person. This inequity in power between the parties can vitiate one party's consent as they are unable to freely exercise their independent will.

Exam Probability: **Low**

49. *Answer choices:*

(see index for correct answer)

- a. Requirements contract
- b. Unenforceable
- c. Undue influence
- d. Pact ink

Guidance: level 1

:: ::

A _____ is the party who initiates a lawsuit before a court. By doing so, the _____ seeks a legal remedy; if this search is successful, the court will issue judgment in favor of the _____ and make the appropriate court order. "_____" is the term used in civil cases in most English-speaking jurisdictions, the notable exception being England and Wales, where a _____ has, since the introduction of the Civil Procedure Rules in 1999, been known as a "claimant", but that term also has other meanings. In criminal cases, the prosecutor brings the case against the defendant, but the key complaining party is often called the "complainant".

Exam Probability: **Medium**

50. *Answer choices:*

(see index for correct answer)

- a. Plaintiff
- b. open system
- c. personal values
- d. similarity-attraction theory

Guidance: level 1

:: ::

_____ is that part of a civil law legal system which is part of the jus commune that involves relationships between individuals, such as the law of contracts or torts, and the law of obligations. It is to be distinguished from public law, which deals with relationships between both natural and artificial persons and the state, including regulatory statutes, penal law and other law that affects the public order. In general terms, _____ involves interactions between private citizens, whereas public law involves interrelations between the state and the general population.

Exam Probability: **Medium**

51. *Answer choices:*

(see index for correct answer)

- a. imperative
- b. similarity-attraction theory
- c. Character
- d. hierarchical

Guidance: level 1

:: ::

At common law, _____ are a remedy in the form of a monetary award to be paid to a claimant as compensation for loss or injury. To warrant the award, the claimant must show that a breach of duty has caused foreseeable loss. To be recognised at law, the loss must involve damage to property, or mental or physical injury; pure economic loss is rarely recognised for the award of _____ .

Exam Probability: **High**

52. *Answer choices:*

(see index for correct answer)

- a. Damages
- b. hierarchical perspective
- c. co-culture
- d. process perspective

Guidance: level 1

:: United States securities law ::

_____ is a legal term for intent or knowledge of wrongdoing. An offending party then has knowledge of the "wrongness" of an act or event prior to committing it.

Exam Probability: **Medium**

53. Answer choices:

(see index for correct answer)

- a. Strike suit
- b. Scienter
- c. Uniform Securities Act
- d. Series 14

Guidance: level 1

:: Insurance terms ::

_____ is the assumption by a third party of another party's legal right to collect a debt or damages. It is a legal doctrine whereby one person is entitled to enforce the subsisting or revived rights of another for one's own benefit. A right of _____ typically arises by operation of law, but can also arise by statute or by agreement. _____ is an equitable remedy, having first developed in the English Court of Chancery. It is a familiar feature of common law systems. Analogous doctrines exist in civil law jurisdictions.

Exam Probability: **High**

54. Answer choices:

(see index for correct answer)

- a. Recoupment
- b. Independent insurance agent

- c. Self-revelation
- d. Adjustment clause

Guidance: level 1

:: Psychometrics ::

_____ is a dynamic, structured, interactive process where a neutral third party assists disputing parties in resolving conflict through the use of specialized communication and negotiation techniques. All participants in _____ are encouraged to actively participate in the process. _____ is a "party-centered" process in that it is focused primarily upon the needs, rights, and interests of the parties. The mediator uses a wide variety of techniques to guide the process in a constructive direction and to help the parties find their optimal solution. A mediator is facilitative in that she/he manages the interaction between parties and facilitates open communication. _____ is also evaluative in that the mediator analyzes issues and relevant norms, while refraining from providing prescriptive advice to the parties.

Exam Probability: **Low**

55. *Answer choices:*
(see index for correct answer)

- a. Mediation
- b. Base rate
- c. Heart Intelligence
- d. Multidimensional scaling

Guidance: level 1

:: Finance ::

_____ is the investigation or exercise of care that a reasonable business or person is expected to take before entering into an agreement or contract with another party, or an act with a certain standard of care.

Exam Probability: **Low**

56. *Answer choices:*

(see index for correct answer)

- a. Undervalued stock
- b. Due diligence
- c. Asset-backed commercial paper
- d. Stub period

Guidance: level 1

:: Business law ::

A _____ is a form of partnership similar to a general partnership except that while a general partnership must have at least two general partners, a _____ must have at least one GP and at least one limited partner.

Exam Probability: **High**

57. *Answer choices:*

(see index for correct answer)

- a. Leave of absence
- b. Advertising regulation
- c. Limited partnership
- d. Unfair competition

Guidance: level 1

:: ::

A _____ is a person or firm who arranges transactions between a buyer and a seller for a commission when the deal is executed. A _____ who also acts as a seller or as a buyer becomes a principal party to the deal. Neither role should be confused with that of an agent—one who acts on behalf of a principal party in a deal.

Exam Probability: **High**

58. *Answer choices:*

(see index for correct answer)

- a. open system
- b. Broker

- c. hierarchical
- d. personal values

Guidance: level 1

:: Data management ::

_____ is a form of intellectual property that grants the creator of an original creative work an exclusive legal right to determine whether and under what conditions this original work may be copied and used by others, usually for a limited term of years. The exclusive rights are not absolute but limited by limitations and exceptions to _____ law, including fair use. A major limitation on _____ on ideas is that _____ protects only the original expression of ideas, and not the underlying ideas themselves.

Exam Probability: **Low**

59. *Answer choices:*

(see index for correct answer)

- a. Sales intelligence
- b. Copyright
- c. Electronic lab notebook
- d. Microsoft Office PerformancePoint Server

Guidance: level 1

Finance

Finance is a field that is concerned with the allocation (investment) of assets and liabilities over space and time, often under conditions of risk or uncertainty. Finance can also be defined as the science of money management. Participants in the market aim to price assets based on their risk level, fundamental value, and their expected rate of return. Finance can be split into three sub-categories: public finance, corporate finance and personal finance.

_____ is the administration of an organization, whether it is a business, a not-for-profit organization, or government body. _____ includes the activities of setting the strategy of an organization and coordinating the efforts of its employees to accomplish its objectives through the application of available resources, such as financial, natural, technological, and human resources. The term "_____" may also refer to those people who manage an organization.

Exam Probability: **High**

1. *Answer choices:*

(see index for correct answer)

- a. Management
- b. Character
- c. functional perspective
- d. surface-level diversity

Guidance: level 1

:: ::

_____ is the withdrawal from one's position or occupation or from one's active working life. A person may also semi-retire by reducing work hours.

Exam Probability: **High**

2. *Answer choices:*

(see index for correct answer)

- a. process perspective
- b. hierarchical perspective
- c. empathy
- d. corporate values

Guidance: level 1

:: Institutional investors ::

A _____ is an investment fund that pools capital from accredited investors or institutional investors and invests in a variety of assets, often with complex portfolio-construction and risk management techniques. It is administered by a professional investment management firm, and often structured as a limited partnership, limited liability company, or similar vehicle. _____ s are generally distinct from mutual funds and regarded as alternative investments, as their use of leverage is not capped by regulators, and distinct from private equity funds, as the majority of _____ s invest in relatively liquid assets. However, funds which operate similarly to _____ s but are regulated similarly to mutual funds are available and known as liquid alternative investments.

Exam Probability: **High**

3. *Answer choices:*

(see index for correct answer)

- a. Sampension
- b. Admiral Administration
- c. Davidson Kempner Capital Management
- d. Gracy Title Company

Guidance: level 1

:: Financial ratios ::

_____ is a measure of how revenue growth translates into growth in operating income. It is a measure of leverage, and of how risky, or volatile, a company's operating income is.

Exam Probability: **Medium**

4. *Answer choices:*

(see index for correct answer)

- a. Diluted earnings per share
- b. Return on net assets
- c. Debt-to-capital ratio
- d. Operating leverage

Guidance: level 1

:: Financial markets ::

A _____ is a market in which people trade financial securities and derivatives such as futures and options at low transaction costs. Securities include stocks and bonds, and precious metals.

Exam Probability: **Medium**

5. *Answer choices:*

(see index for correct answer)

- a. Electronic trade matching
- b. Forward market
- c. Financial market
- d. Future Trading Act

Guidance: level 1

:: International trade ::

In finance, an _____ is the rate at which one currency will be exchanged for another. It is also regarded as the value of one country's currency in relation to another currency. For example, an interbank _____ of 114 Japanese yen to the United States dollar means that ¥114 will be exchanged for each US$1 or that US$1 will be exchanged for each ¥114. In this case it is said that the price of a dollar in relation to yen is ¥114, or equivalently that the price of a yen in relation to dollars is $1/114.

Exam Probability: **Low**

6. Answer choices:

(see index for correct answer)

- a. Banana Framework Agreement
- b. Trade finance
- c. Exchange rate
- d. Omnibus Foreign Trade and Competitiveness Act

Guidance: level 1

:: Business law ::

A _____ is an arrangement where parties, known as partners, agree to cooperate to advance their mutual interests. The partners in a _____ may be individuals, businesses, interest-based organizations, schools, governments or combinations. Organizations may partner to increase the likelihood of each achieving their mission and to amplify their reach. A _____ may result in issuing and holding equity or may be only governed by a contract.

Exam Probability: **Medium**

7. Answer choices:

(see index for correct answer)

- a. United Kingdom commercial law
- b. Fraud deterrence
- c. Chattel mortgage
- d. Negotiable instrument

Guidance: level 1

:: ::

_____ is the collection of mechanisms, processes and relations by which corporations are controlled and operated. Governance structures and principles identify the distribution of rights and responsibilities among different participants in the corporation and include the rules and procedures for making decisions in corporate affairs. _____ is necessary because of the possibility of conflicts of interests between stakeholders, primarily between shareholders and upper management or among shareholders.

Exam Probability: **Low**

8. *Answer choices:*

(see index for correct answer)

- a. imperative
- b. hierarchical perspective
- c. open system
- d. personal values

Guidance: level 1

:: Financial ratios ::

The _____ is a liquidity ratio that measures whether a firm has enough resources to meet its short-term obligations. It compares a firm's current assets to its current liabilities, and is expressed as follows.

Exam Probability: **Low**

9. *Answer choices:*

(see index for correct answer)

- a. Return of capital
- b. efficiency ratio
- c. Like for like
- d. Profit margin

Guidance: level 1

:: Loans ::

In finance, a _____ is the lending of money by one or more individuals, organizations, or other entities to other individuals, organizations etc. The recipient incurs a debt, and is usually liable to pay interest on that debt until it is repaid, and also to repay the principal amount borrowed.

Exam Probability: **Medium**

10. *Answer choices:*

(see index for correct answer)

- a. Interest-only loan
- b. Loan-to-value
- c. Loan
- d. Adjustable rate

Guidance: level 1

:: Financial crises ::

A _____ is any of a broad variety of situations in which some financial assets suddenly lose a large part of their nominal value. In the 19th and early 20th centuries, many financial crises were associated with banking panics, and many recessions coincided with these panics. Other situations that are often called financial crises include stock market crashes and the bursting of other financial bubbles, currency crises, and sovereign defaults. Financial crises directly result in a loss of paper wealth but do not necessarily result in significant changes in the real economy .

Exam Probability: **High**

11. *Answer choices:*

(see index for correct answer)

- a. Panic of 1792
- b. United Copper
- c. Financial crisis
- d. Panic of 1857

Guidance: level 1

:: Generally Accepted Accounting Principles ::

The first published description of the process is found in Luca Pacioli's 1494 work Summa de arithmetica, in the section titled Particularis de Computis et Scripturis. Although he did not use the term, he essentially prescribed a technique similar to a post-closing _____ .

Exam Probability: **Medium**

12. *Answer choices:*

(see index for correct answer)

- a. Paid in capital
- b. Write-off
- c. Fin 48
- d. Trial balance

Guidance: level 1

:: Real estate ::

Amortisation is paying off an amount owed over time by making planned, incremental payments of principal and interest. To amortise a loan means "to kill it off". In accounting, amortisation refers to charging or writing off an intangible asset's cost as an operational expense over its estimated useful life to reduce a company's taxable income.

Exam Probability: **Medium**

13. *Answer choices:*

(see index for correct answer)

- a. Ground rent
- b. Cadastral community
- c. Amortization
- d. Apartment

Guidance: level 1

:: Mereology ::

_____, in the abstract, is what belongs to or with something, whether as an attribute or as a component of said thing. In the context of this article, it is one or more components, whether physical or incorporeal, of a person's estate; or so belonging to, as in being owned by, a person or jointly a group of people or a legal entity like a corporation or even a society. Depending on the nature of the _____, an owner of _____ has the right to consume, alter, share, redefine, rent, mortgage, pawn, sell, exchange, transfer, give away or destroy it, or to exclude others from doing these things, as well as to perhaps abandon it; whereas regardless of the nature of the _____, the owner thereof has the right to properly use it, or at the very least exclusively keep it.

Exam Probability: **Low**

14. *Answer choices:*

(see index for correct answer)

- a. Property
- b. Mereology
- c. Simple
- d. Mereotopology

Guidance: level 1

:: Public finance ::

_____ is the process by which the monetary authority of a country, typically the central bank or currency board, controls either the cost of very short-term borrowing or the money supply, often targeting inflation rate or interest rate to ensure price stability and general trust in the currency.

Exam Probability: **Low**

15. *Answer choices:*

(see index for correct answer)

- a. Contingencies fund
- b. California Municipal Treasurers Association
- c. Budget freeze
- d. Barnett formula

Guidance: level 1

:: Financial markets ::

A _____ is a financial market in which long-term debt or equity-backed securities are bought and sold. _____ s channel the wealth of savers to those who can put it to long-term productive use, such as companies or governments making long-term investments. Financial regulators like the Bank of England and the U.S. Securities and Exchange Commission oversee _____ s to protect investors against fraud, among other duties.

Exam Probability: **High**

16. *Answer choices:*

(see index for correct answer)

- a. Capital market
- b. Price-weighted index
- c. TradersStudio
- d. Portfolios with Purpose

Guidance: level 1

:: Accounting terminology ::

A _____ contains all the accounts for recording transactions relating to a company's assets, liabilities, owners' equity, revenue, and expenses. In modern accounting software or ERP, the _____ works as a central repository for accounting data transferred from all subledgers or modules like accounts payable, accounts receivable, cash management, fixed assets, purchasing and projects. The _____ is the backbone of any accounting system which holds financial and non-financial data for an organization. The collection of all accounts is known as the _____ . Each account is known as a ledger account. In a manual or non-computerized system this may be a large book. The statement of financial position and the statement of income and comprehensive income are both derived from the _____ . Each account in the _____ consists of one or more pages. The _____ is where posting to the accounts occurs. Posting is the process of recording amounts as credits , and amounts as debits , in the pages of the _____ . Additional columns to the right hold a running activity total .

Exam Probability: **High**

17. Answer choices:

(see index for correct answer)

- a. General ledger
- b. profit and loss statement
- c. outstanding balance
- d. Fund accounting

Guidance: level 1

:: ::

A _____ is an individual or institution that legally owns one or more shares of stock in a public or private corporation. _____ s may be referred to as members of a corporation. Legally, a person is not a _____ in a corporation until their name and other details are entered in the corporation's register of _____ s or members.

Exam Probability: **Low**

18. Answer choices:

(see index for correct answer)

- a. information systems assessment
- b. Shareholder
- c. hierarchical perspective
- d. interpersonal communication

Guidance: level 1

:: Personal finance ::

_____ is income not spent, or deferred consumption. Methods of _____ include putting money aside in, for example, a deposit account, a pension account, an investment fund, or as cash. _____ also involves reducing expenditures, such as recurring costs. In terms of personal finance, _____ generally specifies low-risk preservation of money, as in a deposit account, versus investment, wherein risk is a lot higher; in economics more broadly, it refers to any income not used for immediate consumption.

Exam Probability: **Medium**

19. *Answer choices:*

(see index for correct answer)

- a. Financial gerontology
- b. Income protection insurance
- c. Financial infidelity
- d. Saving

Guidance: level 1

:: Accounting systems ::

In bookkeeping, a _____ statement is a process that explains the difference on a specified date between the bank balance shown in an organization's bank statement, as supplied by the bank and the corresponding amount shown in the organization's own accounting records.

Exam Probability: **Medium**

20. *Answer choices:*

(see index for correct answer)

- a. Counting house
- b. control account
- c. Inflation accounting
- d. Unified ledger accounting

Guidance: level 1

:: Elementary geometry ::

The _____ is the front of an animal's head that features three of the head's sense organs, the eyes, nose, and mouth, and through which animals express many of their emotions. The _____ is crucial for human identity, and damage such as scarring or developmental deformities affects the psyche adversely.

Exam Probability: **Medium**

21. *Answer choices:*

(see index for correct answer)

- a. Line segment
- b. Transversal
- c. Sphere
- d. Hinge theorem

Guidance: level 1

:: Income ::

_____ is a ratio between the net profit and cost of investment resulting from an investment of some resources. A high ROI means the investment's gains favorably to its cost. As a performance measure, ROI is used to evaluate the efficiency of an investment or to compare the efficiencies of several different investments. In purely economic terms, it is one way of relating profits to capital invested. _____ is a performance measure used by businesses to identify the efficiency of an investment or number of different investments.

Exam Probability: **Low**

22. *Answer choices:*

(see index for correct answer)

- a. Pay grade
- b. Signing bonus

- c. Aggregate expenditure
- d. Implied level of government service

Guidance: level 1

:: Investment ::

_____ , and investment appraisal, is the planning process used to determine whether an organization's long term investments such as new machinery, replacement of machinery, new plants, new products, and research development projects are worth the funding of cash through the firm's capitalization structure . It is the process of allocating resources for major capital, or investment, expenditures. One of the primary goals of _____ investments is to increase the value of the firm to the shareholders.

Exam Probability: **Low**

23. *Answer choices:*

(see index for correct answer)

- a. Traditional investments
- b. Tax transparent fund
- c. Qirad
- d. Capital budgeting

Guidance: level 1

:: Portfolio theories ::

In finance, the _____ is a model used to determine a theoretically appropriate required rate of return of an asset, to make decisions about adding assets to a well-diversified portfolio.

Exam Probability: **Low**

24. *Answer choices:*

(see index for correct answer)

- a. Post-modern portfolio theory
- b. Tail risk parity
- c. Maslowian portfolio theory
- d. Intertemporal portfolio choice

Guidance: level 1

:: Investment ::

In finance, the benefit from an _____ is called a return. The return may consist of a gain realised from the sale of property or an _____, unrealised capital appreciation, or _____ income such as dividends, interest, rental income etc., or a combination of capital gain and income. The return may also include currency gains or losses due to changes in foreign currency exchange rates.

Exam Probability: **Low**

25. *Answer choices:*

(see index for correct answer)

- a. China International Fair for Investment and Trade
- b. Value premium
- c. Investment advisory
- d. Investment

Guidance: level 1

:: Generally Accepted Accounting Principles ::

In accounting, an economic item's _____ is the original nominal monetary value of that item. _____ accounting involves reporting assets and liabilities at their _____ s, which are not updated for changes in the items' values. Consequently, the amounts reported for these balance sheet items often differ from their current economic or market values.

Exam Probability: **Low**

26. *Answer choices:*

(see index for correct answer)

- a. Deferred income
- b. Paid in capital

- c. Completed-contract method
- d. Historical cost

Guidance: level 1

:: Business ethics ::

In accounting and in most Schools of economic thought, _____ is a rational and unbiased estimate of the potential market price of a good, service, or asset. It takes into account such objectivity factors as.

Exam Probability: **Medium**

27. *Answer choices:*
(see index for correct answer)

- a. Corruption of Foreign Public Officials Act
- b. Fair value
- c. Corporate crime
- d. Ethical consumerism

Guidance: level 1

:: Banking ::

_____ refers to a broad area of finance involving the collection, handling, and usage of cash. It involves assessing market liquidity, cash flow, and investments.

Exam Probability: **High**

28. *Answer choices:*

(see index for correct answer)

- a. Fiscal agent
- b. Cash management
- c. Foreign currency account
- d. Anonymous Internet banking

Guidance: level 1

:: Financial risk ::

_____ is any of various types of risk associated with financing, including financial transactions that include company loans in risk of default. Often it is understood to include only downside risk, meaning the potential for financial loss and uncertainty about its extent.

Exam Probability: **High**

29. *Answer choices:*

(see index for correct answer)

- a. Market portfolio
- b. Risk neutral
- c. Financial risk
- d. Spectral risk measure

Guidance: level 1

:: Funds ::

_____ value is the value of an entity's assets minus the value of its liabilities, often in relation to open-end or mutual funds, since shares of such funds registered with the U.S. Securities and Exchange Commission are redeemed at their _____ value. It is also a key figure with regard to hedge funds and venture capital funds when calculating the value of the underlying investments in these funds by investors. This may also be the same as the book value or the equity value of a business. _____ value may represent the value of the total equity, or it may be divided by the number of shares outstanding held by investors, thereby representing the _____ value per share.

Exam Probability: **Low**

30. *Answer choices:*

(see index for correct answer)

- a. Net asset
- b. The Watch Fund
- c. Partnership for New York City

- d. Gross asset value

Guidance: level 1

:: ::

The _____ is a private, non-profit organization standard-setting body whose primary purpose is to establish and improve Generally Accepted Accounting Principles within the United States in the public's interest. The Securities and Exchange Commission designated the FASB as the organization responsible for setting accounting standards for public companies in the US. The FASB replaced the American Institute of Certified Public Accountants' Accounting Principles Board on July 1, 1973.

Exam Probability: **Medium**

31. *Answer choices:*

(see index for correct answer)

- a. co-culture
- b. imperative
- c. process perspective
- d. Character

Guidance: level 1

:: Basel II ::

A _____ is the risk of default on a debt that may arise from a borrower failing to make required payments. In the first resort, the risk is that of the lender and includes lost principal and interest, disruption to cash flows, and increased collection costs. The loss may be complete or partial. In an efficient market, higher levels of _____ will be associated with higher borrowing costs. Because of this, measures of borrowing costs such as yield spreads can be used to infer _____ levels based on assessments by market participants.

Exam Probability: **High**

32. *Answer choices:*
(see index for correct answer)

- a. Basic indicator approach
- b. Basel II
- c. Market risk
- d. Legal risk

Guidance: level 1

:: Bonds (finance) ::

A _____ is a fund established by an economic entity by setting aside revenue over a period of time to fund a future capital expense, or repayment of a long-term debt.

Exam Probability: **Medium**

33. Answer choices:

(see index for correct answer)

- a. Zero-coupon bond
- b. Sinking fund
- c. Global bond
- d. Securities Industry and Financial Markets Association

Guidance: level 1

:: ::

_____ , often abbreviated as B/E in finance, is the point of balance making neither a profit nor a loss. The term originates in finance but the concept has been applied in other fields.

Exam Probability: **Medium**

34. Answer choices:

(see index for correct answer)

- a. information systems assessment
- b. deep-level diversity
- c. imperative
- d. Break-even

Guidance: level 1

:: Fixed income market ::

The _____ is a financial market where participants can issue new debt, known as the primary market, or buy and sell debt securities, known as the secondary market. This is usually in the form of bonds, but it may include notes, bills, and so on.

Exam Probability: **Low**

35. *Answer choices:*
(see index for correct answer)

- a. Fixed-income attribution
- b. Inter-dealer broker
- c. Bond market
- d. Yield curve

Guidance: level 1

:: Generally Accepted Accounting Principles ::

The _____ principle is a cornerstone of accrual accounting together with the matching principle. They both determine the accounting period in which revenues and expenses are recognized. According to the principle, revenues are recognized when they are realized or realizable, and are earned, no matter when cash is received. In cash accounting – in contrast – revenues are recognized when cash is received no matter when goods or services are sold.

Exam Probability: **Medium**

36. *Answer choices:*

(see index for correct answer)

- a. Statement of recommended practice
- b. Expense
- c. Fin 48
- d. Closing entries

Guidance: level 1

:: ::

A _____ is any person who contracts to acquire an asset in return for some form of consideration.

Exam Probability: **High**

37. *Answer choices:*

(see index for correct answer)

- a. imperative
- b. cultural
- c. corporate values
- d. Buyer

Guidance: level 1

:: Generally Accepted Accounting Principles ::

_____ is the accounting classification of an account. It is part of double-entry book-keeping technique.

Exam Probability: **High**

38. *Answer choices:*

(see index for correct answer)

- a. Generally accepted accounting principles
- b. Revenue recognition
- c. Normal balance
- d. Income statement

Guidance: level 1

:: Accounting terminology ::

In management accounting or _____ , managers use the provisions of accounting information in order to better inform themselves before they decide matters within their organizations, which aids their management and performance of control functions.

Exam Probability: **High**

39. *Answer choices:*

(see index for correct answer)

- a. Record to report
- b. Fair value accounting
- c. Managerial accounting
- d. Statement of financial position

Guidance: level 1

:: Financial markets ::

The _____ is the part of the capital market that deals with the issuance and sale of equity-backed securities to investors directly by the issuer. Investor buy securities that were never traded before. _____ s create long term instruments through which corporate entities raise funds from the capital market. It is also known as the New Issue Market .

Exam Probability: **Medium**

40. *Answer choices:*

(see index for correct answer)

- a. TradersStudio
- b. Primary market
- c. Clearing
- d. Broker-dealer

Guidance: level 1

:: Costs ::

The _____ is computed by dividing the total cost of goods available for sale by the total units available for sale. This gives a weighted-average unit cost that is applied to the units in the ending inventory.

Exam Probability: **Medium**

41. *Answer choices:*

(see index for correct answer)

- a. Opportunity cost of capital
- b. Cost competitiveness of fuel sources
- c. Average Cost
- d. Road Logistics Costing in South Africa

Guidance: level 1

:: Accounting terminology ::

_____ or capital expense is the money a company spends to buy, maintain, or improve its fixed assets, such as buildings, vehicles, equipment, or land. It is considered a _____ when the asset is newly purchased or when money is used towards extending the useful life of an existing asset, such as repairing the roof.

Exam Probability: **Low**

42. *Answer choices:*

(see index for correct answer)

- a. double-entry bookkeeping
- b. Capital expenditure
- c. Accrual
- d. Adjusting entries

Guidance: level 1

:: Accounting terminology ::

_____ of something is, in finance, the adding together of interest or different investments over a period of time. It holds specific meanings in accounting, where it can refer to accounts on a balance sheet that represent liabilities and non-cash-based assets used in _____-based accounting. These types of accounts include, among others, accounts payable, accounts receivable, goodwill, deferred tax liability and future interest expense.

Exam Probability: **Medium**

43. *Answer choices:*

(see index for correct answer)

- a. profit and loss statement
- b. Accounting equation
- c. double-entry bookkeeping
- d. Accrual

Guidance: level 1

:: International Financial Reporting Standards ::

_____ , usually called IFRS, are standards issued by the IFRS Foundation and the International Accounting Standards Board to provide a common global language for business affairs so that company accounts are understandable and comparable across international boundaries. They are a consequence of growing international shareholding and trade and are particularly important for companies that have dealings in several countries. They are progressively replacing the many different national accounting standards. They are the rules to be followed by accountants to maintain books of accounts which are comparable, understandable, reliable and relevant as per the users internal or external. IFRS, with the exception of IAS 29 Financial Reporting in Hyperinflationary Economies and IFRIC 7 Applying the Restatement Approach under IAS 29, are authorized in terms of the historical cost paradigm. IAS 29 and IFRIC 7 are authorized in terms of the units of constant purchasing power paradigm.IAS 2 is related to inventories in this standard we talk about the stock its production process etcIFRS began as an attempt to harmonize accounting across the European Union but the value of harmonization quickly made the concept attractive around the world. However, it has been debated whether or not de facto harmonization has occurred. Standards that were issued by IASC are still within use today and go by the name International Accounting Standards , while standards issued by IASB are called IFRS. IAS were issued between 1973 and 2001 by the Board of the International Accounting Standards Committee . On 1 April 2001, the new International Accounting Standards Board took over from the IASC the responsibility for setting International Accounting Standards. During its first meeting the new Board adopted existing IAS and Standing Interpretations Committee standards . The IASB has continued to develop standards calling the new standards " _____ ".

Exam Probability: **Medium**

44. *Answer choices:*

(see index for correct answer)

- a. International Financial Reporting Standards
- b. IAS 2
- c. IAS 1

- d. IFRS 1

Guidance: level 1

:: ::

A _____, in the word's original meaning, is a sheet of paper on which one performs work. They come in many forms, most commonly associated with children's school work assignments, tax forms, and accounting or other business environments. Software is increasingly taking over the paper-based _____.

Exam Probability: **Medium**

45. *Answer choices:*

(see index for correct answer)

- a. open system
- b. interpersonal communication
- c. functional perspective
- d. deep-level diversity

Guidance: level 1

:: Taxation ::

In a tax system, the _____ is the ratio at which a business or person is taxed. There are several methods used to present a _____: statutory, average, marginal, and effective. These rates can also be presented using different definitions applied to a tax base: inclusive and exclusive.

Exam Probability: **Medium**

46. *Answer choices:*

(see index for correct answer)

- a. African Tax Administration Forum
- b. Tax rate
- c. Voluntary taxation
- d. Privilege tax

Guidance: level 1

:: Business economics ::

In finance, _____ is the risk of losses caused by interest rate changes. The prices of most financial instruments, such as stocks and bonds move inversely with interest rates, so investors are subject to capital loss when rates rise.

Exam Probability: **Medium**

47. *Answer choices:*

(see index for correct answer)

- a. Rate risk
- b. Trade name
- c. Willingness to accept
- d. Kaizen costing

Guidance: level 1

:: Asset ::

_____s, also known as tangible assets or property, plant and equipment, is a term used in accounting for assets and property that cannot easily be converted into cash. This can be compared with current assets such as cash or bank accounts, described as liquid assets. In most cases, only tangible assets are referred to as fixed. IAS 16 defines _____ s as assets whose future economic benefit is probable to flow into the entity, whose cost can be measured reliably. _____ s belong to one of 2 types:"Freehold Assets" – assets which are purchased with legal right of ownership and used,and "Leasehold Assets" – assets used by owner without legal right for a particular period of time.

Exam Probability: **High**

48. *Answer choices:*

(see index for correct answer)

- a. Asset
- b. Fixed asset

Guidance: level 1

:: Business law ::

A _____ is a group of people who jointly supervise the activities of an organization, which can be either a for-profit business, nonprofit organization, or a government agency. Such a board's powers, duties, and responsibilities are determined by government regulations and the organization's own constitution and bylaws. These authorities may specify the number of members of the board, how they are to be chosen, and how often they are to meet.

Exam Probability: **Low**

49. *Answer choices:*

(see index for correct answer)

- a. Board of directors
- b. Contract A
- c. Independent contractor
- d. United States labor law

Guidance: level 1

:: Generally Accepted Accounting Principles ::

A _____, in accrual accounting, is any account where the asset or liability is not realized until a future date, e.g. annuities, charges, taxes, income, etc. The deferred item may be carried, dependent on type of _____, as either an asset or liability. See also accrual.

Exam Probability: **Medium**

50. *Answer choices:*

(see index for correct answer)

- a. net realisable value
- b. Deferral
- c. Matching principle
- d. Engagement letter

Guidance: level 1

:: Basic financial concepts ::

_____ is a sustained increase in the general price level of goods and services in an economy over a period of time. When the general price level rises, each unit of currency buys fewer goods and services; consequently, _____ reflects a reduction in the purchasing power per unit of money a loss of real value in the medium of exchange and unit of account within the economy. The measure of _____ is the _____ rate, the annualized percentage change in a general price index, usually the consumer price index, over time. The opposite of _____ is deflation.

Exam Probability: **Medium**

51. *Answer choices:*

(see index for correct answer)

- a. Leverage cycle
- b. Maturity
- c. Deflation
- d. Inflation

Guidance: level 1

:: Margin policy ::

In finance, a _____ is a standardized forward contract, a legal agreement to buy or sell something at a predetermined price at a specified time in the future, between parties not known to each other. The asset transacted is usually a commodity or financial instrument. The predetermined price the parties agree to buy and sell the asset for is known as the forward price. The specified time in the future—which is when delivery and payment occur—is known as the delivery date. Because it is a function of an underlying asset, a _____ is a derivative product.

Exam Probability: **High**

52. *Answer choices:*

(see index for correct answer)

- a. Futures contract
- b. Regulation T

Guidance: level 1

:: Budgets ::

A _____ is a financial plan for a defined period, often one year. It may also include planned sales volumes and revenues, resource quantities, costs and expenses, assets, liabilities and cash flows. Companies, governments, families and other organizations use it to express strategic plans of activities or events in measurable terms.

Exam Probability: **Low**

53. *Answer choices:*

(see index for correct answer)

- a. Budget
- b. Participatory budgeting
- c. Zero-based budgeting
- d. Marginal budgeting for bottlenecks

Guidance: level 1

:: Government bonds ::

A _____, commonly known as a Muni Bond, is a bond issued by a local government or territory, or one of their agencies. It is generally used to finance public projects such as roads, schools, airports and seaports, and infrastructure-related repairs. The term _____ is commonly used in the United States, which has the largest market of such trade-able securities in the world. As of 2011, the _____ market was valued at $3.7 trillion. Potential issuers of _____ s include states, cities, counties, redevelopment agencies, special-purpose districts, school districts, public utility districts, publicly owned airports and seaports, and other governmental entities at or below the state level having more than a de minimis amount of one of the three sovereign powers: the power of taxation, the power of eminent domain or the police power.

Exam Probability: **Low**

54. *Answer choices:*

(see index for correct answer)

- a. Risk-free bond
- b. Bond vigilante
- c. Sovereign bond
- d. Gilt-edged securities

Guidance: level 1

_____ is a costing method that identifies activities in an organization and assigns the cost of each activity to all products and services according to the actual consumption by each. This model assigns more indirect costs into direct costs compared to conventional costing.

Exam Probability: **Medium**

55. *Answer choices:*

(see index for correct answer)

- a. imperative
- b. levels of analysis
- c. Character
- d. Activity-based costing

Guidance: level 1

:: Expense ::

_____ relates to the cost of borrowing money. It is the price that a lender charges a borrower for the use of the lender's money. On the income statement, _____ can represent the cost of borrowing money from banks, bond investors, and other sources. _____ is different from operating expense and CAPEX, for it relates to the capital structure of a company, and it is usually tax-deductible.

Exam Probability: **Medium**

56. *Answer choices:*

(see index for correct answer)

- a. Business overhead expense disability insurance
- b. Momentem
- c. Operating expense
- d. Interest expense

Guidance: level 1

:: Financial accounting ::

_____ in accounting is the process of treating investments in associate companies. Equity accounting is usually applied where an investor entity holds 20–50% of the voting stock of the associate company. The investor records such investments as an asset on its balance sheet. The investor's proportional share of the associate company's net income increases the investment, and proportional payments of dividends decrease it. In the investor's income statement, the proportional share of the investor's net income or net loss is reported as a single-line item.

Exam Probability: **High**

57. *Answer choices:*

(see index for correct answer)

- a. Certified Public Accountants Association
- b. Equity method

- c. Accounting identity
- d. Exit rate

Guidance: level 1

:: Accounting source documents ::

A _____ or account statement is a summary of financial transactions which have occurred over a given period on a bank account held by a person or business with a financial institution.

Exam Probability: **High**

58. *Answer choices:*
(see index for correct answer)

- a. Air waybill
- b. Credit memorandum
- c. Invoice
- d. Banknote

Guidance: level 1

:: Generally Accepted Accounting Principles ::

_____ is a small amount of discretionary funds in the form of cash used for expenditures where it is not sensible to make any disbursement by cheque, because of the inconvenience and costs of writing, signing, and then cashing the cheque.

Exam Probability: **High**

59. *Answer choices:*

(see index for correct answer)

- a. Revenue recognition
- b. Gross sales
- c. Petty cash
- d. Deferred income

Guidance: level 1

Human resource management

Human resource (HR) management is the strategic approach to the effective management of organization workers so that they help the business gain a competitive advantage. It is designed to maximize employee performance in service of an employer's strategic objectives. HR is primarily concerned with the management of people within organizations, focusing on policies and on systems. HR departments are responsible for overseeing employee-benefits design, employee recruitment, training and development, performance appraisal, and rewarding (e.g., managing pay and benefit systems). HR also concerns itself with organizational change and industrial relations, that is, the balancing of organizational practices with requirements arising from collective bargaining and from governmental laws.

A _____ is a technical analysis of a biological specimen, for example urine, hair, blood, breath, sweat, and/or oral fluid/saliva—to determine the presence or absence of specified parent drugs or their metabolites. Major applications of _____ ing include detection of the presence of performance enhancing steroids in sport, employers and parole/probation officers screening for drugs prohibited by law and police officers testing for the presence and concentration of alcohol in the blood commonly referred to as BAC. BAC tests are typically administered via a breathalyzer while urinalysis is used for the vast majority of _____ ing in sports and the workplace. Numerous other methods with varying degrees of accuracy, sensitivity, and detection periods exist.

Exam Probability: **High**

1. *Answer choices:*

(see index for correct answer)

- a. deep-level diversity
- b. open system
- c. interpersonal communication
- d. Drug test

Guidance: level 1

:: Management ::

_____ or executive pay is composed of the financial compensation and other non-financial awards received by an executive from their firm for their service to the organization. It is typically a mixture of salary, bonuses, shares of or call options on the company stock, benefits, and perquisites, ideally configured to take into account government regulations, tax law, the desires of the organization and the executive, and rewards for performance.

Exam Probability: **Low**

2. *Answer choices:*

(see index for correct answer)

- a. Executive compensation
- b. Toxic leader
- c. Swarm Development Group
- d. PhD in management

Guidance: level 1

:: Cognitive biases ::

The _____ is a type of immediate judgement discrepancy, or cognitive bias, where a person making an initial assessment of another person, place, or thing will assume ambiguous information based upon concrete information. A simplified example of the _____ is when an individual noticing that the person in the photograph is attractive, well groomed, and properly attired, assumes, using a mental heuristic, that the person in the photograph is a good person based upon the rules of that individual's social concept. This constant error in judgment is reflective of the individual's preferences, prejudices, ideology, aspirations, and social perception. The _____ is an evaluation by an individual and can affect the perception of a decision, action, idea, business, person, group, entity, or other whenever concrete data is generalized or influences ambiguous information.

Exam Probability: **High**

3. *Answer choices:*
(see index for correct answer)

- a. Certainty effect
- b. Just-world hypothesis
- c. Illusory truth effect
- d. Halo effect

Guidance: level 1

:: Educational assessment and evaluation ::

An _____ is a component of a competence to do a certain kind of work at a certain level. Outstanding _____ can be considered "talent". An _____ may be physical or mental. _____ is inborn potential to do certain kinds of work whether developed or undeveloped. Ability is developed knowledge, understanding, learned or acquired abilities or attitude. The innate nature of _____ is in contrast to skills and achievement, which represent knowledge or ability that is gained through learning.

Exam Probability: **Medium**

4. *Answer choices:*

(see index for correct answer)

- a. Naglieri Nonverbal Ability Test
- b. Aptitude
- c. Standardized test
- d. Spelling test

Guidance: level 1

:: Organizational behavior ::

_____ is the act of matching attitudes, beliefs, and behaviors to group norms or politics. Norms are implicit, specific rules, shared by a group of individuals, that guide their interactions with others. People often choose to conform to society rather than to pursue personal desires because it is often easier to follow the path others have made already, rather than creating a new one. This tendency to conform occurs in small groups and/or society as a whole, and may result from subtle unconscious influences, or direct and overt social pressure. _____ can occur in the presence of others, or when an individual is alone. For example, people tend to follow social norms when eating or watching television, even when alone.

Exam Probability: **Low**

5. *Answer choices:*
(see index for correct answer)

- a. Organizational retaliatory behavior
- b. Informal organization
- c. Conformity
- d. Organizational citizenship behavior

Guidance: level 1

:: Recruitment ::

_____ is a specialized recruitment service which organizations pay to seek out and recruit highly qualified candidates for senior-level and executive jobs. Headhunters may also seek out and recruit other highly specialized and/or skilled positions in organizations for which there is strong competition in the job market for the top talent, such as senior data analysts or computer programmers. The method usually involves commissioning a third-party organization, typically an _____ firm, but possibly a standalone consultant or consulting firm, to research the availability of suitable qualified candidates working for competitors or related businesses or organizations. Having identified a shortlist of qualified candidates who match the client's requirements, the _____ firm may act as an intermediary to contact the individual and see if they might be interested in moving to a new employer. The _____ firm may also carry out initial screening of the candidate, negotiations on remuneration and benefits, and preparing the employment contract. In some markets there has been a move towards using _____ for lower positions driven by the fact that there are less candidates for some positions even on lower levels than executive.

Exam Probability: **Low**

6. *Answer choices:*

(see index for correct answer)

- a. Curriculum vitae
- b. Executive search
- c. Mobile recruiting
- d. S.I.R. Method of Recruiting

Guidance: level 1

:: Systems thinking ::

In business management, a _____ is a company that facilitates the learning of its members and continuously transforms itself. The concept was coined through the work and research of Peter Senge and his colleagues.

Exam Probability: **Low**

7. *Answer choices:*

(see index for correct answer)

- a. Club of Rome
- b. Thought leader
- c. The Energy and Resources Institute
- d. Learning organization

Guidance: level 1

:: Labor rights ::

A _____ is a wrong or hardship suffered, real or supposed, which forms legitimate grounds of complaint. In the past, the word meant the infliction or cause of hardship.

Exam Probability: **High**

8. *Answer choices:*

(see index for correct answer)

- a. Kate Mullany House
- b. Kim Bobo
- c. Labor rights
- d. Swift raids

Guidance: level 1

:: Labor ::

_____ refers to the process of grouping activities into departments. Division of labour creates specialists who need coordination. This coordination is facilitated by grouping specialists together in departments.

Exam Probability: **Medium**

9. *Answer choices:*

(see index for correct answer)

- a. Departmentalization
- b. Job creep
- c. Labour movement
- d. Affective labor

Guidance: level 1

:: Asset ::

In financial accounting, an _____ is any resource owned by the business. Anything tangible or intangible that can be owned or controlled to produce value and that is held by a company to produce positive economic value is an _____ . Simply stated, _____ s represent value of ownership that can be converted into cash . The balance sheet of a firm records the monetary value of the _____ s owned by that firm. It covers money and other valuables belonging to an individual or to a business.

Exam Probability: **High**

10. *Answer choices:*

(see index for correct answer)

- a. Current asset
- b. Asset

Guidance: level 1

:: Labor ::

The workforce or labour force is the labour pool in employment. It is generally used to describe those working for a single company or industry, but can also apply to a geographic region like a city, state, or country. Within a company, its value can be labelled as its "Workforce in Place". The workforce of a country includes both the employed and the unemployed. The labour force participation rate, LFPR , is the ratio between the labour force and the overall size of their cohort . The term generally excludes the employers or management, and can imply those involved in manual labour. It may also mean all those who are available for work.

Exam Probability: **Low**

11. *Answer choices:*

(see index for correct answer)

- a. Deskilling
- b. Labor force
- c. Quality of working life
- d. Anti-capitalism

Guidance: level 1

:: ::

Refresher/ _____ is the process of learning a new or the same old skill or trade for the same group of personnel. Refresher/ _____ is required to be provided on regular basis to avoid personnel obsolescence due to technological changes & the individuals memory capacity. This short term instruction course shall serve to re-acquaint personnel with skills previously learnt or to bring one's knowledge or skills up-to-date so that skills stay sharp. This kind of training could be provided annually or more frequently as maybe required, based on the importance of consistency of the task of which the skill is involved. Examples of refreshers are cGMP, GDP, HSE trainings. _____ shall also be conducted for an employee, when the employee is rated as 'not qualified' for a skill or knowledge, as determined based on the assessment of answers in the training questionnaire of the employee.

Exam Probability: **Medium**

12. Answer choices:

(see index for correct answer)

- a. Retraining
- b. corporate values
- c. hierarchical perspective
- d. imperative

Guidance: level 1

:: Human resource management ::

_____ are the people who make up the workforce of an organization, business sector, or economy. "Human capital" is sometimes used synonymously with " _____ ", although human capital typically refers to a narrower effect . Likewise, other terms sometimes used include manpower, talent, labor, personnel, or simply people.

Exam Probability: **Low**

13. Answer choices:

(see index for correct answer)

- a. Idea portal
- b. Human resources
- c. Training and development
- d. Perceived organizational support

Guidance: level 1

:: Labour law ::

In law, _____ is to give an immediately secured right of present or future deployment. One has a vested right to an asset that cannot be taken away by any third party, even though one may not yet possess the asset. When the right, interest, or title to the present or future possession of a legal estate can be transferred to any other party, it is termed a vested interest.

Exam Probability: **Medium**

14. *Answer choices:*
(see index for correct answer)

- a. Vesting
- b. Maximum medical improvement
- c. Bosman ruling
- d. Core Labor Standards

Guidance: level 1

:: Income ::

A _____ is a unit in systems of monetary compensation for employment. It is commonly used in public service, both civil and military, but also for companies of the private sector. _____s facilitate the employment process by providing a fixed framework of salary ranges, as opposed to a free negotiation. Typically, _____s encompass two dimensions: a "vertical" range where each level corresponds to the responsibility of, and requirements needed for a certain position; and a "horizontal" range within this scale to allow for monetary incentives rewarding the employee's quality of performance or length of service. Thus, an employee progresses within the horizontal and vertical ranges upon achieving positive appraisal on a regular basis. In most cases, evaluation is done annually and encompasses more than one method.

Exam Probability: **Low**

15. *Answer choices:*

(see index for correct answer)

- a. Aggregate income
- b. Pay grade
- c. Income Per User
- d. Return on investment

Guidance: level 1

:: Social psychology ::

_____ is a type of nonverbal communication in which physical behaviors, as opposed to words, are used to express or convey information. Such behavior includes facial expressions, body posture, gestures, eye movement, touch and the use of space. _____ exists in both animals and humans, but this article focuses on interpretations of human _____ . It is also known as kinesics.

Exam Probability: **Medium**

16. *Answer choices:*

(see index for correct answer)

- a. objectification
- b. sociometer
- c. brainwriting
- d. coercive persuasion

Guidance: level 1

:: ::

_____ is a labor union representing almost 1.9 million workers in over 100 occupations in the United States and Canada. SEIU is focused on organizing workers in three sectors: health care , including hospital, home care and nursing home workers; public services ; and property services .

Exam Probability: **Medium**

17. *Answer choices:*

(see index for correct answer)

- a. surface-level diversity
- b. cultural
- c. corporate values
- d. deep-level diversity

Guidance: level 1

:: ::

_____ is a form of government characterized by strong central power and limited political freedoms. Individual freedoms are subordinate to the state and there is no constitutional accountability and rule of law under an authoritarian regime. Authoritarian regimes can be autocratic with power concentrated in one person or it can be more spread out between multiple officials and government institutions. Juan Linz's influential 1964 description of _____ characterized authoritarian political systems by four qualities.

Exam Probability: **Low**

18. *Answer choices:*

(see index for correct answer)

- a. hierarchical
- b. Authoritarianism
- c. surface-level diversity

- d. open system

Guidance: level 1

:: Occupations ::

An _____ is a person who has a position of authority in a hierarchical organization. The term derives from the late Latin from officiarius, meaning "official".

Exam Probability: **High**

19. *Answer choices:*
(see index for correct answer)

- a. Officer
- b. Mixing engineer
- c. Sailmaker
- d. Carpentry

Guidance: level 1

:: Information systems ::

_____ is the process of creating, sharing, using and managing the knowledge and information of an organisation. It refers to a multidisciplinary approach to achieving organisational objectives by making the best use of knowledge.

Exam Probability: **Low**

20. *Answer choices:*

(see index for correct answer)

- a. Knowledge management
- b. Enhanced publication
- c. Validis
- d. UK Academy for Information Systems

Guidance: level 1

:: Behaviorism ::

In behavioral psychology, _____ is a consequence applied that will strengthen an organism's future behavior whenever that behavior is preceded by a specific antecedent stimulus. This strengthening effect may be measured as a higher frequency of behavior, longer duration, greater magnitude, or shorter latency. There are two types of _____, known as positive _____ and negative _____; positive is where by a reward is offered on expression of the wanted behaviour and negative is taking away an undesirable element in the persons environment whenever the desired behaviour is achieved.

Exam Probability: **Low**

21. *Answer choices:*

(see index for correct answer)

- a. Matching Law
- b. Reinforcement
- c. Systematic desensitization
- d. social facilitation

Guidance: level 1

:: ::

_____ consists of using generic or ad hoc methods in an orderly manner to find solutions to problems. Some of the problem-solving techniques developed and used in philosophy, artificial intelligence, computer science, engineering, mathematics, or medicine are related to mental problem-solving techniques studied in psychology.

Exam Probability: **Medium**

22. *Answer choices:*

(see index for correct answer)

- a. Sarbanes-Oxley act of 2002
- b. hierarchical

- c. open system
- d. Problem solving

Guidance: level 1

:: Organizational theory ::

_____ is the process of creating, retaining, and transferring knowledge within an organization. An organization improves over time as it gains experience. From this experience, it is able to create knowledge. This knowledge is broad, covering any topic that could better an organization. Examples may include ways to increase production efficiency or to develop beneficial investor relations. Knowledge is created at four different units: individual, group, organizational, and inter organizational.

Exam Probability: **Low**

23. *Answer choices:*

(see index for correct answer)

- a. Network-centric organization
- b. Organizational learning
- c. Staff augmentation
- d. Participatory organization

Guidance: level 1

:: Human resource management ::

_____ is the corporate management term for the act of reorganizing the legal, ownership, operational, or other structures of a company for the purpose of making it more profitable, or better organized for its present needs. Other reasons for _____ include a change of ownership or ownership structure, demerger, or a response to a crisis or major change in the business such as bankruptcy, repositioning, or buyout. _____ may also be described as corporate _____ , debt _____ and financial _____ .

Exam Probability: **High**

24. *Answer choices:*

(see index for correct answer)

- a. Workforce modeling
- b. Restructuring
- c. Employee value proposition
- d. Skill mix

Guidance: level 1

:: ::

An _____ is a period of work experience offered by an organization for a limited period of time. Once confined to medical graduates, the term is now used for a wide range of placements in businesses, non-profit organizations and government agencies. They are typically undertaken by students and graduates looking to gain relevant skills and experience in a particular field. Employers benefit from these placements because they often recruit employees from their best interns, who have known capabilities, thus saving time and money in the long run. _____ s are usually arranged by third-party organizations which recruit interns on behalf of industry groups. Rules vary from country to country about when interns should be regarded as employees. The system can be open to exploitation by unscrupulous employers.

Exam Probability: **High**

25. *Answer choices:*

(see index for correct answer)

- a. Internship
- b. cultural
- c. information systems assessment
- d. personal values

Guidance: level 1

:: Human resource management ::

_____ means increasing the scope of a job through extending the range of its job duties and responsibilities generally within the same level and periphery. _____ involves combining various activities at the same level in the organization and adding them to the existing job. It is also called the horizontal expansion of job activities. This contradicts the principles of specialisation and the division of labour whereby work is divided into small units, each of which is performed repetitively by an individual worker and the responsibilities are always clear. Some motivational theories suggest that the boredom and alienation caused by the division of labour can actually cause efficiency to fall. Thus, _____ seeks to motivate workers through reversing the process of specialisation. A typical approach might be to replace assembly lines with modular work; instead of an employee repeating the same step on each product, they perform several tasks on a single item. In order for employees to be provided with _____ they will need to be retrained in new fields to understand how each field works.

Exam Probability: **Medium**

26. *Answer choices:*

(see index for correct answer)

- a. Administrative services organization
- b. Skills management
- c. war for talent
- d. Employee silence

Guidance: level 1

:: Production and manufacturing ::

_____ is a theory of management that analyzes and synthesizes workflows. Its main objective is improving economic efficiency, especially labor productivity. It was one of the earliest attempts to apply science to the engineering of processes and to management. _____ is sometimes known as Taylorism after its founder, Frederick Winslow Taylor.

Exam Probability: **Medium**

27. *Answer choices:*

(see index for correct answer)

- a. Enterprise control
- b. Master production schedule
- c. Industrial engineering
- d. Scientific management

Guidance: level 1

:: Unemployment ::

The _____ is the negative relationship between the levels of unemployment and wages that arises when these variables are expressed in local terms. According to David Blanchflower and Andrew Oswald, the _____ summarizes the fact that "A worker who is employed in an area of high unemployment earns less than an identical individual who works in a region with low joblessness."

Exam Probability: **Low**

28. *Answer choices:*

(see index for correct answer)

- a. Wage curve
- b. Structural unemployment
- c. Youth unemployment
- d. Growth recession

Guidance: level 1

:: Foreign workers ::

> A _____ or guest worker is a human who works in a country other than the one of which he or she is a citizen. Some _____s are using a guest worker program in a country with more preferred job prospects than their home country. Guest workers are often either sent or invited to work outside their home country, or have acquired a job before they left their home country, whereas migrant workers often leave their home country without having a specific job at hand.

Exam Probability: **Medium**

29. *Answer choices:*

(see index for correct answer)

- a. Kalayaan
- b. Migrant domestic workers
- c. Foreign worker

- d. Ten Pound Poms

Guidance: level 1

:: Employment compensation ::

A _____ is pay and benefits employees receive when they leave employment at a company unwillfully. In addition to their remaining regular pay, it may include some of the following.

Exam Probability: **High**

30. *Answer choices:*

(see index for correct answer)

- a. ADP, LLC
- b. Annual leave
- c. Severance package
- d. Spiff

Guidance: level 1

:: ::

_____ is overt or covert, often harmful, social interaction with the intention of inflicting damage or other unpleasantness upon another individual. It may occur either reactively or without provocation. In humans, frustration due to blocked goals can cause _____. Human _____ can be classified into direct and indirect _____; whilst the former is characterized by physical or verbal behavior intended to cause harm to someone, the latter is characterized by behavior intended to harm the social relations of an individual or group.

Exam Probability: **Low**

31. *Answer choices:*

(see index for correct answer)

- a. levels of analysis
- b. Aggression
- c. Character
- d. cultural

Guidance: level 1

:: Human resource management ::

The _____ is a free online database that contains hundreds of occupational definitions to help students, job seekers, businesses and workforce development professionals to understand today's world of work in the United States. It was developed under the sponsorship of the US Department of Labor/Employment and Training Administration through a grant to the North Carolina Employment Security Commission during the 1990s. John L. Holland's vocational model, often referred to as the Holland Codes, is used in the "Interests" section of the O*NET.

Exam Probability: **Medium**

32. *Answer choices:*

(see index for correct answer)

- a. Co-determination
- b. Job enlargement
- c. Vendor on premises
- d. Skill mix

Guidance: level 1

:: Validity (statistics) ::

In psychometrics, _____ refers to the extent to which a measure represents all facets of a given construct. For example, a depression scale may lack _____ if it only assesses the affective dimension of depression but fails to take into account the behavioral dimension. An element of subjectivity exists in relation to determining _____, which requires a degree of agreement about what a particular personality trait such as extraversion represents. A disagreement about a personality trait will prevent the gain of a high _____.

Exam Probability: **Low**

33. *Answer choices:*

(see index for correct answer)

- a. Content validity
- b. Validation
- c. Ecological validity
- d. Internal validity

Guidance: level 1

:: Human resource management ::

_____ involves improving the effectiveness of organizations and the individuals and teams within them. Training may be viewed as related to immediate changes in organizational effectiveness via organized instruction, while development is related to the progress of longer-term organizational and employee goals. While _____ technically have differing definitions, the two are oftentimes used interchangeably and/or together. _____ has historically been a topic within applied psychology but has within the last two decades become closely associated with human resources management, talent management, human resources development, instructional design, human factors, and knowledge management.

Exam Probability: **Medium**

34. *Answer choices:*

(see index for correct answer)

- a. Employee value proposition
- b. Selection ratio
- c. Training and development
- d. Autonomous work group

Guidance: level 1

:: ::

The U.S. _____ is a federal agency that administers and enforces civil rights laws against workplace discrimination. The EEOC investigates discrimination complaints based on an individual's race, children, national origin, religion, sex, age, disability, sexual orientation, gender identity, genetic information, and retaliation for reporting, participating in, and/or opposing a discriminatory practice.

Exam Probability: **Medium**

35. *Answer choices:*
(see index for correct answer)

- a. hierarchical perspective
- b. Equal Employment Opportunity Commission
- c. open system
- d. deep-level diversity

Guidance: level 1

:: Production and manufacturing ::

_____ consists of organization-wide efforts to "install and make permanent climate where employees continuously improve their ability to provide on demand products and services that customers will find of particular value." "Total" emphasizes that departments in addition to production are obligated to improve their operations; "management" emphasizes that executives are obligated to actively manage quality through funding, training, staffing, and goal setting. While there is no widely agreed-upon approach, TQM efforts typically draw heavily on the previously developed tools and techniques of quality control. TQM enjoyed widespread attention during the late 1980s and early 1990s before being overshadowed by ISO 9000, Lean manufacturing, and Six Sigma.

Exam Probability: **Medium**

36. *Answer choices:*

(see index for correct answer)

- a. Six Sigma
- b. ORiN
- c. Total productive maintenance
- d. Total Quality Management

Guidance: level 1

:: ::

_____ is a belief that hard work and diligence have a moral benefit and an inherent ability, virtue or value to strengthen character and individual abilities. It is a set of values centered on importance of work and manifested by determination or desire to work hard. Social ingrainment of this value is considered to enhance character through hard work that is respective to an individual's field of work.

Exam Probability: **High**

37. *Answer choices:*

(see index for correct answer)

- a. Work ethic
- b. Sarbanes-Oxley act of 2002
- c. imperative
- d. personal values

Guidance: level 1

:: Business ethics ::

_____ is a persistent pattern of mistreatment from others in the workplace that causes either physical or emotional harm. It can include such tactics as verbal, nonverbal, psychological, physical abuse and humiliation. This type of workplace aggression is particularly difficult because, unlike the typical school bully, workplace bullies often operate within the established rules and policies of their organization and their society. In the majority of cases, bullying in the workplace is reported as having been by someone who has authority over their victim. However, bullies can also be peers, and occasionally subordinates. Research has also investigated the impact of the larger organizational context on bullying as well as the group-level processes that impact on the incidence and maintenance of bullying behaviour. Bullying can be covert or overt. It may be missed by superiors; it may be known by many throughout the organization. Negative effects are not limited to the targeted individuals, and may lead to a decline in employee morale and a change in organizational culture. It can also take place as overbearing supervision, constant criticism, and blocking promotions.

Exam Probability: **High**

38. *Answer choices:*

(see index for correct answer)

- a. Society of Corporate Compliance and Ethics
- b. Global Reporting Initiative
- c. Moral hazard
- d. TG Soft

Guidance: level 1

_____ is the administration of an organization, whether it is a business, a not-for-profit organization, or government body. _____ includes the activities of setting the strategy of an organization and coordinating the efforts of its employees to accomplish its objectives through the application of available resources, such as financial, natural, technological, and human resources. The term "_____" may also refer to those people who manage an organization.

Exam Probability: **High**

39. *Answer choices:*

(see index for correct answer)

- a. Management
- b. interpersonal communication
- c. surface-level diversity
- d. cultural

Guidance: level 1

:: Business law ::

A _____ is an arrangement where parties, known as partners, agree to cooperate to advance their mutual interests. The partners in a _____ may be individuals, businesses, interest-based organizations, schools, governments or combinations. Organizations may partner to increase the likelihood of each achieving their mission and to amplify their reach. A _____ may result in issuing and holding equity or may be only governed by a contract.

Exam Probability: **Low**

40. *Answer choices:*

(see index for correct answer)

- a. Participation
- b. Unfair Commercial Practices Directive
- c. Novated lease
- d. Partnership

Guidance: level 1

:: Labour law ::

A _____ is a legal contract that is meant to limit the liability of an employer whose employees are romantically involved. An employer may choose to require a _____ when a romantic relationship within the company becomes known, in order to indemnify the company in case the employees' romantic relationship fails, primarily so that one party can't bring a sexual harassment lawsuit against the company. To that end, the _____ states that the relationship is consensual, and both parties of the relationship must sign it. The _____ may also stipulate rules for acceptable romantic behavior in the workplace.

Exam Probability: **High**

41. *Answer choices:*

(see index for correct answer)

- a. Maximum medical improvement
- b. Victimisation
- c. Bosman ruling
- d. Conditional dismissal

Guidance: level 1

:: Fundamental analysis ::

_____, also known as letter stock or restricted securities, is stock of a company that is not fully transferable until certain conditions have been met. Upon satisfaction of those conditions, the stock is no longer restricted, and becomes transferable to the person holding the award. _____ is often used as a form of employee compensation, in which case it typically becomes transferrable upon the satisfaction of certain conditions, such as continued employment for a period of time or the achievement of particular product-development milestones, earnings per share goals or other financial targets. _____ is a popular alternative to stock options, particularly for executives, due to favorable accounting rules and income tax treatment.

Exam Probability: **High**

42. *Answer choices:*

(see index for correct answer)

- a. Growth stock
- b. Restricted stock
- c. Terminal value
- d. Enterprise value

Guidance: level 1

:: Human resource management ::

_____, Inc. is an American office staffing company that operates globally. The company places employees at all levels in various sectors including financial services, information technology, and law. Also, its professional services include human resource and management consulting, outsourcing, recruitment, career transition, and vendor management. _____ was founded by William Russell Kelly in 1946 and is headquartered in Troy, Michigan. In 2015, the company reported 8,100 employees, $5.5 billion in revenue, and placed 550,000 employees to work in positions in various sectors, making it one of the world's largest staffing firms.

Exam Probability: **High**

43. *Answer choices:*

(see index for correct answer)

- a. Kelly Services
- b. Income bracket
- c. Competency-based management
- d. Selection ratio

Guidance: level 1

:: ::

A _____ is a systematic way of determining the value/worth of a job in relation to other jobs in an organization. It tries to make a systematic comparison between jobs to assess their relative worth for the purpose of establishing a rational pay structure. _____ needs to be differentiated from job analysis. Job analysis is a systematic way of gathering information about a job. Every _____ method requires at least some basic job analysis in order to provide factual information about the jobs concerned. Thus, _____ begins with job analysis and ends at that point where the worth of a job is ascertained for achieving pay equity between jobs and different roles.

Exam Probability: **High**

44. *Answer choices:*

(see index for correct answer)

- a. Job evaluation
- b. surface-level diversity
- c. empathy
- d. imperative

Guidance: level 1

:: Validity (statistics) ::

In psychometrics, _____ is the extent to which a score on a scale or test predicts scores on some criterion measure.

Exam Probability: **Low**

45. Answer choices:

(see index for correct answer)

- a. Face validity
- b. Criterion validity
- c. Predictive validity
- d. Statistical conclusion

Guidance: level 1

:: Parental leave ::

_____ is a type of employment discrimination that occurs when expectant women are fired, not hired, or otherwise discriminated against due to their pregnancy or intention to become pregnant. Common forms of _____ include not being hired due to visible pregnancy or likelihood of becoming pregnant, being fired after informing an employer of one's pregnancy, being fired after maternity leave, and receiving a pay dock due to pregnancy. Convention on the Elimination of All Forms of Discrimination against Women prohibits dismissal on the grounds of maternity or pregnancy and ensures right to maternity leave or comparable social benefits. The Maternity Protection Convention C 183 proclaims adequate protection for pregnancy as well. Though women have some protection in the United States because of the _____ Act of 1978, it has not completely curbed the incidence of _____ . The Equal Rights Amendment could ensure more robust sex equality ensuring that women and men could both work and have children at the same time.

Exam Probability: **Low**

46. Answer choices:

(see index for correct answer)

- a. Pregnant Workers Directive
- b. Motherhood penalty
- c. Pregnancy discrimination
- d. Sara Hlupekile Longwe

Guidance: level 1

:: Persuasion techniques ::

_____ is a psychological technique in which an individual attempts to influence another person by becoming more likeable to their target. This term was coined by social psychologist Edward E. Jones, who further defined _____ as "a class of strategic behaviors illicitly designed to influence a particular other person concerning the attractiveness of one's personal qualities." _____ research has identified some specific tactics of employing _____ .

Exam Probability: **High**

47. *Answer choices:*

(see index for correct answer)

- a. Ingratiation
- b. Fairy tale
- c. Flattery
- d. Modes of persuasion

Guidance: level 1

:: Workplace ::

A _____ is a process through which feedback from an employee's subordinates, colleagues, and supervisor, as well as a self-evaluation by the employee themselves is gathered. Such feedback can also include, when relevant, feedback from external sources who interact with the employee, such as customers and suppliers or other interested stakeholders. _____ is so named because it solicits feedback regarding an employee's behavior from a variety of points of view. It therefore may be contrasted with "downward feedback", or "upward feedback" delivered to supervisory or management employees by subordinates only.

Exam Probability: **Medium**

48. *Answer choices:*

(see index for correct answer)

- a. Queen bee syndrome
- b. Counterproductive work behavior
- c. 360-degree feedback
- d. Workplace incivility

Guidance: level 1

:: Corporate governance ::

An _____ is generally a person responsible for running an organization, although the exact nature of the role varies depending on the organization. In many militaries, an _____, or "XO," is the second-in-command, reporting to the commanding officer. The XO is typically responsible for the management of day-to-day activities, freeing the commander to concentrate on strategy and planning the unit's next move.

Exam Probability: **Low**

49. *Answer choices:*

(see index for correct answer)

- a. Chief operating officer
- b. King Report on Corporate Governance
- c. Executive officer
- d. Chief governance officer

Guidance: level 1

:: United States employment discrimination case law ::

_____, 641 F.2d 934, was a D.C. Circuit opinion, written by Judge Skelly Wright, that held that workplace sexual harassment could constitute employment discrimination under the Civil Rights Act of 1964.

Exam Probability: **High**

50. *Answer choices:*

(see index for correct answer)

- a. Bundy v. Jackson
- b. Executive Order 11375
- c. New York City Transit Authority v. Beazer
- d. Glenn v. Brumby

Guidance: level 1

:: Employment ::

_____ is the probability that an individual will keep his/her job; a job with a high level of _____ is such that a person with the job would have a small chance of losing it.

Exam Probability: **High**

51. *Answer choices:*

(see index for correct answer)

- a. Extra role performance
- b. Job security
- c. Payroll tax
- d. Work-in

Guidance: level 1

:: Legal terms ::

_____ , a form of alternative dispute resolution , is a way to resolve disputes outside the courts. The dispute will be decided by one or more persons , which renders the "_____ award". An _____ award is legally binding on both sides and enforceable in the courts.

Exam Probability: **High**

52. *Answer choices:*

(see index for correct answer)

- a. Goonda
- b. Arbitration
- c. Felony
- d. Last antecedent rule

Guidance: level 1

:: ::

The causes of _____ are heavily debated. Classical economics, new classical economics, and the Austrian School of economics argued that market mechanisms are reliable means of resolving _____ . These theories argue against interventions imposed on the labor market from the outside, such as unionization, bureaucratic work rules, minimum wage laws, taxes, and other regulations that they claim discourage the hiring of workers. Keynesian economics emphasizes the cyclical nature of _____ and recommends government interventions in the economy that it claims will reduce _____ during recessions. This theory focuses on recurrent shocks that suddenly reduce aggregate demand for goods and services and thus reduce demand for workers. Keynesian models recommend government interventions designed to increase demand for workers; these can include financial stimuli, publicly funded job creation, and expansionist monetary policies. Its namesake economist, John Maynard Keynes, believed that the root cause of _____ is the desire of investors to receive more money rather than produce more products, which is not possible without public bodies producing new money. A third group of theories emphasize the need for a stable supply of capital and investment to maintain full employment. On this view, government should guarantee full employment through fiscal policy, monetary policy and trade policy as stated, for example, in the US Employment Act of 1946, by counteracting private sector or trade investment volatility, and reducing inequality.

Exam Probability: **High**

53. *Answer choices:*

(see index for correct answer)

- a. corporate values
- b. Unemployment
- c. process perspective
- d. open system

Guidance: level 1

:: Employment ::

_____ is a relationship between two parties, usually based on a contract where work is paid for, where one party, which may be a corporation, for profit, not-for-profit organization, co-operative or other entity is the employer and the other is the employee. Employees work in return for payment, which may be in the form of an hourly wage, by piecework or an annual salary, depending on the type of work an employee does or which sector she or he is working in. Employees in some fields or sectors may receive gratuities, bonus payment or stock options. In some types of _____, employees may receive benefits in addition to payment. Benefits can include health insurance, housing, disability insurance or use of a gym. _____ is typically governed by _____ laws, regulations or legal contracts.

Exam Probability: **High**

54. *Answer choices:*

(see index for correct answer)

- a. Employment
- b. Workgang
- c. Performance improvement
- d. Dead-end job

Guidance: level 1

:: Employment compensation ::

A _____ , also known as a flexible spending arrangement, is one of a number of tax-advantaged financial accounts, resulting in payroll tax savings. Before the Patient Protection and Affordable Care Act, one significant disadvantage to using an FSA was that funds not used by the end of the plan year were forfeited to the employer, known as the "use it or lose it" rule. Under the terms of the Affordable Care Act, a plan may permit an employee to carry over up to $500 into the following year without losing the funds.

Exam Probability: **Medium**

55. *Answer choices:*

(see index for correct answer)

- a. Employee assistance program
- b. Flexible spending account
- c. Commission
- d. Golden parachute

Guidance: level 1

:: Psychometrics ::

A _____ is a set of categories designed to elicit information about a quantitative or a qualitative attribute. In the social sciences, particularly psychology, common examples are the Likert response scale and 1-10 _____ s in which a person selects the number which is considered to reflect the perceived quality of a product.

Exam Probability: **Low**

56. *Answer choices:*

(see index for correct answer)

- a. Standards for Educational and Psychological Testing
- b. Figure rating scale
- c. Bias in Mental Testing
- d. Research %26 Education Association

Guidance: level 1

:: ::

_____ involves the development of an action plan designed to motivate and guide a person or group toward a goal. _____ can be guided by goal-setting criteria such as SMART criteria. _____ is a major component of personal-development and management literature.

Exam Probability: **High**

57. *Answer choices:*

(see index for correct answer)

- a. process perspective
- b. information systems assessment
- c. Goal setting

- d. levels of analysis

Guidance: level 1

:: ::

From an accounting perspective, _____ is crucial because _____ and _____ taxes considerably affect the net income of most companies and because they are subject to laws and regulations .

Exam Probability: **Low**

58. *Answer choices:*

(see index for correct answer)

- a. Payroll
- b. surface-level diversity
- c. functional perspective
- d. hierarchical

Guidance: level 1

:: Lean manufacturing ::

_____ is the Sino-Japanese word for "improvement". In business, _____ refers to activities that continuously improve all functions and involve all employees from the CEO to the assembly line workers. It also applies to processes, such as purchasing and logistics, that cross organizational boundaries into the supply chain. It has been applied in healthcare, psychotherapy, life-coaching, government, and banking.

Exam Probability: **Medium**

59. *Answer choices:*

(see index for correct answer)

- a. Lean services
- b. Lean Government
- c. Computer-aided lean management
- d. Muri

Guidance: level 1

Information systems

Information systems (IS) are formal, sociotechnical, organizational systems designed to collect, process, store, and distribute information. In a sociotechnical perspective Information Systems are composed by four components: technology, process, people and organizational structure.

:: Management ::

_____ is the kind of knowledge that is difficult to transfer to another person by means of writing it down or verbalizing it. For example, that London is in the United Kingdom is a piece of explicit knowledge that can be written down, transmitted, and understood by a recipient. However, the ability to speak a language, ride a bicycle, knead dough, play a musical instrument, or design and use complex equipment requires all sorts of knowledge that is not always known explicitly, even by expert practitioners, and which is difficult or impossible to explicitly transfer to other people.

Exam Probability: **Low**

1. *Answer choices:*

(see index for correct answer)

- a. Tacit knowledge
- b. Business workflow analysis
- c. Topple rate
- d. Failure demand

Guidance: level 1

:: Outsourcing ::

A service-level agreement is a commitment between a service provider and a client. Particular aspects of the service – quality, availability, responsibilities – are agreed between the service provider and the service user. The most common component of SLA is that the services should be provided to the customer as agreed upon in the contract. As an example, Internet service providers and telcos will commonly include _____ s within the terms of their contracts with customers to define the level of service being sold in plain language terms. In this case the SLA will typically have a technical definition in mean time between failures , mean time to repair or mean time to recovery ; identifying which party is responsible for reporting faults or paying fees; responsibility for various data rates; throughput; jitter; or similar measurable details.

Exam Probability: **Low**

2. *Answer choices:*

(see index for correct answer)

- a. Request for proposal
- b. Toronto-Dominion Bank
- c. Sourcing agent
- d. Service level agreement

Guidance: level 1

:: Information technology management ::

An _____ , acceptable usage policy or fair use policy, is a set of rules applied by the owner, creator or administrator of a network, website, or service, that restrict the ways in which the network, website or system may be used and sets guidelines as to how it should be used. AUP documents are written for corporations, businesses, universities, schools, internet service providers , and website owners, often to reduce the potential for legal action that may be taken by a user, and often with little prospect of enforcement.

Exam Probability: **Low**

3. *Answer choices:*

(see index for correct answer)

- a. Early-arriving fact
- b. Configuration management database
- c. Digital asset management
- d. Telematics

Guidance: level 1

:: SQL ::

SQL is a domain-specific language used in programming and designed for managing data held in a relational database management system , or for stream processing in a relational data stream management system . It is particularly useful in handling structured data where there are relations between different entities/variables of the data. SQL offers two main advantages over older read/write APIs like ISAM or VSAM. First, it introduced the concept of accessing many records with one single command; and second, it eliminates the need to specify how to reach a record, e.g. with or without an index.

Exam Probability: **Medium**

4. *Answer choices:*

(see index for correct answer)

- a. Varchar
- b. Object-oriented SQL
- c. Windows Internal Database
- d. Structured query language

Guidance: level 1

:: E-commerce ::

Electronic governance or e-governance is the application of information and communication technology for delivering government services, exchange of information, communication transactions, integration of various stand-alone systems and services between government-to-citizen, government-to-business, _____, government-to-employees as well as back-office processes and interactions within the entire government framework. Through e-governance, government services are made available to citizens in a convenient, efficient, and transparent manner. The three main target groups that can be distinguished in governance concepts are government, citizens, andbusinesses/interest groups. In e-governance, there are no distinct boundaries.

Exam Probability: **Medium**

5. *Answer choices:*

(see index for correct answer)

- a. Hukkster
- b. DVD-by-mail
- c. USAePay
- d. FastSpring

Guidance: level 1

:: ::

A _____ or data centre is a building, dedicated space within a building, or a group of buildings used to house computer systems and associated components, such as telecommunications and storage systems.

Exam Probability: **Low**

6. *Answer choices:*

(see index for correct answer)

- a. hierarchical perspective
- b. information systems assessment
- c. cultural
- d. Sarbanes-Oxley act of 2002

Guidance: level 1

:: Internet advertising ::

_____ is software that aims to gather information about a person or organization, sometimes without their knowledge, that may send such information to another entity without the consumer's consent, that asserts control over a device without the consumer's knowledge, or it may send such information to another entity with the consumer's consent, through cookies.

Exam Probability: **Medium**

7. *Answer choices:*

(see index for correct answer)

- a. Joe job
- b. Cultural encoding

- c. VoloMedia
- d. Spyware

Guidance: level 1

:: ::

_____ is a set of values of subjects with respect to qualitative or quantitative variables.

Exam Probability: **Medium**

8. *Answer choices:*

(see index for correct answer)

- a. co-culture
- b. deep-level diversity
- c. imperative
- d. personal values

Guidance: level 1

:: Google services ::

_____ is a web mapping service developed by Google. It offers satellite imagery, aerial photography, street maps, 360° panoramic views of streets, real-time traffic conditions, and route planning for traveling by foot, car, bicycle and air, or public transportation.

Exam Probability: **High**

9. *Answer choices:*

(see index for correct answer)

- a. AdSense
- b. Google Friend Connect
- c. Google Gadgets API
- d. Google Moderator

Guidance: level 1

:: Human–computer interaction ::

_____ is a database query language for relational databases. It was devised by Moshé M. Zloof at IBM Research during the mid-1970s, in parallel to the development of SQL. It is the first graphical query language, using visual tables where the user would enter commands, example elements and conditions. Many graphical front-ends for databases use the ideas from QBE today. Originally limited only for the purpose of retrieving data, QBE was later extended to allow other operations, such as inserts, deletes and updates, as well as creation of temporary tables.

Exam Probability: **Medium**

10. *Answer choices:*

(see index for correct answer)

- a. ELMER guidelines
- b. Query by Example
- c. Volunia
- d. CMN-GOMS

Guidance: level 1

:: Fraud ::

_____ is the deliberate use of someone else's identity, usually as a method to gain a financial advantage or obtain credit and other benefits in the other person's name, and perhaps to the other person's disadvantage or loss. The person whose identity has been assumed may suffer adverse consequences, especially if they are held responsible for the perpetrator's actions.
_____ occurs when someone uses another's personally identifying information, like their name, identifying number, or credit card number, without their permission, to commit fraud or other crimes. The term _____ was coined in 1964. Since that time, the definition of _____ has been statutorily prescribed throughout both the U.K. and the United States as the theft of personally identifying information, generally including a person's name, date of birth, social security number, driver's license number, bank account or credit card numbers, PIN numbers, electronic signatures, fingerprints, passwords, or any other information that can be used to access a person's financial resources.

Exam Probability: **High**

11. *Answer choices:*

(see index for correct answer)

- a. Hijacked journal
- b. Voice phishing
- c. Tunneling
- d. Fraud

Guidance: level 1

:: Computer networking ::

_____ is a method of grouping data that is transmitted over a digital network into packets. Packets are made of a header and a payload. Data in the header are used by networking hardware to direct the packet to its destination where the payload is extracted and used by application software. _____ is the primary basis for data communications in computer networks worldwide.

Exam Probability: **Low**

12. *Answer choices:*

(see index for correct answer)

- a. Peer group
- b. Promiscuous traffic

- c. Local Management Interface
- d. Path length

Guidance: level 1

:: Multi-agent systems ::

> A _____ is a number of Internet-connected devices, each of which is running one or more bots. _____ s can be used to perform distributed denial-of-service attack, steal data, send spam, and allows the attacker to access the device and its connection. The owner can control the _____ using command and control software. The word " _____ " is a combination of the words "robot" and "network". The term is usually used with a negative or malicious connotation.

Exam Probability: **High**

13. *Answer choices:*

(see index for correct answer)

- a. Golaem Crowd
- b. Botnet
- c. Multi-agent planning
- d. Multi-agent system

Guidance: level 1

:: Data analysis ::

_____ is a process of inspecting, cleansing, transforming, and modeling data with the goal of discovering useful information, informing conclusions, and supporting decision-making. _____ has multiple facets and approaches, encompassing diverse techniques under a variety of names, and is used in different business, science, and social science domains. In today's business world, _____ plays a role in making decisions more scientific and helping businesses operate more effectively.

Exam Probability: **Medium**

14. *Answer choices:*

(see index for correct answer)

- a. Data analysis
- b. Oversampling and undersampling in data analysis
- c. TinkerPlots
- d. Visual comparison

Guidance: level 1

:: Automatic identification and data capture ::

_____ uses electromagnetic fields to automatically identify and track tags attached to objects. The tags contain electronically stored information. Passive tags collect energy from a nearby RFID reader's interrogating radio waves. Active tags have a local power source and may operate hundreds of meters from the RFID reader. Unlike a barcode, the tag need not be within the line of sight of the reader, so it may be embedded in the tracked object. RFID is one method of automatic identification and data capture.

Exam Probability: **Low**

15. *Answer choices:*

(see index for correct answer)

- a. Transmitter hunting
- b. Barcode
- c. RFIQin
- d. Radio-frequency identification

Guidance: level 1

:: Policy ::

A _____ is a statement or a legal document that discloses some or all of the ways a party gathers, uses, discloses, and manages a customer or client's data. It fulfills a legal requirement to protect a customer or client's privacy. Personal information can be anything that can be used to identify an individual, not limited to the person's name, address, date of birth, marital status, contact information, ID issue, and expiry date, financial records, credit information, medical history, where one travels, and intentions to acquire goods and services. In the case of a business it is often a statement that declares a party's policy on how it collects, stores, and releases personal information it collects. It informs the client what specific information is collected, and whether it is kept confidential, shared with partners, or sold to other firms or enterprises. Privacy policies typically represent a broader, more generalized treatment, as opposed to data use statements, which tend to be more detailed and specific.

Exam Probability: **Medium**

16. *Answer choices:*

(see index for correct answer)

- a. Perverse incentive
- b. Science policy
- c. Privacy policy
- d. Nosokinetics

Guidance: level 1

:: Computer networking ::

A backbone is a part of computer network that interconnects various pieces of network, providing a path for the exchange of information between different LANs or subnetworks. A backbone can tie together diverse networks in the same building, in different buildings in a campus environment, or over wide areas. Normally, the backbone's capacity is greater than the networks connected to it.

Exam Probability: **Medium**

17. *Answer choices:*

(see index for correct answer)

- a. Network forensics
- b. Wireless Andrew
- c. Backbone network
- d. Frenetic

Guidance: level 1

:: E-commerce ::

_____ , and its now-deprecated predecessor, Secure Sockets Layer , are cryptographic protocols designed to provide communications security over a computer network. Several versions of the protocols find widespread use in applications such as web browsing, email, instant messaging, and voice over IP . Websites can use TLS to secure all communications between their servers and web browsers.

Exam Probability: **Low**

18. *Answer choices:*

(see index for correct answer)

- a. Standard Interchange Language
- b. Trymedia
- c. Transport Layer Security
- d. ESewa

Guidance: level 1

:: Fraud ::

In law, _____ is intentional deception to secure unfair or unlawful gain, or to deprive a victim of a legal right. _____ can violate civil law, a criminal law, or it may cause no loss of money, property or legal right but still be an element of another civil or criminal wrong. The purpose of _____ may be monetary gain or other benefits, for example by obtaining a passport, travel document, or driver's license, or mortgage _____, where the perpetrator may attempt to qualify for a mortgage by way of false statements.

Exam Probability: **High**

19. *Answer choices:*

(see index for correct answer)

- a. Insurance fraud
- b. Fraud

- c. Accreditation mill
- d. Voice phishing

Guidance: level 1

:: Market research ::

_____ is the action of defining, gathering, analyzing, and distributing intelligence about products, customers, competitors, and any aspect of the environment needed to support executives and managers in strategic decision making for an organization.

Exam Probability: **Medium**

20. *Answer choices:*

(see index for correct answer)

- a. Vehicle Dependability Study
- b. Email marketing
- c. Demographic marketer
- d. Competitive intelligence

Guidance: level 1

:: Network analyzers ::

A _____ , meaning "meat eater", is an organism that derives its energy and nutrient requirements from a diet consisting mainly or exclusively of animal tissue, whether through predation or scavenging. Animals that depend solely on animal flesh for their nutrient requirements are called obligate _____ s while those that also consume non-animal food are called facultative _____ s. Omnivores also consume both animal and non-animal food, and, apart from the more general definition, there is no clearly defined ratio of plant to animal material that would distinguish a facultative _____ from an omnivore. A _____ at the top of the food chain, not preyed upon by other animals, is termed an apex predator.

Exam Probability: **Medium**

21. *Answer choices:*

(see index for correct answer)

- a. Zx Sniffer
- b. Capsa
- c. AirSnort
- d. Openkore

Guidance: level 1

:: Information technology management ::

In information technology to _____ means to move from one place to another, information to detailed data by focusing in on something. In a GUI-environment, "drilling-down" may involve clicking on some representation in order to reveal more detail.

Exam Probability: **Low**

22. *Answer choices:*

(see index for correct answer)

- a. Central Computer and Telecommunications Agency
- b. Drill down
- c. Electronic document and records management system
- d. EFx Factory

Guidance: level 1

:: Knowledge engineering ::

> The _____ is an extension of the World Wide Web through standards by the World Wide Web Consortium. The standards promote common data formats and exchange protocols on the Web, most fundamentally the Resource Description Framework. According to the W3C, "The _____ provides a common framework that allows data to be shared and reused across application, enterprise, and community boundaries". The _____ is therefore regarded as an integrator across different content, information applications and systems.

Exam Probability: **Medium**

23. *Answer choices:*

(see index for correct answer)

- a. Knowledge engineer

- b. Knowledge Acquisition and Documentation Structuring
- c. CSHALS
- d. Knowledge Engineering Environment

Guidance: level 1

:: Data security ::

_____, sometimes shortened to InfoSec, is the practice of preventing unauthorized access, use, disclosure, disruption, modification, inspection, recording or destruction of information. The information or data may take any form, e.g. electronic or physical. _____'s primary focus is the balanced protection of the confidentiality, integrity and availability of data while maintaining a focus on efficient policy implementation, all without hampering organization productivity. This is largely achieved through a multi-step risk management process that identifies assets, threat sources, vulnerabilities, potential impacts, and possible controls, followed by assessment of the effectiveness of the risk management plan.

Exam Probability: **High**

24. *Answer choices:*

(see index for correct answer)

- a. MyDLP
- b. Doxing
- c. Information security
- d. WISeKey

Guidance: level 1

:: Google services ::

_____ is a word processor included as part of a free, web-based software office suite offered by Google within its Google Drive service. This service also includes Google Sheets and Google Slides, a spreadsheet and presentation program respectively. _____ is available as a web application, mobile app for Android, iOS, Windows, BlackBerry, and as a desktop application on Google's ChromeOS. The app is compatible with Microsoft Office file formats. The application allows users to create and edit files online while collaborating with other users in real-time. Edits are tracked by user with a revision history presenting changes. An editor's position is highlighted with an editor-specific color and cursor. A permissions system regulates what users can do. Updates have introduced features using machine learning, including "Explore", offering search results based on the contents of a document, and "Action items", allowing users to assign tasks to other users.

Exam Probability: **High**

25. *Answer choices:*

(see index for correct answer)

- a. Knowledge Graph
- b. Google Blog Search
- c. Google Mars
- d. Google Docs

Guidance: level 1

:: Supply chain management ::

ERP is usually referred to as a category of business management software — typically a suite of integrated applications—that an organization can use to collect, store, manage, and interpret data from these many business activities.

Exam Probability: **Low**

26. *Answer choices:*
(see index for correct answer)

- a. Scan-based trading
- b. Supply chain cyber security
- c. Enterprise resource planning
- d. Supply chain engineering

Guidance: level 1

:: Market structure and pricing ::

_____ is a term denoting that a product includes permission to use its source code, design documents, or content. It most commonly refers to the open-source model, in which open-source software or other products are released under an open-source license as part of the open-source-software movement. Use of the term originated with software, but has expanded beyond the software sector to cover other open content and forms of open collaboration.

Exam Probability: **High**

27. *Answer choices:*

(see index for correct answer)

- a. Open source
- b. Installed base
- c. Liberalization
- d. Market structure

Guidance: level 1

:: Information technology management ::

_____ s or pop-ups are forms of online advertising on the World Wide Web. A pop-up is a graphical user interface display area, usually a small window, that suddenly appears in the foreground of the visual interface. The pop-up window containing an advertisement is usually generated by JavaScript that uses cross-site scripting, sometimes with a secondary payload that uses Adobe Flash. They can also be generated by other vulnerabilities/security holes in browser security.

Exam Probability: **Medium**

28. *Answer choices:*

(see index for correct answer)

- a. Bachelor in Information Management

- b. Web commerce
- c. Global delivery model
- d. Pop-up ad

Guidance: level 1

:: Information technology management ::

_____ is the use of software to control machine tools and related ones in the manufacturing of workpieces. This is not the only definition for CAM, but it is the most common; CAM may also refer to the use of a computer to assist in all operations of a manufacturing plant, including planning, management, transportation and storage. Its primary purpose is to create a faster production process and components and tooling with more precise dimensions and material consistency, which in some cases, uses only the required amount of raw material, while simultaneously reducing energy consumption. CAM is now a system used in schools and lower educational purposes. CAM is a subsequent computer-aided process after computer-aided design and sometimes computer-aided engineering, as the model generated in CAD and verified in CAE can be input into CAM software, which then controls the machine tool. CAM is used in many schools alongside Computer-Aided Design to create objects.

Exam Probability: **High**

29. *Answer choices:*

(see index for correct answer)

- a. Computer-aided manufacturing
- b. ISO/IEC JTC 1/SC 40

- c. E-Booking
- d. Storage hypervisor

Guidance: level 1

:: Virtual economies ::

_____ Inc. is an American social game developer running social video game services founded in April 2007 and headquartered in San Francisco, California, United States. The company primarily focuses on mobile and social networking platforms. _____ states its mission as "connecting the world through games."

Exam Probability: **Low**

30. *Answer choices:*

(see index for correct answer)

- a. Zynga
- b. Pioneer
- c. Evony
- d. Mudflation

Guidance: level 1

:: Asset ::

In financial accounting, an _____ is any resource owned by the business. Anything tangible or intangible that can be owned or controlled to produce value and that is held by a company to produce positive economic value is an _____ . Simply stated, _____ s represent value of ownership that can be converted into cash . The balance sheet of a firm records the monetary value of the _____ s owned by that firm. It covers money and other valuables belonging to an individual or to a business.

Exam Probability: **Medium**

31. *Answer choices:*

(see index for correct answer)

- a. Current asset
- b. Fixed asset

Guidance: level 1

:: Financial markets ::

The _____ business model is a business model in which a customer must pay a recurring price at regular intervals for access to a product or service. The model was pioneered by publishers of books and periodicals in the 17th century, and is now used by many businesses and websites.

Exam Probability: **Low**

32. *Answer choices:*

(see index for correct answer)

- a. Price-weighted index
- b. Convertible arbitrage
- c. Subscription
- d. Arbitrage

Guidance: level 1

:: E-commerce ::

Customer to customer markets provide an innovative way to allow customers to interact with each other. Traditional markets require business to customer relationships, in which a customer goes to the business in order to purchase a product or service. In customer to customer markets, the business facilitates an environment where customers can sell goods or services to each other. Other types of markets include business to business and business to customer .

Exam Probability: **Low**

33. *Answer choices:*

(see index for correct answer)

- a. Live banner
- b. Digital currency
- c. CA/Browser Forum
- d. Donna Hoffman

Guidance: level 1

:: ::

A database is an organized collection of data, generally stored and accessed electronically from a computer system. Where databases are more complex they are often developed using formal design and modeling techniques.

Exam Probability: **High**

34. *Answer choices:*

(see index for correct answer)

- a. hierarchical perspective
- b. Database management system
- c. open system
- d. levels of analysis

Guidance: level 1

:: Information science ::

In discourse-based grammatical theory, _____ is any tracking of referential information by speakers. Information may be new, just introduced into the conversation; given, already active in the speakers' consciousness; or old, no longer active. The various types of activation, and how these are defined, are model-dependent.

Exam Probability: **High**

35. *Answer choices:*

(see index for correct answer)

- a. Information flow
- b. Neuroheuristics
- c. Semantic Sensor Web
- d. Information literacy

Guidance: level 1

:: Computer memory ::

_____ is an electronic non-volatile computer storage medium that can be electrically erased and reprogrammed.

Exam Probability: **Low**

36. *Answer choices:*

(see index for correct answer)

- a. Rambus
- b. Flash memory
- c. Disk space
- d. Regenerative capacitor memory

Guidance: level 1

:: Distribution, retailing, and wholesaling ::

_____ measures the performance of a system. Certain goals are defined and the _____ gives the percentage to which those goals should be achieved. Fill rate is different from _____ .

Exam Probability: **Medium**

37. *Answer choices:*

(see index for correct answer)

- a. Service level
- b. New Leaf Distributing Company
- c. Direct market
- d. National

Guidance: level 1

:: Virtual economies ::

_____ is an online virtual world, developed and owned by the San Francisco-based firm Linden Lab and launched on June 23, 2003. By 2013, _____ had approximately one million regular users; at the end of 2017 active user count totals "between 800,000 and 900,000". In many ways, _____ is similar to massively multiplayer online role-playing games; however, Linden Lab is emphatic that their creation is not a game: "There is no manufactured conflict, no set objective".

Exam Probability: **Low**

38. *Answer choices:*

(see index for correct answer)

- a. Habbo
- b. Pioneer
- c. Second Life
- d. Monopoly money

Guidance: level 1

:: E-commerce ::

_____ generally refer to payment services operated under financial regulation and performed from or via a mobile device. Instead of paying with cash, cheque, or credit cards, a consumer can use a mobile to pay for a wide range of services and digital or hard goods. Although the concept of using non-coin-based currency systems has a long history, it is only recently that the technology to support such systems has become widely available.

Exam Probability: **Low**

39. *Answer choices:*

(see index for correct answer)

- a. Online food ordering
- b. UN/CEFACT
- c. Mobile payment
- d. Variable pricing

Guidance: level 1

:: Network management ::

_____ is the process of administering and managing computer networks. Services provided by this discipline include fault analysis, performance management, provisioning of networks and maintaining the quality of service. Software that enables network administrators to perform their functions is called _____ software.

Exam Probability: **High**

40. *Answer choices:*

(see index for correct answer)

- a. Network management
- b. AiScaler
- c. Telecommunication Management Network model
- d. OAMP

Guidance: level 1

:: Telecommunications engineering ::

A _____ is a computer processor that incorporates the functions of a central processing unit on a single integrated circuit, or at most a few integrated circuits. The _____ is a multipurpose, clock driven, register based, digital integrated circuit that accepts binary data as input, processes it according to instructions stored in its memory and provides results as output. _____ s contain both combinational logic and sequential digital logic. _____ s operate on numbers and symbols represented in the binary number system.

Exam Probability: **Medium**

41. *Answer choices:*

(see index for correct answer)

- a. Computer network
- b. Microprocessor

Guidance: level 1

:: ::

_____ is an American video-sharing website headquartered in San Bruno, California. Three former PayPal employees—Chad Hurley, Steve Chen, and Jawed Karim—created the service in February 2005. Google bought the site in November 2006 for US$1.65 billion; _____ now operates as one of Google's subsidiaries.

Exam Probability: **Low**

42. *Answer choices:*

(see index for correct answer)

- a. YouTube
- b. corporate values
- c. surface-level diversity
- d. empathy

Guidance: level 1

:: Data ::

_____ is viewed by many disciplines as a modern equivalent of visual communication. It involves the creation and study of the visual representation of data.

Exam Probability: **High**

43. *Answer choices:*

(see index for correct answer)

- a. Data visualization
- b. Raw data
- c. One Source Networks
- d. Metro Chicago Information Center

Guidance: level 1

:: ::

In communications and information processing, _____ is a system of rules to convert information—such as a letter, word, sound, image, or gesture—into another form or representation, sometimes shortened or secret, for communication through a communication channel or storage in a storage medium. An early example is the invention of language, which enabled a person, through speech, to communicate what they saw, heard, felt, or thought to others. But speech limits the range of communication to the distance a voice can carry, and limits the audience to those present when the speech is uttered. The invention of writing, which converted spoken language into visual symbols, extended the range of communication across space and time.

Exam Probability: **Medium**

44. *Answer choices:*

(see index for correct answer)

- a. corporate values
- b. open system
- c. information systems assessment
- d. Sarbanes-Oxley act of 2002

Guidance: level 1

:: Procurement practices ::

_____ or commercially available off-the-shelf products are packaged solutions which are then adapted to satisfy the needs of the purchasing organization, rather than the commissioning of custom-made, or bespoke, solutions. A related term, Mil-COTS, refers to COTS products for use by the U.S. military.

Exam Probability: **Low**

45. *Answer choices:*

(see index for correct answer)

- a. Syndicated procurement
- b. Commercial off-the-shelf

Guidance: level 1

:: Business ::

_____ is a sourcing model in which individuals or organizations obtain goods and services, including ideas and finances, from a large, relatively open and often rapidly-evolving group of internet users; it divides work between participants to achieve a cumulative result. The word _____ itself is a portmanteau of crowd and outsourcing, and was coined in 2005. As a mode of sourcing, _____ existed prior to the digital age.

Exam Probability: **Low**

46. *Answer choices:*

(see index for correct answer)

- a. Lean dynamics
- b. CyberAlert, Inc.
- c. Countertrade
- d. Crowdsourcing

Guidance: level 1

:: IT risk management ::

_____ involves a set of policies, tools and procedures to enable the recovery or continuation of vital technology infrastructure and systems following a natural or human-induced disaster. _____ focuses on the IT or technology systems supporting critical business functions, as opposed to business continuity, which involves keeping all essential aspects of a business functioning despite significant disruptive events. _____ can therefore be considered as a subset of business continuity.

Exam Probability: **Medium**

47. *Answer choices:*

(see index for correct answer)

- a. Information assurance
- b. Business continuity
- c. Incident response team

Guidance: level 1

:: Virtual reality ::

An _____, a concept in Hinduism that means "descent", refers to the material appearance or incarnation of a deity on earth. The relative verb to "alight, to make one's appearance" is sometimes used to refer to any guru or revered human being.

Exam Probability: **High**

48. *Answer choices:*

(see index for correct answer)

- a. Quake II engine
- b. Stroker Serpentine
- c. Avatar
- d. Virtual artifact

Guidance: level 1

:: Information systems ::

A _____ is an information system used for decision-making, and for the coordination, control, analysis, and visualization of information in an organization; especially in a company.

Exam Probability: **Medium**

49. *Answer choices:*

(see index for correct answer)

- a. Information filtering system
- b. Management information system
- c. CarWings
- d. Legal expert system

Guidance: level 1

:: ::

A _____ is server software, or hardware dedicated to running said software, that can satisfy World Wide Web client requests. A _____ can, in general, contain one or more websites. A _____ processes incoming network requests over HTTP and several other related protocols.

Exam Probability: **Low**

50. *Answer choices:*

(see index for correct answer)

- a. open system
- b. information systems assessment
- c. interpersonal communication
- d. personal values

Guidance: level 1

:: Human–computer interaction ::

_____ is the ease of use and learnability of a human-made object such as a tool or device. In software engineering, _____ is the degree to which a software can be used by specified consumers to achieve quantified objectives with effectiveness, efficiency, and satisfaction in a quantified context of use.

Exam Probability: **Low**

51. *Answer choices:*

(see index for correct answer)

- a. Usability
- b. Christopher Ahlberg
- c. Interactive computing
- d. The Magical Number Seven, Plus or Minus Two

Guidance: level 1

:: ::

_____ is a kind of action that occur as two or more objects have an effect upon one another. The idea of a two-way effect is essential in the concept of _____ , as opposed to a one-way causal effect. A closely related term is interconnectivity, which deals with the _____ s of _____ s within systems: combinations of many simple _____ s can lead to surprising emergent phenomena. _____ has different tailored meanings in various sciences. Changes can also involve _____ .

Exam Probability: **High**

52. *Answer choices:*

(see index for correct answer)

- a. interpersonal communication

- b. functional perspective
- c. hierarchical
- d. Interaction

Guidance: level 1

:: Confidence tricks ::

_____ is the fraudulent attempt to obtain sensitive information such as usernames, passwords and credit card details by disguising oneself as a trustworthy entity in an electronic communication. Typically carried out by email spoofing or instant messaging, it often directs users to enter personal information at a fake website which matches the look and feel of the legitimate site.

Exam Probability: **High**

53. *Answer choices:*

(see index for correct answer)

- a. Ponzi scheme
- b. Sucker list
- c. Phishing
- d. Badger game

Guidance: level 1

:: Information science ::

_____ is the resolution of uncertainty; it is that which answers the question of "what an entity is" and thus defines both its essence and nature of its characteristics. _____ relates to both data and knowledge, as data is meaningful _____ representing values attributed to parameters, and knowledge signifies understanding of a concept. _____ is uncoupled from an observer, which is an entity that can access _____ and thus discern what it specifies; _____ exists beyond an event horizon for example. In the case of knowledge, the _____ itself requires a cognitive observer to be obtained.

Exam Probability: **Medium**

54. *Answer choices:*
(see index for correct answer)

- a. Five laws of library science
- b. Legal informatics
- c. ISO 15926
- d. American Documentation Institute

Guidance: level 1

:: Information technology ::

_____ is the use of computers to store, retrieve, transmit, and manipulate data, or information, often in the context of a business or other enterprise. IT is considered to be a subset of information and communications technology. An _____ system is generally an information system, a communications system or, more specifically speaking, a computer system – including all hardware, software and peripheral equipment – operated by a limited group of users.

Exam Probability: **Medium**

55. *Answer choices:*

(see index for correct answer)

- a. Information revolution
- b. PC Supporters
- c. Information technology
- d. Localization Industry Standards Association

Guidance: level 1

:: ::

The _____, commonly known as the Web, is an information system where documents and other web resources are identified by Uniform Resource Locators, which may be interlinked by hypertext, and are accessible over the Internet. The resources of the WWW may be accessed by users by a software application called a web browser.

Exam Probability: **Medium**

56. *Answer choices:*

(see index for correct answer)

- a. personal values
- b. functional perspective
- c. open system
- d. World Wide Web

Guidance: level 1

:: Information science ::

The United States National Forum on _____ defines _____ as "... the hyper ability to know when there is a need for information, to be able to identify, locate, evaluate, and effectively use that information for the issue or problem at hand." The American Library Association defines " _____ " as a set of abilities requiring individuals to "recognize when information is needed and have the ability to locate, evaluate, and use effectively the needed information. Other definitions incorporate aspects of "skepticism, judgement, free thinking, questioning, and understanding..." or incorporate competencies that an informed citizen of an information society ought to possess to participate intelligently and actively in that society.

Exam Probability: **Medium**

57. *Answer choices:*

(see index for correct answer)

- a. Ontology engineering
- b. Journal of the Association for Information Science and Technology
- c. Archetype
- d. Information scientist

Guidance: level 1

:: Fault tolerance ::

_____ is the property that enables a system to continue operating properly in the event of the failure of some of its components. If its operating quality decreases at all, the decrease is proportional to the severity of the failure, as compared to a naively designed system, in which even a small failure can cause total breakdown. _____ is particularly sought after in high-availability or life-critical systems. The ability of maintaining functionality when portions of a system break down is referred to as graceful degradation.

Exam Probability: **High**

58. *Answer choices:*

(see index for correct answer)

- a. Fault tolerance
- b. Random fault
- c. Byzantine fault tolerance
- d. Recovery procedure

Guidance: level 1

:: ::

_____, Inc. is an American online social media and social networking service company based in Menlo Park, California. It was founded by Mark Zuckerberg, along with fellow Harvard College students and roommates Eduardo Saverin, Andrew McCollum, Dustin Moskovitz and Chris Hughes. It is considered one of the Big Four technology companies along with Amazon, Apple, and Google.

Exam Probability: **Medium**

59. *Answer choices:*

(see index for correct answer)

- a. Facebook
- b. cultural
- c. empathy
- d. information systems assessment

Guidance: level 1

Marketing

Marketing is the study and management of exchange relationships. Marketing is the business process of creating relationships with and satisfying customers. With its focus on the customer, marketing is one of the premier components of business management.

Marketing is defined by the American Marketing Association as "the activity, set of institutions, and processes for creating, communicating, delivering, and exchanging offerings that have value for customers, clients, partners, and society at large."

_____ is a marketing communication that employs an openly sponsored, non-personal message to promote or sell a product, service or idea. Sponsors of _____ are typically businesses wishing to promote their products or services. _____ is differentiated from public relations in that an advertiser pays for and has control over the message. It differs from personal selling in that the message is non-personal, i.e., not directed to a particular individual. _____ is communicated through various mass media, including traditional media such as newspapers, magazines, television, radio, outdoor _____ or direct mail; and new media such as search results, blogs, social media, websites or text messages. The actual presentation of the message in a medium is referred to as an advertisement, or "ad" or advert for short.

Exam Probability: **Medium**

1. *Answer choices:*

(see index for correct answer)

- a. similarity-attraction theory
- b. interpersonal communication
- c. functional perspective
- d. Advertising

Guidance: level 1

:: Management accounting ::

In economics, _____ s, indirect costs or overheads are business expenses that are not dependent on the level of goods or services produced by the business. They tend to be time-related, such as interest or rents being paid per month, and are often referred to as overhead costs. This is in contrast to variable costs, which are volume-related and unknown at the beginning of the accounting year. For a simple example, such as a bakery, the monthly rent for the baking facilities, and the monthly payments for the security system and basic phone line are _____ s, as they do not change according to how much bread the bakery produces and sells. On the other hand, the wage costs of the bakery are variable, as the bakery will have to hire more workers if the production of bread increases. Economists reckon _____ as a entry barrier for new entrepreneurs.

Exam Probability: **High**

2. *Answer choices:*

(see index for correct answer)

- a. Fixed cost
- b. Hedge accounting
- c. Responsibility center
- d. Revenue center

Guidance: level 1

:: Marketing ::

_____ is the percentage of a market accounted for by a specific entity. In a survey of nearly 200 senior marketing managers, 67% responded that they found the revenue- "dollar _____" metric very useful, while 61% found "unit _____" very useful.

Exam Probability: **Medium**

3. *Answer choices:*

(see index for correct answer)

- a. Market share
- b. Marketing myopia
- c. Breakthrough Moments
- d. Factor analysis

Guidance: level 1

:: Television commercials ::

_____ is a phenomenon whereby something new and somehow valuable is formed. The created item may be intangible or a physical object.

Exam Probability: **Low**

4. *Answer choices:*

(see index for correct answer)

- a. Hotel Hell Vacation
- b. Revolving Door
- c. BK Dinner Baskets
- d. Universal Business Adapter

Guidance: level 1

:: Market research ::

_____ is an organized effort to gather information about target markets or customers. It is a very important component of business strategy. The term is commonly interchanged with marketing research; however, expert practitioners may wish to draw a distinction, in that marketing research is concerned specifically about marketing processes, while _____ is concerned specifically with markets.

Exam Probability: **Low**

5. *Answer choices:*

(see index for correct answer)

- a. A/B testing
- b. Market research
- c. AbsolutData
- d. Brand elections

Guidance: level 1

:: Advertising techniques ::

In promotion and of advertising, a _____ or show consists of a person's written or spoken statement extolling the virtue of a product. The term "_____" most commonly applies to the sales-pitches attributed to ordinary citizens, whereas the word "endorsement" usually applies to pitches by celebrities. _____ s can be part of communal marketing. Sometimes, the cartoon character can be a _____ in a commercial.

Exam Probability: **Medium**

6. *Answer choices:*

(see index for correct answer)

- a. Testimonial
- b. Trojan horse
- c. Display window
- d. Retail Radio

Guidance: level 1

:: Materials ::

A _____ , also known as a feedstock, unprocessed material, or primary commodity, is a basic material that is used to produce goods, finished products, energy, or intermediate materials which are feedstock for future finished products. As feedstock, the term connotes these materials are bottleneck assets and are highly important with regard to producing other products. An example of this is crude oil, which is a _____ and a feedstock used in the production of industrial chemicals, fuels, plastics, and pharmaceutical goods; lumber is a _____ used to produce a variety of products including all types of furniture. The term " _____ " denotes materials in minimally processed or unprocessed in states; e.g., raw latex, crude oil, cotton, coal, raw biomass, iron ore, air, logs, or water i.e. "...any product of agriculture, forestry, fishing and any other mineral that is in its natural form or which has undergone the transformation required to prepare it for internationally marketing in substantial volumes."

Exam Probability: **High**

7. *Answer choices:*

(see index for correct answer)

- a. FDU materials
- b. Glass microsphere
- c. Radar-absorbent material
- d. Layered double hydroxides

Guidance: level 1

:: Brand management ::

_____ refers to the extent to which customers are able to recall or recognise a brand. _____ is a key consideration in consumer behavior, advertising management, brand management and strategy development. The consumer's ability to recognise or recall a brand is central to purchasing decision-making. Purchasing cannot proceed unless a consumer is first aware of a product category and a brand within that category. Awareness does not necessarily mean that the consumer must be able to recall a specific brand name, but he or she must be able to recall sufficient distinguishing features for purchasing to proceed. For instance, if a consumer asks her friend to buy her some gum in a "blue pack", the friend would be expected to know which gum to buy, even though neither friend can recall the precise brand name at the time.

Exam Probability: **High**

8. *Answer choices:*

(see index for correct answer)

- a. Symbol-intensive brand
- b. Brand valuation
- c. Brand Finance
- d. Brand aversion

Guidance: level 1

:: Brokered programming ::

An _____ is a form of television commercial, which generally includes a toll-free telephone number or website. Most often used as a form of direct response television, long-form _____ s are typically 28:30 or 58:30 minutes in length. _____ s are also known as paid programming. This phenomenon started in the United States, where _____ s were typically shown overnight, outside peak prime time hours for commercial broadcasters. Some television stations chose to air _____ s as an alternative to the former practice of signing off. Some channels air _____ s 24 hours. Some stations also choose to air _____ s during the daytime hours mostly on weekends to fill in for unscheduled network or syndicated programming. By 2009, most _____ spending in the U.S. occurred during the early morning, daytime and evening hours, or in the afternoon. Stations in most countries around the world have instituted similar media structures. The _____ industry is worth over $200 billion.

Exam Probability: **High**

9. *Answer choices:*

(see index for correct answer)

- a. Toonzai
- b. One Magnificent Morning
- c. Leased access
- d. Infomercial

Guidance: level 1

:: Market research ::

A _____ is a small, but demographically diverse group of people and whose reactions are studied especially in market research or political analysis in guided or open discussions about a new product or something else to determine the reactions that can be expected from a larger population. It is a form of qualitative research consisting of interviews in which a group of people are asked about their perceptions, opinions, beliefs, and attitudes towards a product, service, concept, advertisement, idea, or packaging. Questions are asked in an interactive group setting where participants are free to talk with other group members. During this process, the researcher either takes notes or records the vital points he or she is getting from the group. Researchers should select members of the _____ carefully for effective and authoritative responses.

Exam Probability: **Medium**

10. *Answer choices:*

(see index for correct answer)

- a. Focus group
- b. Competitive intelligence
- c. Sectoral analysis
- d. New economic order

Guidance: level 1

In business and engineering, new _____ covers the complete process of bringing a new product to market. A central aspect of NPD is product design, along with various business considerations. New _____ is described broadly as the transformation of a market opportunity into a product available for sale. The product can be tangible or intangible, though sometimes services and other processes are distinguished from "products." NPD requires an understanding of customer needs and wants, the competitive environment, and the nature of the market.Cost, time and quality are the main variables that drive customer needs. Aiming at these three variables, innovative companies develop continuous practices and strategies to better satisfy customer requirements and to increase their own market share by a regular development of new products. There are many uncertainties and challenges which companies must face throughout the process. The use of best practices and the elimination of barriers to communication are the main concerns for the management of the NPD.

Exam Probability: **Low**

11. *Answer choices:*

(see index for correct answer)

- a. Product development
- b. corporate values
- c. levels of analysis
- d. similarity-attraction theory

Guidance: level 1

_____ is the provision of service to customers before, during and after a purchase. The perception of success of such interactions is dependent on employees "who can adjust themselves to the personality of the guest". _____ concerns the priority an organization assigns to _____ relative to components such as product innovation and pricing. In this sense, an organization that values good _____ may spend more money in training employees than the average organization or may proactively interview customers for feedback.

Exam Probability: **Medium**

12. *Answer choices:*

(see index for correct answer)

- a. cultural
- b. imperative
- c. levels of analysis
- d. open system

Guidance: level 1

:: Data management ::

In computing, a _____ , also known as an enterprise _____ , is a system used for reporting and data analysis, and is considered a core component of business intelligence. DWs are central repositories of integrated data from one or more disparate sources. They store current and historical data in one single place that are used for creating analytical reports for workers throughout the enterprise.

Exam Probability: **Medium**

13. *Answer choices:*

(see index for correct answer)

- a. World Wide Molecular Matrix
- b. Signed overpunch
- c. Data warehouse
- d. Data set

Guidance: level 1

:: ::

A _____ is the process of presenting a topic to an audience. It is typically a demonstration, introduction, lecture, or speech meant to inform, persuade, inspire, motivate, or to build good will or to present a new idea or product. The term can also be used for a formal or ritualized introduction or offering, as with the _____ of a debutante. _____ s in certain formats are also known as keynote address.

Exam Probability: **Medium**

14. *Answer choices:*

(see index for correct answer)

- a. cultural
- b. Character

- c. Presentation
- d. process perspective

Guidance: level 1

:: Direct marketing ::

> _____ is a form of advertising where organizations communicate directly to customers through a variety of media including cell phone text messaging, email, websites, online adverts, database marketing, fliers, catalog distribution, promotional letters, targeted television, newspapers, magazine advertisements, and outdoor advertising. Among practitioners, it is also known as direct response marketing.

Exam Probability: **Low**

15. *Answer choices:*

(see index for correct answer)

- a. Direct marketing
- b. DVD club
- c. Berlin promotion agency
- d. Time Reading Program

Guidance: level 1

:: ::

Retail is the process of selling consumer goods or services to customers through multiple channels of distribution to earn a profit. Retailers satisfy demand identified through a supply chain. The term "retailer" is typically applied where a service provider fills the small orders of a large number of individuals, who are end-users, rather than large orders of a small number of wholesale, corporate or government clientele. Shopping generally refers to the act of buying products. Sometimes this is done to obtain final goods, including necessities such as food and clothing; sometimes it takes place as a recreational activity. Recreational shopping often involves window shopping and browsing: it does not always result in a purchase.

Exam Probability: **Medium**

16. *Answer choices:*

(see index for correct answer)

- a. interpersonal communication
- b. hierarchical
- c. Retailing
- d. functional perspective

Guidance: level 1

:: Consumer theory ::

_____ is the quantity of a good that consumers are willing and able to purchase at various prices during a given period of time.

Exam Probability: **Low**

17. *Answer choices:*

(see index for correct answer)

- a. Engel curve
- b. Demand
- c. End-of-life
- d. Consumption

Guidance: level 1

:: Consumer behaviour ::

Convenient procedures, products and services are those intended to increase ease in accessibility, save resources and decrease frustration. A modern _____ is a labor-saving device, service or substance which make a task easier or more efficient than a traditional method. _____ is a relative concept, and depends on context. For example, automobiles were once considered a _____, yet today are regarded as a normal part of life.

Exam Probability: **Medium**

18. *Answer choices:*

(see index for correct answer)

- a. University of Michigan Consumer Sentiment Index
- b. Convenience

- c. Geodemography
- d. Social norms approach

Guidance: level 1

:: Industrial design ::

In physics and mathematics, the _____ of a mathematical space is informally defined as the minimum number of coordinates needed to specify any point within it. Thus a line has a _____ of one because only one coordinate is needed to specify a point on it for example, the point at 5 on a number line. A surface such as a plane or the surface of a cylinder or sphere has a _____ of two because two coordinates are needed to specify a point on it for example, both a latitude and longitude are required to locate a point on the surface of a sphere. The inside of a cube, a cylinder or a sphere is three- _____ al because three coordinates are needed to locate a point within these spaces.

Exam Probability: **Medium**

19. *Answer choices:*

(see index for correct answer)

- a. Oxide jacking
- b. Sky-Sailor
- c. Australian International Design Awards
- d. Industrial Designers Society of America

Guidance: level 1

:: Production economics ::

In microeconomics, _____ are the cost advantages that enterprises obtain due to their scale of operation, with cost per unit of output decreasing with increasing scale.

Exam Probability: **Low**

20. *Answer choices:*

(see index for correct answer)

- a. Economies of scale
- b. Cost-of-production theory of value
- c. Robinson Crusoe economy
- d. HMI quality

Guidance: level 1

:: ::

_____ is a concept of English common law and is a necessity for simple contracts but not for special contracts. The concept has been adopted by other common law jurisdictions, including the US.

Exam Probability: **High**

21. Answer choices:

(see index for correct answer)

- a. Sarbanes-Oxley act of 2002
- b. similarity-attraction theory
- c. Consideration
- d. co-culture

Guidance: level 1

:: Supply chain management terms ::

In business and finance, _____ is a system of organizations, people, activities, information, and resources involved in moving a product or service from supplier to customer. _____ activities involve the transformation of natural resources, raw materials, and components into a finished product that is delivered to the end customer. In sophisticated _____ systems, used products may re-enter the _____ at any point where residual value is recyclable. _____ s link value chains.

Exam Probability: **High**

22. Answer choices:

(see index for correct answer)

- a. inventory management
- b. Stockout
- c. Price look-up code

- d. Last mile

Guidance: level 1

:: ::

Consumer behaviour is the study of individuals, groups, or organizations and all the activities associated with the purchase, use and disposal of goods and services, including the consumer's emotional, mental and behavioural responses that precede or follow these activities. Consumer behaviour emerged in the 1940s and 50s as a distinct sub-discipline in the marketing area.

Exam Probability: **Medium**

23. *Answer choices:*

(see index for correct answer)

- a. imperative
- b. Consumer behavior
- c. information systems assessment
- d. corporate values

Guidance: level 1

:: Marketing ::

The _____ is a foundation model for businesses. The _____ has been defined as the "set of marketing tools that the firm uses to pursue its marketing objectives in the target market". Thus the _____ refers to four broad levels of marketing decision, namely: product, price, place, and promotion. Marketing practice has been occurring for millennia, but marketing theory emerged in the early twentieth century. The contemporary _____, or the 4 Ps, which has become the dominant framework for marketing management decisions, was first published in 1960. In services marketing, an extended _____ is used, typically comprising 7 Ps, made up of the original 4 Ps extended by process, people, and physical evidence. Occasionally service marketers will refer to 8 Ps, comprising these 7 Ps plus performance.

Exam Probability: **Medium**

24. *Answer choices:*

(see index for correct answer)

- a. Net idol
- b. Fourth screen
- c. Marketing mix
- d. Patronage concentration

Guidance: level 1

:: Marketing ::

_____ is a growth strategy that identifies and develops new market segments for current products. A _____ strategy targets non-buying customers in currently targeted segments. It also targets new customers in new segments.

Exam Probability: **Medium**

25. *Answer choices:*

(see index for correct answer)

- a. LIDA
- b. Fan loyalty
- c. Advertiser-funded programming
- d. customer-perceived value

Guidance: level 1

:: ::

In sales, commerce and economics, a _____ is the recipient of a good, service, product or an idea - obtained from a seller, vendor, or supplier via a financial transaction or exchange for money or some other valuable consideration.

Exam Probability: **Low**

26. *Answer choices:*

(see index for correct answer)

- a. surface-level diversity
- b. levels of analysis
- c. Sarbanes-Oxley act of 2002
- d. functional perspective

Guidance: level 1

:: Business ::

The seller, or the provider of the goods or services, completes a sale in response to an acquisition, appropriation, requisition or a direct interaction with the buyer at the point of sale. There is a passing of title of the item, and the settlement of a price, in which agreement is reached on a price for which transfer of ownership of the item will occur. The seller, not the purchaser typically executes the sale and it may be completed prior to the obligation of payment. In the case of indirect interaction, a person who sells goods or service on behalf of the owner is known as a _____ man or _____ woman or _____ person, but this often refers to someone selling goods in a store/shop, in which case other terms are also common, including _____ clerk, shop assistant, and retail clerk.

Exam Probability: **Low**

27. *Answer choices:*
(see index for correct answer)

- a. Sales

- b. Attribution
- c. Corporate services
- d. Functional sourcing

Guidance: level 1

:: Human resource management ::

_____ encompasses values and behaviors that contribute to the unique social and psychological environment of a business. The _____ influences the way people interact, the context within which knowledge is created, the resistance they will have towards certain changes, and ultimately the way they share knowledge. _____ represents the collective values, beliefs and principles of organizational members and is a product of factors such as history, product, market, technology, strategy, type of employees, management style, and national culture; culture includes the organization's vision, values, norms, systems, symbols, language, assumptions, environment, location, beliefs and habits.

Exam Probability: **High**

28. *Answer choices:*

(see index for correct answer)

- a. war for talent
- b. Bonus payment
- c. Organizational culture
- d. Chief human resources officer

Guidance: level 1

:: Public relations ::

_____ is the public visibility or awareness for any product, service or company. It may also refer to the movement of information from its source to the general public, often but not always via the media. The subjects of _____ include people, goods and services, organizations, and works of art or entertainment.

Exam Probability: **Low**

29. *Answer choices:*

(see index for correct answer)

- a. European Public Relations Education and Research Association
- b. Cunningham Communication
- c. Media monitoring service
- d. Public Relations Inquiry

Guidance: level 1

:: Supply chain management ::

The _____ is a barcode symbology that is widely used in the United States, Canada, United Kingdom, Australia, New Zealand, in Europe and other countries for tracking trade items in stores.

Exam Probability: **Medium**

30. *Answer choices:*

(see index for correct answer)

- a. Supply Chain Management Review
- b. JDA Software
- c. Transportation management system
- d. Universal Product Code

Guidance: level 1

:: Marketing ::

_____ is a marketing practice of individuals or organizations. It allows them to sell products or services to other companies or organizations that resell them, use them in their products or services or use them to support their works.

Exam Probability: **Medium**

31. *Answer choices:*

(see index for correct answer)

- a. Corporate anniversary
- b. Business marketing
- c. Market sector
- d. Presentation folder

Guidance: level 1

:: ::

A _____ consists of one people who live in the same dwelling and share meals. It may also consist of a single family or another group of people. A dwelling is considered to contain multiple _____ s if meals or living spaces are not shared. The _____ is the basic unit of analysis in many social, microeconomic and government models, and is important to economics and inheritance.

Exam Probability: **Medium**

32. *Answer choices:*
(see index for correct answer)

- a. information systems assessment
- b. interpersonal communication
- c. Household
- d. deep-level diversity

Guidance: level 1

:: ::

_____ is a term frequently used in marketing. It is a measure of how products and services supplied by a company meet or surpass customer expectation. _____ is defined as "the number of customers, or percentage of total customers, whose reported experience with a firm, its products, or its services exceeds specified satisfaction goals."

Exam Probability: **Medium**

33. *Answer choices:*

(see index for correct answer)

- a. deep-level diversity
- b. co-culture
- c. functional perspective
- d. Customer satisfaction

Guidance: level 1

:: Marketing ::

A business can use a variety of _____ when selling a product or service. The price can be set to maximize profitability for each unit sold or from the market overall. It can be used to defend an existing market from new entrants, to increase market share within a market or to enter a new market.

Exam Probability: **Low**

34. *Answer choices:*

(see index for correct answer)

- a. Pricing strategies
- b. Pink money
- c. Licensing International Expo
- d. Aftersales

Guidance: level 1

:: Consumer theory ::

A _____ is a technical term in psychology, economics and philosophy usually used in relation to choosing between alternatives. For example, someone prefers A over B if they would rather choose A than B.

Exam Probability: **Medium**

35. *Answer choices:*

(see index for correct answer)

- a. Demand
- b. Permanent income hypothesis
- c. Expenditure function
- d. Snob effect

Guidance: level 1

:: Project management ::

A _____ is a source or supply from which a benefit is produced and it has some utility. _____s can broadly be classified upon their availability—they are classified into renewable and non-renewable _____s. Examples of non renewable _____s are coal ,crude oil natural gas nuclear energy etc. Examples of renewable _____s are air,water,wind,solar energy etc. They can also be classified as actual and potential on the basis of level of development and use, on the basis of origin they can be classified as biotic and abiotic, and on the basis of their distribution, as ubiquitous and localized . An item becomes a _____ with time and developing technology. Typically, _____s are materials, energy, services, staff, knowledge, or other assets that are transformed to produce benefit and in the process may be consumed or made unavailable. Benefits of _____ utilization may include increased wealth, proper functioning of a system, or enhanced well-being. From a human perspective a natural _____ is anything obtained from the environment to satisfy human needs and wants. From a broader biological or ecological perspective a _____ satisfies the needs of a living organism .

Exam Probability: **High**

36. *Answer choices:*

(see index for correct answer)

- a. Constructability
- b. Iteration
- c. project triangle
- d. Resource

Guidance: level 1

:: ::

_____ , or auditory perception, is the ability to perceive sounds by detecting vibrations, changes in the pressure of the surrounding medium through time, through an organ such as the ear. The academic field concerned with _____ is auditory science.

Exam Probability: **Medium**

37. *Answer choices:*

(see index for correct answer)

- a. hierarchical perspective
- b. interpersonal communication
- c. personal values
- d. similarity-attraction theory

Guidance: level 1

:: Marketing ::

_____ or stock is the goods and materials that a business holds for the ultimate goal of resale.

Exam Probability: **Low**

38. *Answer choices:*

(see index for correct answer)

- a. Inventory
- b. Brand
- c. Adobe Social
- d. Online lead generation

Guidance: level 1

:: ::

In a supply chain, a _____ , or a seller, is an enterprise that contributes goods or services. Generally, a supply chain _____ manufactures inventory/stock items and sells them to the next link in the chain. Today, these terms refer to a supplier of any good or service.

Exam Probability: **Low**

39. *Answer choices:*

(see index for correct answer)

- a. hierarchical perspective
- b. surface-level diversity
- c. Vendor

- d. cultural

Guidance: level 1

:: Packaging ::

In work place, _____ or job _____ means good ranking with the hypothesized conception of requirements of a role. There are two types of job _____ s: contextual and task. Task _____ is related to cognitive ability while contextual _____ is dependent upon personality. Task _____ are behavioral roles that are recognized in job descriptions and by remuneration systems, they are directly related to organizational _____ , whereas, contextual _____ are value based and additional behavioral roles that are not recognized in job descriptions and covered by compensation; they are extra roles that are indirectly related to organizational _____ . Citizenship _____ like contextual _____ means a set of individual activity/contribution that supports the organizational culture.

Exam Probability: **Low**

40. *Answer choices:*
(see index for correct answer)

- a. Octabin
- b. Performance
- c. Bag-in-box
- d. Discbox Slider

Guidance: level 1

:: Competition (economics) ::

_____ arises whenever at least two parties strive for a goal which cannot be shared: where one's gain is the other's loss.

Exam Probability: **Medium**

41. *Answer choices:*

(see index for correct answer)

- a. Competition
- b. National Competitiveness Report of Armenia
- c. School choice
- d. Wantrapreneur

Guidance: level 1

:: Management ::

In business, a _____ is the attribute that allows an organization to outperform its competitors. A _____ may include access to natural resources, such as high-grade ores or a low-cost power source, highly skilled labor, geographic location, high entry barriers, and access to new technology.

Exam Probability: **Low**

42. *Answer choices:*

(see index for correct answer)

- a. Opera management
- b. Competitive advantage
- c. Systems analysis
- d. Certified management consultant

Guidance: level 1

:: Health promotion ::

_____ , as defined by the World _____ Organization , is "a state of complete physical, mental and social well-being and not merely the absence of disease or infirmity." This definition has been subject to controversy, as it may have limited value for implementation. _____ may be defined as the ability to adapt and manage physical, mental and social challenges throughout life.

Exam Probability: **Medium**

43. *Answer choices:*

(see index for correct answer)

- a. Health promotion
- b. Black Report
- c. Health care reform
- d. 10 Essential Public Health Services

Guidance: level 1

:: Stock market ::

_____ is freedom from, or resilience against, potential harm caused by others. Beneficiaries of _____ may be of persons and social groups, objects and institutions, ecosystems or any other entity or phenomenon vulnerable to unwanted change by its environment.

Exam Probability: **High**

44. *Answer choices:*

(see index for correct answer)

- a. Security
- b. Central limit order book
- c. Stock Catalyst
- d. Shareholders

Guidance: level 1

:: Promotion and marketing communications ::

A _____ is the intended audience or readership of a publication, advertisement, or other message. In marketing and advertising, it is a particular group of consumers within the predetermined target market, identified as the targets or recipients for a particular advertisement or message. Businesses that have a wide target market will focus on a specific _____ for certain messages to send, such as The Body Shops Mother's Day advertisements, which were aimed at the children and spouses of women, rather than the whole market which would have included the women themselves.

Exam Probability: **Low**

45. *Answer choices:*

(see index for correct answer)

- a. Target audience
- b. Sales force automation
- c. Wordmark
- d. Infoganda

Guidance: level 1

In regulatory jurisdictions that provide for it, _____ is a group of laws and organizations designed to ensure the rights of consumers as well as fair trade, competition and accurate information in the marketplace. The laws are designed to prevent the businesses that engage in fraud or specified unfair practices from gaining an advantage over competitors. They may also provides additional protection for those most vulnerable in society. _____ laws are a form of government regulation that aim to protect the rights of consumers. For example, a government may require businesses to disclose detailed information about products—particularly in areas where safety or public health is an issue, such as food.

Exam Probability: **Low**

46. *Answer choices:*

(see index for correct answer)

- a. imperative
- b. Consumer Protection
- c. Sarbanes-Oxley act of 2002
- d. open system

Guidance: level 1

:: Stock market ::

The _____ of a corporation is all of the shares into which ownership of the corporation is divided. In American English, the shares are commonly known as "_____s". A single share of the _____ represents fractional ownership of the corporation in proportion to the total number of shares. This typically entitles the _____ holder to that fraction of the company's earnings, proceeds from liquidation of assets , or voting power, often dividing these up in proportion to the amount of money each _____ holder has invested. Not all _____ is necessarily equal, as certain classes of _____ may be issued for example without voting rights, with enhanced voting rights, or with a certain priority to receive profits or liquidation proceeds before or after other classes of shareholders.

Exam Probability: **High**

47. *Answer choices:*

(see index for correct answer)

- a. Non-voting stock
- b. BATS Chi-X Europe
- c. Registered share
- d. Stock

Guidance: level 1

:: Management ::

_____ is the process of thinking about the activities required to achieve a desired goal. It is the first and foremost activity to achieve desired results. It involves the creation and maintenance of a plan, such as psychological aspects that require conceptual skills. There are even a couple of tests to measure someone's capability of _____ well. As such, _____ is a fundamental property of intelligent behavior. An important further meaning, often just called "_____" is the legal context of permitted building developments.

Exam Probability: **Low**

48. *Answer choices:*

(see index for correct answer)

- a. Business process mapping
- b. Identity formation
- c. Target operating model
- d. Supply chain sustainability

Guidance: level 1

:: Budgets ::

A _____ is a financial plan for a defined period, often one year. It may also include planned sales volumes and revenues, resource quantities, costs and expenses, assets, liabilities and cash flows. Companies, governments, families and other organizations use it to express strategic plans of activities or events in measurable terms.

Exam Probability: **High**

49. *Answer choices:*

(see index for correct answer)

- a. Personal budget
- b. Budgeted cost of work scheduled
- c. Zero budget
- d. Public budgeting

Guidance: level 1

:: ::

_____ consists of using generic or ad hoc methods in an orderly manner to find solutions to problems. Some of the problem-solving techniques developed and used in philosophy, artificial intelligence, computer science, engineering, mathematics, or medicine are related to mental problem-solving techniques studied in psychology.

Exam Probability: **High**

50. *Answer choices:*

(see index for correct answer)

- a. Character
- b. functional perspective

- c. corporate values
- d. co-culture

Guidance: level 1

:: Services management and marketing ::

_____ is a specialised branch of marketing. _____ emerged as a separate field of study in the early 1980s, following the recognition that the unique characteristics of services required different strategies compared with the marketing of physical goods.

Exam Probability: **Low**

51. *Answer choices:*
(see index for correct answer)

- a. Services marketing
- b. Automated attendant
- c. The Experience Economy
- d. Internet hosting service

Guidance: level 1

:: Monopoly (economics) ::

A _____ is a form of intellectual property that gives its owner the legal right to exclude others from making, using, selling, and importing an invention for a limited period of years, in exchange for publishing an enabling public disclosure of the invention. In most countries _____ rights fall under civil law and the _____ holder needs to sue someone infringing the _____ in order to enforce his or her rights. In some industries _____ s are an essential form of competitive advantage; in others they are irrelevant.

Exam Probability: **Low**

52. *Answer choices:*
(see index for correct answer)

- a. Ramsey problem
- b. Patent
- c. Legal monopoly
- d. Sherman Antitrust Act

Guidance: level 1

:: Product management ::

A _____, trade mark, or trade-mark is a recognizable sign, design, or expression which identifies products or services of a particular source from those of others, although _____ s used to identify services are usually called service marks. The _____ owner can be an individual, business organization, or any legal entity. A _____ may be located on a package, a label, a voucher, or on the product itself. For the sake of corporate identity, _____ s are often displayed on company buildings. It is legally recognized as a type of intellectual property.

Exam Probability: **Medium**

53. *Answer choices:*

(see index for correct answer)

- a. Product cost management
- b. Pareto chart
- c. Trademark
- d. Mature technology

Guidance: level 1

:: ::

An _____ is a systematic and independent examination of books, accounts, statutory records, documents and vouchers of an organization to ascertain how far the financial statements as well as non-financial disclosures present a true and fair view of the concern. It also attempts to ensure that the books of accounts are properly maintained by the concern as required by law. _____ ing has become such a ubiquitous phenomenon in the corporate and the public sector that academics started identifying an " _____ Society". The _____ or perceives and recognises the propositions before them for examination, obtains evidence, evaluates the same and formulates an opinion on the basis of his judgement which is communicated through their _____ ing report.

Exam Probability: **High**

54. *Answer choices:*

(see index for correct answer)

- a. deep-level diversity
- b. corporate values
- c. interpersonal communication
- d. Audit

Guidance: level 1

:: Consumer behaviour ::

_____ refers to the ability of a company or product to retain its customers over some specified period. High _____ means customers of the product or business tend to return to, continue to buy or in some other way not defect to another product or business, or to non-use entirely. Selling organizations generally attempt to reduce customer defections. _____ starts with the first contact an organization has with a customer and continues throughout the entire lifetime of a relationship and successful retention efforts take this entire lifecycle into account. A company's ability to attract and retain new customers is related not only to its product or services, but also to the way it services its existing customers, the value the customers actually generate as a result of utilizing the solutions, and the reputation it creates within and across the marketplace.

Exam Probability: **High**

55. *Answer choices:*

(see index for correct answer)

- a. Conspicuous expression
- b. Customer retention
- c. Shopping while black
- d. Consumer ethnocentrism

Guidance: level 1

:: Graphic design ::

An _____ is an artifact that depicts visual perception, such as a photograph or other two-dimensional picture, that resembles a subject—usually a physical object—and thus provides a depiction of it. In the context of signal processing, an _____ is a distributed amplitude of color.

Exam Probability: **Medium**

56. *Answer choices:*

(see index for correct answer)

- a. Book design
- b. Image
- c. Manga Studio
- d. 99designs

Guidance: level 1

:: ::

An _____, often referred to as a creative agency or an ad agency, is a business dedicated to creating, planning, and handling advertising and sometimes other forms of promotion and marketing for its clients. An ad agency is generally independent from the client; it may be an internal department or agency that provides an outside point of view to the effort of selling the client's products or services, or an outside firm. An agency can also handle overall marketing and branding strategies promotions for its clients, which may include sales as well.

Exam Probability: **Medium**

57. *Answer choices:*

(see index for correct answer)

- a. functional perspective
- b. personal values
- c. co-culture
- d. corporate values

Guidance: level 1

:: Marketing ::

_____ comes from the Latin neg and otsia referring to businessmen who, unlike the patricians, had no leisure time in their industriousness; it held the meaning of business until the 17th century when it took on the diplomatic connotation as a dialogue between two or more people or parties intended to reach a beneficial outcome over one or more issues where a conflict exists with respect to at least one of these issues. Thus, _____ is a process of combining divergent positions into a joint agreement under a decision rule of unanimity.

Exam Probability: **Low**

58. *Answer choices:*

(see index for correct answer)

- a. Marketing supply chain
- b. Patronage concentration
- c. Movie packaging
- d. Postmodern communication

Guidance: level 1

:: Commerce ::

_____ relates to "the exchange of goods and services, especially on a large scale". It includes legal, economic, political, social, cultural and technological systems that operate in a country or in international trade.

Exam Probability: **High**

59. *Answer choices:*
(see index for correct answer)

- a. Video rental shop
- b. DataCash
- c. Third-party source
- d. Sales quote

Guidance: level 1

Manufacturing

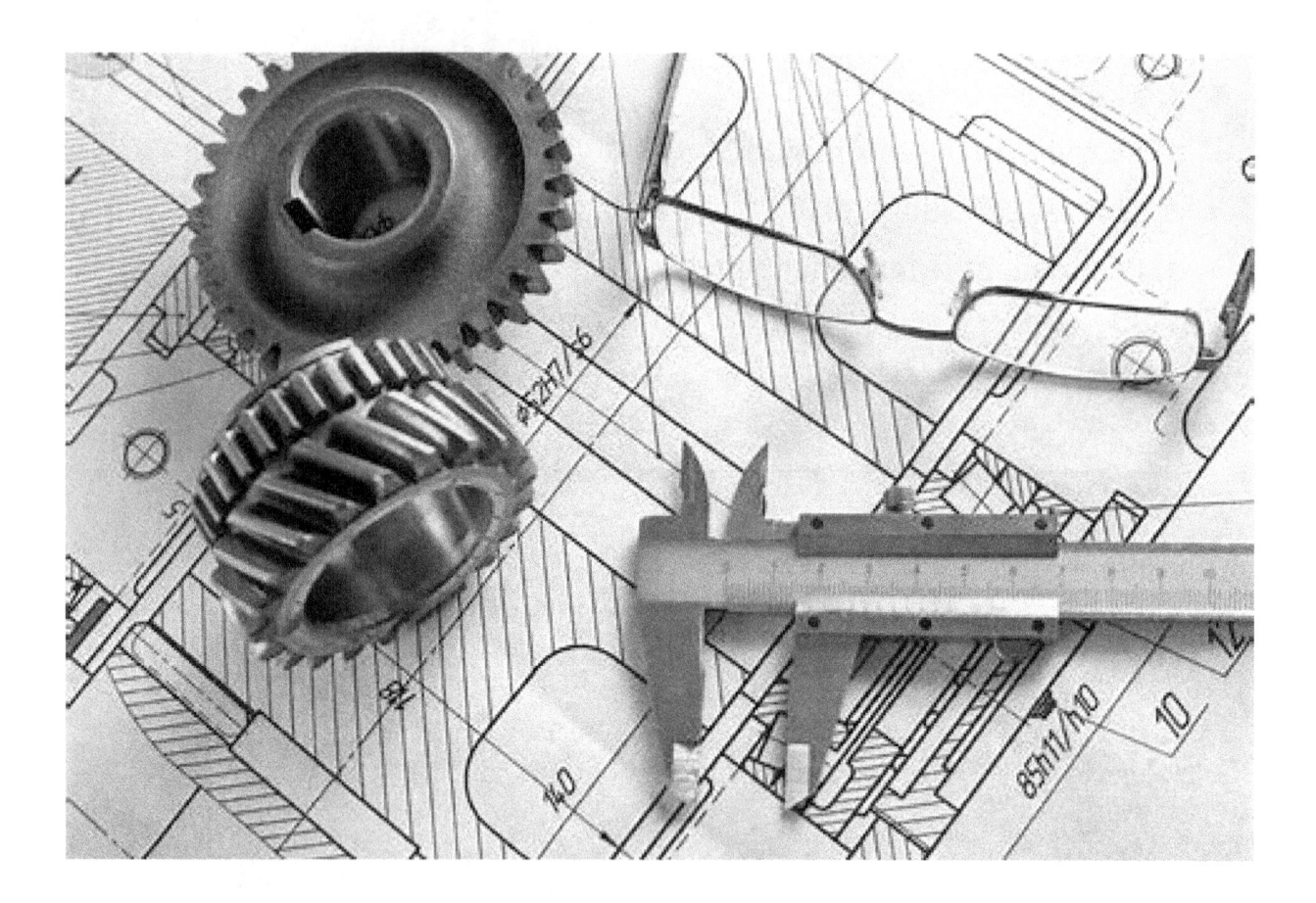

Manufacturing is the production of merchandise for use or sale using labor and machines, tools, chemical and biological processing, or formulation. The term may refer to a range of human activity, from handicraft to high tech, but is most commonly applied to industrial design , in which raw materials are transformed into finished goods on a large scale. Such finished goods may be sold to other manufacturers for the production of other, more complex products, such as aircraft, household appliances, furniture, sports equipment or automobiles, or sold to wholesalers, who in turn sell them to retailers, who then sell them to end users and consumers.

:: Gas technologies ::

A _____ is a device used to transfer heat between two or more fluids. _____ s are used in both cooling and heating processes. The fluids may be separated by a solid wall to prevent mixing or they may be in direct contact. They are widely used in space heating, refrigeration, air conditioning, power stations, chemical plants, petrochemical plants, petroleum refineries, natural-gas processing, and sewage treatment. The classic example of a _____ is found in an internal combustion engine in which a circulating fluid known as engine coolant flows through radiator coils and air flows past the coils, which cools the coolant and heats the incoming air. Another example is the heat sink, which is a passive _____ that transfers the heat generated by an electronic or a mechanical device to a fluid medium, often air or a liquid coolant.

Exam Probability: **Medium**

1. *Answer choices:*

(see index for correct answer)

- a. Micropump
- b. Heat exchanger
- c. Carbon dioxide scrubber
- d. Oxygen tank

Guidance: level 1

:: Business process ::

A _____ or business method is a collection of related, structured activities or tasks by people or equipment which in a specific sequence produce a service or product for a particular customer or customers. _____ es occur at all organizational levels and may or may not be visible to the customers. A _____ may often be visualized as a flowchart of a sequence of activities with interleaving decision points or as a process matrix of a sequence of activities with relevance rules based on data in the process. The benefits of using _____ es include improved customer satisfaction and improved agility for reacting to rapid market change. Process-oriented organizations break down the barriers of structural departments and try to avoid functional silos.

Exam Probability: **High**

2. *Answer choices:*

(see index for correct answer)

- a. Information technology outsourcing
- b. Business communication
- c. Sales process engineering
- d. Bizagi

Guidance: level 1

:: Monopoly (economics) ::

_____ are "efficiencies formed by variety, not volume". For example, a gas station that sells gasoline can sell soda, milk, baked goods, etc through their customer service representatives and thus achieve gasoline companies _____.

Exam Probability: **Medium**

3. *Answer choices:*
(see index for correct answer)

- a. Ownership unbundling
- b. Privatization
- c. Patent portfolio
- d. Motion Picture Patents Company

Guidance: level 1

:: Production and manufacturing ::

_____ is a theory of management that analyzes and synthesizes workflows. Its main objective is improving economic efficiency, especially labor productivity. It was one of the earliest attempts to apply science to the engineering of processes and to management. _____ is sometimes known as Taylorism after its founder, Frederick Winslow Taylor.

Exam Probability: **Medium**

4. *Answer choices:*

(see index for correct answer)

- a. product lifecycle
- b. Process layout
- c. Scientific management
- d. First pass yield

Guidance: level 1

:: Distribution, retailing, and wholesaling ::

The _____ is a distribution channel phenomenon in which forecasts yield supply chain inefficiencies. It refers to increasing swings in inventory in response to shifts in customer demand as one moves further up the supply chain. The concept first appeared in Jay Forrester's Industrial Dynamics and thus it is also known as the Forrester effect. The _____ was named for the way the amplitude of a whip increases down its length. The further from the originating signal, the greater the distortion of the wave pattern. In a similar manner, forecast accuracy decreases as one moves upstream along the supply chain. For example, many consumer goods have fairly consistent consumption at retail but this signal becomes more chaotic and unpredictable as the focus moves away from consumer purchasing behavior.

Exam Probability: **High**

5. *Answer choices:*

(see index for correct answer)

- a. Pacific Comics
- b. Pallet rack mover
- c. Bullwhip effect
- d. Silenzio Music

Guidance: level 1

:: Information technology management ::

_____ is the discipline of engineering concerned with the principles and practice of product and service quality assurance and control. In the software development, it is the management, development, operation and maintenance of IT systems and enterprise architectures with a high quality standard.

Exam Probability: **High**

6. *Answer choices:*

(see index for correct answer)

- a. Information technology operations
- b. ODMA
- c. Quality Engineering
- d. NetIQ

Guidance: level 1

:: Information technology management ::

_____ concerns a cycle of organizational activity: the acquisition of information from one or more sources, the custodianship and the distribution of that information to those who need it, and its ultimate disposition through archiving or deletion.

Exam Probability: **Medium**

7. *Answer choices:*

(see index for correct answer)

- a. Operational-level agreement
- b. IT Interaction Model
- c. Information management
- d. Drill down

Guidance: level 1

:: Project management ::

A _____ is a team whose members usually belong to different groups, functions and are assigned to activities for the same project. A team can be divided into sub-teams according to need. Usually _____ s are only used for a defined period of time. They are disbanded after the project is deemed complete. Due to the nature of the specific formation and disbandment, _____ s are usually in organizations.

Exam Probability: **Low**

8. *Answer choices:*

(see index for correct answer)

- a. Deployment Plan
- b. TELOS
- c. Schedule
- d. Gantt chart

Guidance: level 1

:: Product management ::

_____ s, also known as Shewhart charts or process-behavior charts, are a statistical process control tool used to determine if a manufacturing or business process is in a state of control.

Exam Probability: **Low**

9. *Answer choices:*

(see index for correct answer)

- a. Product management
- b. Brand extension
- c. Electronic registration mark
- d. Control chart

Guidance: level 1

:: Production economics ::

In economics and related disciplines, a _____ is a cost in making any economic trade when participating in a market.

Exam Probability: **High**

10. *Answer choices:*

(see index for correct answer)

- a. Transaction cost
- b. Isoquant
- c. Industrial production index
- d. Marginal rate of technical substitution

Guidance: level 1

:: Gas technologies ::

A _____ is a rotary mechanical device that extracts energy from a fluid flow and converts it into useful work. The work produced by a _____ can be used for generating electrical power when combined with a generator. A _____ is a turbomachine with at least one moving part called a rotor assembly, which is a shaft or drum with blades attached. Moving fluid acts on the blades so that they move and impart rotational energy to the rotor. Early _____ examples are windmills and waterwheels.

Exam Probability: **Low**

11. *Answer choices:*

(see index for correct answer)

- a. Liquid ring pump
- b. The Oval Gasholders
- c. Turbine
- d. Hydrogen storage

Guidance: level 1

:: Data interchange standards ::

_____ is the concept of businesses electronically communicating information that was traditionally communicated on paper, such as purchase orders and invoices. Technical standards for EDI exist to facilitate parties transacting such instruments without having to make special arrangements.

Exam Probability: **Low**

12. *Answer choices:*

(see index for correct answer)

- a. ASC X12
- b. Domain Application Protocol
- c. Common Alerting Protocol
- d. Electronic data interchange

Guidance: level 1

:: ::

The _____ is a project plan of how the production budget will be spent over a given timescale, for every phase of a business project.

Exam Probability: **Medium**

13. *Answer choices:*

(see index for correct answer)

- a. empathy
- b. cultural
- c. hierarchical
- d. similarity-attraction theory

Guidance: level 1

:: Fault-tolerant computer systems ::

_____ decision-making is a group decision-making process in which group members develop, and agree to support a decision in the best interest of the whole group or common goal. _____ may be defined professionally as an acceptable resolution, one that can be supported, even if not the "favourite" of each individual. It has its origin in the Latin word consensus, which is from consentio meaning literally feel together. It is used to describe both the decision and the process of reaching a decision. _____ decision-making is thus concerned with the process of deliberating and finalizing a decision, and the social, economic, legal, environmental and political effects of applying this process.

Exam Probability: **Low**

14. *Answer choices:*

(see index for correct answer)

- a. Round-robin DNS
- b. Lockstep
- c. Uptime
- d. Single point of failure

Guidance: level 1

:: Management ::

A supply-chain network is an evolution of the basic supply chain. Due to rapid technological advancement, organisations with a basic supply chain can develop this chain into a more complex structure involving a higher level of interdependence and connectivity between more organisations, this constitutes a supply-chain network.

Exam Probability: **Medium**

15. *Answer choices:*

(see index for correct answer)

- a. Virtual customer environment
- b. Certified Energy Manager
- c. Project management
- d. Supply chain network

Guidance: level 1

:: Supply chain management ::

A _____ is a type of auction in which the traditional roles of buyer and seller are reversed. Thus, there is one buyer and many potential sellers. In an ordinary auction, buyers compete to obtain goods or services by offering increasingly higher prices. In contrast, in a _____ , the sellers compete to obtain business from the buyer and prices will typically decrease as the sellers underbid each other.

Exam Probability: **High**

16. *Answer choices:*

(see index for correct answer)

- a. Supply chain management software
- b. ThoughtSpeed Corporation
- c. RevPAR
- d. Reverse auction

Guidance: level 1

:: Natural resources ::

_____ s are resources that exist without actions of humankind. This includes all valued characteristics such as magnetic, gravitational, electrical properties and forces etc. On Earth it includes sunlight, atmosphere, water, land along with all vegetation, crops and animal life that naturally subsists upon or within the heretofore identified characteristics and substances.

Exam Probability: **High**

17. *Answer choices:*

(see index for correct answer)

- a. Natural resource
- b. Automated mineralogy
- c. Natural Resources Acts
- d. Natural Resources Forum

Guidance: level 1

:: Information technology management ::

The term _____ is used to refer to periods when a system is unavailable. _____ or outage duration refers to a period of time that a system fails to provide or perform its primary function. Reliability, availability, recovery, and unavailability are related concepts. The unavailability is the proportion of a time-span that a system is unavailable or offline. This is usually a result of the system failing to function because of an unplanned event, or because of routine maintenance.

Exam Probability: **High**

18. *Answer choices:*

(see index for correct answer)

- a. Infoblox
- b. Capacity management
- c. Configuration Management
- d. Downtime

Guidance: level 1

:: Metalworking ::

A _____ is a round object with various uses. It is used in _____ games, where the play of the game follows the state of the _____ as it is hit, kicked or thrown by players. _____ s can also be used for simpler activities, such as catch or juggling. _____ s made from hard-wearing materials are used in engineering applications to provide very low friction bearings, known as _____ bearings. Black-powder weapons use stone and metal _____ s as projectiles.

Exam Probability: **Medium**

19. *Answer choices:*

(see index for correct answer)

- a. Mill finish
- b. Moving crack
- c. Low plasticity burnishing
- d. Cast iron

Guidance: level 1

:: ::

An _____ is a company that produces parts and equipment that may be marketed by another manufacturer. For example, Foxconn, a Taiwanese electronics contract manufacturing company, which produces a variety of parts and equipment for companies such as Apple Inc., Dell, Google, Huawei, Nintendo, etc., is the largest OEM company in the world by both scale and revenue.

Exam Probability: **Medium**

20. *Answer choices:*

(see index for correct answer)

- a. Original equipment manufacturer
- b. empathy
- c. information systems assessment
- d. cultural

Guidance: level 1

:: Supply chain management ::

_____ is a core supply chain function and includes supply chain planning and supply chain execution capabilities. Specifically, _____ is the capability firms use to plan total material requirements. The material requirements are communicated to procurement and other functions for sourcing. _____ is also responsible for determining the amount of material to be deployed at each stocking location across the supply chain, establishing material replenishment plans, determining inventory levels to hold for each type of inventory, and communicating information regarding material needs throughout the extended supply chain.

Exam Probability: **Medium**

21. *Answer choices:*

(see index for correct answer)

- a. XIO Strategies
- b. Mobile asset management
- c. ISO/PAS 28000
- d. Materials management

Guidance: level 1

:: Management ::

In organizational studies, _____ is the efficient and effective development of an organization's resources when they are needed. Such resources may include financial resources, inventory, human skills, production resources, or information technology and natural resources.

Exam Probability: **Low**

22. *Answer choices:*

(see index for correct answer)

- a. Product life-cycle management
- b. Instruction creep
- c. Management fad
- d. Resource management

Guidance: level 1

:: Project management ::

Some scenarios associate "this kind of planning" with learning "life skills". _____ s are necessary, or at least useful, in situations where individuals need to know what time they must be at a specific location to receive a specific service, and where people need to accomplish a set of goals within a set time period.

Exam Probability: **Low**

23. *Answer choices:*
(see index for correct answer)

- a. Schedule
- b. Outcomes theory
- c. System anatomy
- d. Code name

Guidance: level 1

:: Costs ::

The _____ is computed by dividing the total cost of goods available for sale by the total units available for sale. This gives a weighted-average unit cost that is applied to the units in the ending inventory.

Exam Probability: **High**

24. Answer choices:

(see index for correct answer)

- a. Cost of poor quality
- b. Cost curve
- c. Average cost
- d. Implicit cost

Guidance: level 1

:: ::

In a supply chain, a _____, or a seller, is an enterprise that contributes goods or services. Generally, a supply chain _____ manufactures inventory/stock items and sells them to the next link in the chain. Today, these terms refer to a supplier of any good or service.

Exam Probability: **Low**

25. Answer choices:

(see index for correct answer)

- a. Vendor
- b. Character
- c. levels of analysis
- d. process perspective

Guidance: level 1

:: Finance ::

_____ is a financial estimate intended to help buyers and owners determine the direct and indirect costs of a product or system. It is a management accounting concept that can be used in full cost accounting or even ecological economics where it includes social costs.

Exam Probability: **Medium**

26. *Answer choices:*

(see index for correct answer)

- a. Bauer Financial
- b. Remote deposit
- c. Total cost of ownership
- d. Net operating assets

Guidance: level 1

:: Supply chain management terms ::

In business and finance, _____ is a system of organizations, people, activities, information, and resources involved in moving a product or service from supplier to customer. _____ activities involve the transformation of natural resources, raw materials, and components into a finished product that is delivered to the end customer. In sophisticated _____ systems, used products may re-enter the _____ at any point where residual value is recyclable. _____ s link value chains.

Exam Probability: **Low**

27. *Answer choices:*

(see index for correct answer)

- a. Last mile
- b. Stockout
- c. Will call
- d. Direct shipment

Guidance: level 1

:: Outsourcing ::

A _____ is a document that solicits proposal, often made through a bidding process, by an agency or company interested in procurement of a commodity, service, or valuable asset, to potential suppliers to submit business proposals. It is submitted early in the procurement cycle, either at the preliminary study, or procurement stage.

Exam Probability: **Medium**

28. *Answer choices:*

(see index for correct answer)

- a. Oregon Bridge Delivery Partners
- b. Talentica Software
- c. Affiliated Computer Services
- d. Transition methodology

Guidance: level 1

:: Marketing techniques ::

A _____ is an award to be given to a person, a group of people like a sports team, or organization to recognise and reward actions or achievements. Official _____ s often involve monetary rewards as well as the fame that comes with them. Some _____ s are also associated with extravagant awarding ceremonies, such as the Academy Awards.

Exam Probability: **Low**

29. *Answer choices:*

(see index for correct answer)

- a. Virtual event
- b. Appeal to fear

- c. Prize
- d. Premium

Guidance: level 1

:: Accounting source documents ::

A _____ is a commercial document and first official offer issued by a buyer to a seller indicating types, quantities, and agreed prices for products or services. It is used to control the purchasing of products and services from external suppliers. _____s can be an essential part of enterprise resource planning system orders.

Exam Probability: **Medium**

30. *Answer choices:*

(see index for correct answer)

- a. Bank statement
- b. Purchase order
- c. Credit memo
- d. Superbill

Guidance: level 1

:: Packaging ::

In work place, _____ or job _____ means good ranking with the hypothesized conception of requirements of a role. There are two types of job _____ s: contextual and task. Task _____ is related to cognitive ability while contextual _____ is dependent upon personality. Task _____ are behavioral roles that are recognized in job descriptions and by remuneration systems, they are directly related to organizational _____, whereas, contextual _____ are value based and additional behavioral roles that are not recognized in job descriptions and covered by compensation; they are extra roles that are indirectly related to organizational _____ . Citizenship _____ like contextual _____ means a set of individual activity/contribution that supports the organizational culture.

Exam Probability: **Medium**

31. *Answer choices:*

(see index for correct answer)

- a. Permeation
- b. UN Recommendations on the Transport of Dangerous Goods
- c. Oxygen scavenger
- d. Wrap rage

Guidance: level 1

:: ::

In production, research, retail, and accounting, a _____ is the value of money that has been used up to produce something or deliver a service, and hence is not available for use anymore. In business, the _____ may be one of acquisition, in which case the amount of money expended to acquire it is counted as _____ . In this case, money is the input that is gone in order to acquire the thing. This acquisition _____ may be the sum of the _____ of production as incurred by the original producer, and further _____ s of transaction as incurred by the acquirer over and above the price paid to the producer. Usually, the price also includes a mark-up for profit over the _____ of production.

Exam Probability: **High**

32. *Answer choices:*

(see index for correct answer)

- a. hierarchical perspective
- b. empathy
- c. co-culture
- d. Cost

Guidance: level 1

:: Supply chain management ::

_____ is the process of finding and agreeing to terms, and acquiring goods, services, or works from an external source, often via a tendering or competitive bidding process. _____ is used to ensure the buyer receives goods, services, or works at the best possible price when aspects such as quality, quantity, time, and location are compared. Corporations and public bodies often define processes intended to promote fair and open competition for their business while minimizing risks such as exposure to fraud and collusion.

Exam Probability: **Low**

33. *Answer choices:*

(see index for correct answer)

- a. Avercast
- b. Cross-border leasing
- c. Procurement
- d. Enterprise carbon accounting

Guidance: level 1

:: Management ::

Business _____ is a discipline in operations management in which people use various methods to discover, model, analyze, measure, improve, optimize, and automate business processes. BPM focuses on improving corporate performance by managing business processes. Any combination of methods used to manage a company's business processes is BPM. Processes can be structured and repeatable or unstructured and variable. Though not required, enabling technologies are often used with BPM.

Exam Probability: **High**

34. *Answer choices:*

(see index for correct answer)

- a. Process management
- b. Industrial democracy
- c. Value proposition
- d. Resource management

Guidance: level 1

:: Production and manufacturing ::

_____ is a comprehensive and rigorous industrial process by which a previously sold, leased, used, worn or non-functional product or part is returned to a 'like-new' or 'better-than-new' condition, from both a quality and performance perspective, through a controlled, reproducible and sustainable process.

Exam Probability: **Low**

35. *Answer choices:*

(see index for correct answer)

- a. Pre-shipment inspection
- b. Process layout

- c. production planning
- d. Safety Network International e.V.

Guidance: level 1

:: Promotion and marketing communications ::

The _____ of American Manufacturers, now ThomasNet, is an online platform for supplier discovery and product sourcing in the US and Canada. It was once known as the "big green books" and "Thomas Registry", and was a multi-volume directory of industrial product information covering 650,000 distributors, manufacturers and service companies within 67,000-plus industrial categories that is now published on ThomasNet.

Exam Probability: **High**

36. *Answer choices:*

(see index for correct answer)

- a. They Go On
- b. Thomas Register
- c. ACNielsen
- d. Nielsen Broadcast Data Systems

Guidance: level 1

:: Waste ::

_____ are unwanted or unusable materials. _____ is any substance which is discarded after primary use, or is worthless, defective and of no use. A by-product by contrast is a joint product of relatively minor economic value. A _____ product may become a by-product, joint product or resource through an invention that raises a _____ product's value above zero.

Exam Probability: **High**

37. *Answer choices:*

(see index for correct answer)

- a. Fly ash
- b. Waste
- c. Red mud
- d. Green waste

Guidance: level 1

:: Process management ::

_____ is a statistics package developed at the Pennsylvania State University by researchers Barbara F. Ryan, Thomas A. Ryan, Jr., and Brian L. Joiner in 1972. It began as a light version of OMNITAB 80, a statistical analysis program by NIST. Statistical analysis software such as _____ automates calculations and the creation of graphs, allowing the user to focus more on the analysis of data and the interpretation of results. It is compatible with other _____, Inc. software.

Exam Probability: **Low**

38. *Answer choices:*

(see index for correct answer)

- a. Minitab
- b. Process modeling
- c. Business process discovery
- d. Business process modeling

Guidance: level 1

:: Production and manufacturing ::

_____ is the process of determining the production capacity needed by an organization to meet changing demands for its products. In the context of _____ , design capacity is the maximum amount of work that an organization is capable of completing in a given period. Effective capacity is the maximum amount of work that an organization is capable of completing in a given period due to constraints such as quality problems, delays, material handling, etc.

Exam Probability: **Low**

39. *Answer choices:*

(see index for correct answer)

- a. LPA512
- b. Order to cash

- c. Capacity planning
- d. Job shop

Guidance: level 1

:: ::

An _____ is, most an organized examination or formal evaluation exercise. In engineering activities _____ involves the measurements, tests, and gauges applied to certain characteristics in regard to an object or activity. The results are usually compared to specified requirements and standards for determining whether the item or activity is in line with these targets, often with a Standard _____ Procedure in place to ensure consistent checking. _____ s are usually non-destructive.

Exam Probability: **High**

40. *Answer choices:*

(see index for correct answer)

- a. personal values
- b. co-culture
- c. Sarbanes-Oxley act of 2002
- d. interpersonal communication

Guidance: level 1

:: Computer memory companies ::

_____ Corporation is a Japanese multinational conglomerate headquartered in Tokyo, Japan. Its diversified products and services include information technology and communications equipment and systems, electronic components and materials, power systems, industrial and social infrastructure systems, consumer electronics, household appliances, medical equipment, office equipment, as well as lighting and logistics.

Exam Probability: **Low**

41. *Answer choices:*

(see index for correct answer)

- a. Crocus Technology
- b. Saffron Technology
- c. Micron Technology
- d. Virage Logic

Guidance: level 1

:: Management ::

_____ is an iterative four-step management method used in business for the control and continuous improvement of processes and products. It is also known as the Deming circle/cycle/wheel, the Shewhart cycle, the control circle/cycle, or plan–do–study–act . Another version of this _____ cycle is O _____ . The added "O" stands for observation or as some versions say: "Observe the current condition." This emphasis on observation and current condition has currency with the literature on lean manufacturing and the Toyota Production System. The _____ cycle, with Ishikawa's changes, can be traced back to S. Mizuno of the Tokyo Institute of Technology in 1959.

Exam Probability: **Medium**

42. *Answer choices:*

(see index for correct answer)

- a. PDCA
- b. Sensemaking
- c. DMSMS
- d. Functional management

Guidance: level 1

:: Project management ::

A _____ is a type of bar chart that illustrates a project schedule, named after its inventor, Henry Gantt , who designed such a chart around the years 1910–1915. Modern _____ s also show the dependency relationships between activities and current schedule status.

Exam Probability: **Medium**

43. *Answer choices:*

(see index for correct answer)

- a. Gantt chart
- b. Team performance management
- c. Theory X and Theory Y
- d. Project engineering

Guidance: level 1

:: Asset ::

In financial accounting, an _____ is any resource owned by the business. Anything tangible or intangible that can be owned or controlled to produce value and that is held by a company to produce positive economic value is an _____ . Simply stated, _____ s represent value of ownership that can be converted into cash . The balance sheet of a firm records the monetary value of the _____ s owned by that firm. It covers money and other valuables belonging to an individual or to a business.

Exam Probability: **Low**

44. *Answer choices:*

(see index for correct answer)

- a. Fixed asset

- b. Asset

Guidance: level 1

:: Industrial organization ::

In economics, specifically general equilibrium theory, a perfect market is defined by several idealizing conditions, collectively called _____ . In theoretical models where conditions of _____ hold, it has been theoretically demonstrated that a market will reach an equilibrium in which the quantity supplied for every product or service, including labor, equals the quantity demanded at the current price. This equilibrium would be a Pareto optimum.

Exam Probability: **Medium**

45. *Answer choices:*

(see index for correct answer)

- a. Industrial organization
- b. Hold-up problem
- c. Path dependence
- d. Switching barriers

Guidance: level 1

:: Project management ::

_____ is a process of setting goals, planning and/or controlling the organizing and leading the execution of any type of activity, such as.

Exam Probability: **High**

46. *Answer choices:*

(see index for correct answer)

- a. Management process
- b. Front-end loading
- c. Agile management
- d. Executive sponsor

Guidance: level 1

:: Production and manufacturing ::

_____ was a management-led program to eliminate defects in industrial production that enjoyed brief popularity in American industry from 1964 to the early 1970s. Quality expert Philip Crosby later incorporated it into his "Absolutes of Quality Management" and it enjoyed a renaissance in the American automobile industry—as a performance goal more than as a program—in the 1990s. Although applicable to any type of enterprise, it has been primarily adopted within supply chains wherever large volumes of components are being purchased.

Exam Probability: **High**

47. Answer choices:

(see index for correct answer)

- a. Shop foreman
- b. Zero Defects
- c. ISO/IEC 17025
- d. Methods-time measurement

Guidance: level 1

:: Production and manufacturing ::

_____ is a production planning, scheduling, and inventory control system used to manage manufacturing processes. Most MRP systems are software-based, but it is possible to conduct MRP by hand as well.

Exam Probability: **High**

48. Answer choices:

(see index for correct answer)

- a. Transfer cars
- b. Profibus
- c. Highly accelerated stress audit
- d. Material requirements planning

Guidance: level 1

:: Quality management ::

_____ is a not-for-profit membership foundation in Brussels, established in 1989 to increase the competitiveness of the European economy. The initial impetus for forming _____ was a response to the work of W. Edwards Deming and the development of the concepts of Total Quality Management.

Exam Probability: **Low**

49. *Answer choices:*
(see index for correct answer)

- a. Quality circle
- b. European Quality in Social Services
- c. Test bay
- d. EFQM

Guidance: level 1

:: Materials ::

A _____ , also known as a feedstock, unprocessed material, or primary commodity, is a basic material that is used to produce goods, finished products, energy, or intermediate materials which are feedstock for future finished products. As feedstock, the term connotes these materials are bottleneck assets and are highly important with regard to producing other products. An example of this is crude oil, which is a _____ and a feedstock used in the production of industrial chemicals, fuels, plastics, and pharmaceutical goods; lumber is a _____ used to produce a variety of products including all types of furniture. The term " _____ " denotes materials in minimally processed or unprocessed in states; e.g., raw latex, crude oil, cotton, coal, raw biomass, iron ore, air, logs, or water i.e. "...any product of agriculture, forestry, fishing and any other mineral that is in its natural form or which has undergone the transformation required to prepare it for internationally marketing in substantial volumes."

Exam Probability: **High**

50. *Answer choices:*

(see index for correct answer)

- a. Materials World
- b. Slurry
- c. Raw material
- d. Lute

Guidance: level 1

:: Software testing ::

_____ 1 was the first artificial Earth satellite. The Soviet Union launched it into an elliptical low Earth orbit on 4 October 1957, orbiting for three weeks before its batteries died, then silently for two more months before falling back into the atmosphere. It was a 58 cm diameter polished metal sphere, with four external radio antennas to broadcast radio pulses. Its radio signal was easily detectable even by radio amateurs, and the 65° inclination and duration of its orbit made its flight path cover virtually the entire inhabited Earth. This surprise success precipitated the American _____ crisis and triggered the Space Race, a part of the Cold War. The launch was the beginning of a new era of political, military, technological, and scientific developments.

Exam Probability: **High**

51. *Answer choices:*

(see index for correct answer)

- a. BS 7925-2
- b. System under test
- c. Sputnik
- d. Security bug

Guidance: level 1

:: Debt ::

_____ is the trust which allows one party to provide money or resources to another party wherein the second party does not reimburse the first party immediately, but promises either to repay or return those resources at a later date. In other words, _____ is a method of making reciprocity formal, legally enforceable, and extensible to a large group of unrelated people.

Exam Probability: **Medium**

52. *Answer choices:*

(see index for correct answer)

- a. Credit
- b. Vulture fund
- c. Debt relief
- d. Credit crunch

Guidance: level 1

:: Lean manufacturing ::

_____ is the Sino-Japanese word for "improvement". In business, _____ refers to activities that continuously improve all functions and involve all employees from the CEO to the assembly line workers. It also applies to processes, such as purchasing and logistics, that cross organizational boundaries into the supply chain. It has been applied in healthcare, psychotherapy, life-coaching, government, and banking.

Exam Probability: **High**

53. *Answer choices:*

(see index for correct answer)

- a. The Machine That Changed the World
- b. Kaizen
- c. takt
- d. Manufacturing supermarket

Guidance: level 1

:: Project management ::

In economics and business decision-making, a sunk cost is a cost that has already been incurred and cannot be recovered.

Exam Probability: **Low**

54. *Answer choices:*

(see index for correct answer)

- a. Project management office
- b. Sunk costs
- c. Critical path drag
- d. Budgeted cost of work performed

Guidance: level 1

:: Chemical processes ::

_____ is the understanding and application of the fundamental principles and laws of nature that allow us to transform raw material and energy into products that are useful to society, at an industrial level. By taking advantage of the driving forces of nature such as pressure, temperature and concentration gradients, as well as the law of conservation of mass, process engineers can develop methods to synthesize and purify large quantities of desired chemical products. _____ focuses on the design, operation, control, optimization and intensification of chemical, physical, and biological processes. _____ encompasses a vast range of industries, such as agriculture, automotive, biotechnical, chemical, food, material development, mining, nuclear, petrochemical, pharmaceutical, and software development. The application of systematic computer-based methods to _____ is "process systems engineering".

Exam Probability: **Low**

55. *Answer choices:*

(see index for correct answer)

- a. Aludel
- b. Efflorescence
- c. Process engineering
- d. Brin process

Guidance: level 1

:: Data management ::

_____ is the ability of a physical product to remain functional, without requiring excessive maintenance or repair, when faced with the challenges of normal operation over its design lifetime. There are several measures of _____ in use, including years of life, hours of use, and number of operational cycles. In economics, goods with a long usable life are referred to as durable goods.

Exam Probability: **Medium**

56. *Answer choices:*

(see index for correct answer)

- a. Data classification
- b. CA Gen
- c. EU Open Data Portal
- d. Durability

Guidance: level 1

:: ::

In sales, commerce and economics, a _____ is the recipient of a good, service, product or an idea - obtained from a seller, vendor, or supplier via a financial transaction or exchange for money or some other valuable consideration.

Exam Probability: **High**

57. *Answer choices:*

(see index for correct answer)

- a. co-culture
- b. Customer
- c. open system
- d. Character

Guidance: level 1

:: Building materials ::

_____ is an alloy of iron and carbon, and sometimes other elements. Because of its high tensile strength and low cost, it is a major component used in buildings, infrastructure, tools, ships, automobiles, machines, appliances, and weapons.

Exam Probability: **Low**

58. *Answer choices:*

(see index for correct answer)

- a. Vinyl siding
- b. Harl
- c. Pantile

- d. Steel

Guidance: level 1

:: ::

_____ refers to the confirmation of certain characteristics of an object, person, or organization. This confirmation is often, but not always, provided by some form of external review, education, assessment, or audit. Accreditation is a specific organization's process of _____ . According to the National Council on Measurement in Education, a _____ test is a credentialing test used to determine whether individuals are knowledgeable enough in a given occupational area to be labeled "competent to practice" in that area.

Exam Probability: **Medium**

59. *Answer choices:*

(see index for correct answer)

- a. hierarchical perspective
- b. Certification
- c. process perspective
- d. levels of analysis

Guidance: level 1

Commerce

Commerce relates to "the exchange of goods and services, especially on a large scale." It includes legal, economic, political, social, cultural and technological systems that operate in any country or internationally.

:: ::

_____, also referred to as orthostasis, is a human position in which the body is held in an upright position and supported only by the feet.

Exam Probability: **Low**

1. Answer choices:

(see index for correct answer)

- a. functional perspective
- b. deep-level diversity
- c. Standing
- d. open system

Guidance: level 1

:: ::

_____ is the provision of service to customers before, during and after a purchase. The perception of success of such interactions is dependent on employees "who can adjust themselves to the personality of the guest". _____ concerns the priority an organization assigns to _____ relative to components such as product innovation and pricing. In this sense, an organization that values good _____ may spend more money in training employees than the average organization or may proactively interview customers for feedback.

Exam Probability: **Low**

2. Answer choices:

(see index for correct answer)

- a. process perspective
- b. levels of analysis

- c. hierarchical perspective
- d. open system

Guidance: level 1

:: Minimum wage ::

A _____ is the lowest remuneration that employers can legally pay their workers—the price floor below which workers may not sell their labor. Most countries had introduced _____ legislation by the end of the 20th century.

Exam Probability: **High**

3. *Answer choices:*
(see index for correct answer)

- a. Minimum Wage Fairness Act
- b. Minimum wage
- c. Minimum wage in the United States
- d. Working poor

Guidance: level 1

:: ::

A _____ is a person or firm who arranges transactions between a buyer and a seller for a commission when the deal is executed. A _____ who also acts as a seller or as a buyer becomes a principal party to the deal. Neither role should be confused with that of an agent—one who acts on behalf of a principal party in a deal.

Exam Probability: **Low**

4. *Answer choices:*

(see index for correct answer)

- a. similarity-attraction theory
- b. Broker
- c. levels of analysis
- d. cultural

Guidance: level 1

:: Securities (finance) ::

A _____ is a container that is traditionally constructed from stiff fibers, and can be made from a range of materials, including wood splints, runners, and cane. While most _____ s are made from plant materials, other materials such as horsehair, baleen, or metal wire can be used. _____ s are generally woven by hand. Some _____ s are fitted with a lid, while others are left open on top.

Exam Probability: **Medium**

5. *Answer choices:*

(see index for correct answer)

- a. Listing
- b. Canadian Depository for Securities
- c. Basket
- d. Trade date

Guidance: level 1

:: Economic globalization ::

_____ is an agreement in which one company hires another company to be responsible for a planned or existing activity that is or could be done internally, and sometimes involves transferring employees and assets from one firm to another.

Exam Probability: **Medium**

6. *Answer choices:*

(see index for correct answer)

- a. reshoring
- b. Outsourcing

Guidance: level 1

:: ::

Business Model Canvas is a strategic management and lean startup template for developing new or documenting existing business models. It is a visual chart with elements describing a firm's or product's value proposition, infrastructure, customers, and finances. It assists firms in aligning their activities by illustrating potential trade-offs.

Exam Probability: **Medium**

7. *Answer choices:*

(see index for correct answer)

- a. information systems assessment
- b. hierarchical perspective
- c. personal values
- d. Cost structure

Guidance: level 1

:: ::

A _____ is a structured form of play, usually undertaken for enjoyment and sometimes used as an educational tool. _____ s are distinct from work, which is usually carried out for remuneration, and from art, which is more often an expression of aesthetic or ideological elements. However, the distinction is not clear-cut, and many _____ s are also considered to be work or art.

Exam Probability: **High**

8. *Answer choices:*

(see index for correct answer)

- a. process perspective
- b. levels of analysis
- c. functional perspective
- d. Game

Guidance: level 1

:: Information technology management ::

B2B is often contrasted with business-to-consumer. In B2B commerce, it is often the case that the parties to the relationship have comparable negotiating power, and even when they do not, each party typically involves professional staff and legal counsel in the negotiation of terms, whereas B2C is shaped to a far greater degree by economic implications of information asymmetry. However, within a B2B context, large companies may have many commercial, resource and information advantages over smaller businesses. The United Kingdom government, for example, created the post of Small Business Commissioner under the Enterprise Act 2016 to "enable small businesses to resolve disputes" and "consider complaints by small business suppliers about payment issues with larger businesses that they supply."

Exam Probability: **Medium**

9. *Answer choices:*

(see index for correct answer)

- a. VFinity
- b. Business-to-business
- c. Computerized maintenance management system
- d. Computer-aided manufacturing

Guidance: level 1

:: ::

In Christian denominations that practice infant baptism, confirmation is seen as the sealing of Christianity created in baptism. Those being _____ are known as confirmands. In some denominations, such as the Anglican Communion and Methodist Churches, confirmation bestows full membership in a local congregation upon the recipient. In others, such as the Roman Catholic Church, Confirmation "renders the bond with the Church more perfect", because, while a baptized person is already a member, "reception of the sacrament of Confirmation is necessary for the completion of baptismal grace".

Exam Probability: **Low**

10. *Answer choices:*

(see index for correct answer)

- a. cultural
- b. open system
- c. imperative

- d. Confirmed

Guidance: level 1

:: ::

A _____ is any person who contracts to acquire an asset in return for some form of consideration.

Exam Probability: **Medium**

11. *Answer choices:*

(see index for correct answer)

- a. similarity-attraction theory
- b. surface-level diversity
- c. Buyer
- d. co-culture

Guidance: level 1

:: Behavior modification ::

In psychotherapy and mental health, _____ has a positive sense of empowering individuals, or a negative sense of encouraging dysfunctional behavior.

Exam Probability: **Medium**

12. *Answer choices:*

(see index for correct answer)

- a. behavioural change
- b. Enabling

Guidance: level 1

:: ::

In a supply chain, a _____, or a seller, is an enterprise that contributes goods or services. Generally, a supply chain _____ manufactures inventory/stock items and sells them to the next link in the chain. Today, these terms refer to a supplier of any good or service.

Exam Probability: **High**

13. *Answer choices:*

(see index for correct answer)

- a. information systems assessment

- b. Vendor
- c. corporate values
- d. interpersonal communication

Guidance: level 1

:: Supply chain management ::

_____ is the removal of intermediaries in economics from a supply chain, or cutting out the middlemen in connection with a transaction or a series of transactions. Instead of going through traditional distribution channels, which had some type of intermediary, companies may now deal with customers directly, for example via the Internet. Hence, the use of factory direct and direct from the factory to mean the same thing.

Exam Probability: **High**

14. *Answer choices:*

(see index for correct answer)

- a. Supplier enablement
- b. Pharmacode
- c. Strategic material
- d. Netchain analysis

Guidance: level 1

:: Dot-com bubble ::

Yahoo! _____ was a web hosting service. It was founded in November 1994 by David Bohnett and John Rezner, and was called Beverly Hills Internet for a very short time before being named _____ .

Exam Probability: **Medium**

15. *Answer choices:*

(see index for correct answer)

- a. Webvan
- b. GeoCities
- c. Internet time
- d. Irrational exuberance

Guidance: level 1

:: ::

A _____ is monetary compensation paid by an employer to an employee in exchange for work done. Payment may be calculated as a fixed amount for each task completed , or at an hourly or daily rate , or based on an easily measured quantity of work done.

Exam Probability: **Medium**

16. *Answer choices:*

(see index for correct answer)

- a. interpersonal communication
- b. surface-level diversity
- c. corporate values
- d. Wage

Guidance: level 1

:: ::

_____ Corporation is an American multinational technology company with headquarters in Redmond, Washington. It develops, manufactures, licenses, supports and sells computer software, consumer electronics, personal computers, and related services. Its best known software products are the _____ Windows line of operating systems, the _____ Office suite, and the Internet Explorer and Edge Web browsers. Its flagship hardware products are the Xbox video game consoles and the _____ Surface lineup of touchscreen personal computers. As of 2016, it is the world's largest software maker by revenue, and one of the world's most valuable companies. The word "_____" is a portmanteau of "microcomputer" and "software". _____ is ranked No. 30 in the 2018 Fortune 500 rankings of the largest United States corporations by total revenue.

Exam Probability: **High**

17. *Answer choices:*

(see index for correct answer)

- a. levels of analysis
- b. Microsoft
- c. hierarchical perspective
- d. similarity-attraction theory

Guidance: level 1

:: ::

_____ is the process of removing or reducing state regulations, typically in the economic sphere. It is the repeal of governmental regulation of the economy. It became common in advanced industrial economies in the 1970s and 1980s, as a result of new trends in economic thinking about the inefficiencies of government regulation, and the risk that regulatory agencies would be controlled by the regulated industry to its benefit, and thereby hurt consumers and the wider economy.

Exam Probability: **Medium**

18. *Answer choices:*

(see index for correct answer)

- a. open system
- b. corporate values
- c. surface-level diversity
- d. empathy

Guidance: level 1

A trade fair is an exhibition organized so that companies in a specific industry can showcase and demonstrate their latest products and services, meet with industry partners and customers, study activities of rivals, and examine recent market trends and opportunities. In contrast to consumer fairs, only some trade fairs are open to the public, while others can only be attended by company representatives and members of the press, therefore _____ s are classified as either "public" or "trade only". A few fairs are hybrids of the two; one example is the Frankfurt Book Fair, which is trade only for its first three days and open to the general public on its final two days. They are held on a continuing basis in virtually all markets and normally attract companies from around the globe. For example, in the U.S., there are currently over 10,000 _____ s held every year, and several online directories have been established to help organizers, attendees, and marketers identify appropriate events.

Exam Probability: **High**

19. *Answer choices:*

(see index for correct answer)

- a. Trade show
- b. deep-level diversity
- c. interpersonal communication
- d. similarity-attraction theory

Guidance: level 1

:: ::

Senior management, executive management, upper management, or a _____ is generally a team of individuals at the highest level of management of an organization who have the day-to-day tasks of managing that organization — sometimes a company or a corporation.

Exam Probability: **High**

20. *Answer choices:*

(see index for correct answer)

- a. cultural
- b. Management team
- c. hierarchical perspective
- d. corporate values

Guidance: level 1

:: ::

_____ is a qualitative measure used to relate the quality of motor vehicle traffic service. LOS is used to analyze roadways and intersections by categorizing traffic flow and assigning quality levels of traffic based on performance measure like vehicle speed, density, congestion, etc.

Exam Probability: **High**

21. *Answer choices:*

(see index for correct answer)

- a. Level of service
- b. Character
- c. functional perspective
- d. hierarchical perspective

Guidance: level 1

:: Game theory ::

To _____ is to make a deal between different parties where each party gives up part of their demand. In arguments, _____ is a concept of finding agreement through communication, through a mutual acceptance of terms—often involving variations from an original goal or desires.

Exam Probability: **High**

22. *Answer choices:*

(see index for correct answer)

- a. Matching pennies
- b. Focal point
- c. Compromise
- d. General equilibrium

Guidance: level 1

:: Marketing ::

A _____ is an overall experience of a customer that distinguishes an organization or product from its rivals in the eyes of the customer. _____ s are used in business, marketing, and advertising. Name _____ s are sometimes distinguished from generic or store _____ s.

Exam Probability: **High**

23. *Answer choices:*

(see index for correct answer)

- a. Product literature
- b. Brand
- c. Adobe Target
- d. Pharmaceutical marketing

Guidance: level 1

:: Free market ::

In economics, a _____ is a system in which the prices for goods and services are determined by the open market and by consumers. In a _____, the laws and forces of supply and demand are free from any intervention by a government or other authority and from all forms of economic privilege, monopolies and artificial scarcities. Proponents of the concept of _____ contrast it with a regulated market in which a government intervenes in supply and demand through various methods, such as tariffs, used to restrict trade and to protect the local economy. In an idealized free-market economy, prices for goods and services are set freely by the forces of supply and demand and are allowed to reach their point of equilibrium without intervention by government policy.

Exam Probability: **High**

24. *Answer choices:*

(see index for correct answer)

- a. Regulated market
- b. Piece rate

Guidance: level 1

:: ::

An _____ is a systematic and independent examination of books, accounts, statutory records, documents and vouchers of an organization to ascertain how far the financial statements as well as non-financial disclosures present a true and fair view of the concern. It also attempts to ensure that the books of accounts are properly maintained by the concern as required by law. _____ing has become such a ubiquitous phenomenon in the corporate and the public sector that academics started identifying an " _____ Society". The _____ or perceives and recognises the propositions before them for examination, obtains evidence, evaluates the same and formulates an opinion on the basis of his judgement which is communicated through their _____ing report.

Exam Probability: **Medium**

25. *Answer choices:*

(see index for correct answer)

- a. deep-level diversity
- b. Audit
- c. personal values
- d. cultural

Guidance: level 1

:: Consortia ::

A _____ is an association of two or more individuals, companies, organizations or governments with the objective of participating in a common activity or pooling their resources for achieving a common goal.

Exam Probability: **Low**

26. *Answer choices:*

(see index for correct answer)

- a. World Information Technology and Services Alliance
- b. Lex Mundi
- c. Consortium
- d. Data Processing and Analysis Consortium

Guidance: level 1

:: Information retrieval ::

_____ is a technique used by recommender systems. _____ has two senses, a narrow one and a more general one.

Exam Probability: **Medium**

27. *Answer choices:*

(see index for correct answer)

- a. Music information retrieval
- b. Collaborative filtering
- c. Artificial Solutions
- d. Isearch

Guidance: level 1

:: E-commerce ::

A _____ is a hosted service offering that acts as an intermediary between business partners sharing standards based or proprietary data via shared business processes. The offered service is referred to as " _____ services".

Exam Probability: **Medium**

28. *Answer choices:*

(see index for correct answer)

- a. Coinye
- b. Authorize.Net
- c. Helpling
- d. Virtual goods

Guidance: level 1

:: Insolvency ::

_____ is the process in accounting by which a company is brought to an end in the United Kingdom, Republic of Ireland and United States. The assets and property of the company are redistributed. _____ is also sometimes referred to as winding-up or dissolution, although dissolution technically refers to the last stage of _____. The process of _____ also arises when customs, an authority or agency in a country responsible for collecting and safeguarding customs duties, determines the final computation or ascertainment of the duties or drawback accruing on an entry.

Exam Probability: **High**

29. *Answer choices:*

(see index for correct answer)

- a. Debt consolidation
- b. Official Committee of Equity Security Holders
- c. Liquidation
- d. Financial distress

Guidance: level 1

:: ::

_____ is the administration of an organization, whether it is a business, a not-for-profit organization, or government body. _____ includes the activities of setting the strategy of an organization and coordinating the efforts of its employees to accomplish its objectives through the application of available resources, such as financial, natural, technological, and human resources. The term "_____" may also refer to those people who manage an organization.

Exam Probability: **Medium**

30. *Answer choices:*

(see index for correct answer)

- a. co-culture
- b. information systems assessment
- c. Management
- d. personal values

Guidance: level 1

:: ::

The _____ of 1990 is a civil rights law that prohibits discrimination based on disability. It affords similar protections against discrimination to Americans with disabilities as the Civil Rights Act of 1964, which made discrimination based on race, religion, sex, national origin, and other characteristics illegal. In addition, unlike the Civil Rights Act, the ADA also requires covered employers to provide reasonable accommodations to employees with disabilities, and imposes accessibility requirements on public accommodations.

Exam Probability: **Low**

31. *Answer choices:*

(see index for correct answer)

- a. hierarchical perspective
- b. co-culture
- c. personal values
- d. Sarbanes-Oxley act of 2002

Guidance: level 1

:: Generally Accepted Accounting Principles ::

In accounting, _____ is the income that a business have from its normal business activities, usually from the sale of goods and services to customers. _____ is also referred to as sales or turnover. Some companies receive _____ from interest, royalties, or other fees. _____ may refer to business income in general, or it may refer to the amount, in a monetary unit, earned during a period of time, as in "Last year, Company X had _____ of $42 million". Profits or net income generally imply total _____ minus total expenses in a given period. In accounting, in the balance statement it is a subsection of the Equity section and _____ increases equity, it is often referred to as the "top line" due to its position on the income statement at the very top. This is to be contrasted with the "bottom line" which denotes net income.

Exam Probability: **High**

32. *Answer choices:*

(see index for correct answer)

- a. Revenue
- b. Chinese accounting standards
- c. Financial position of the United States
- d. Operating income before depreciation and amortization

Guidance: level 1

:: ::

_____ is the collaborative effort of a team to achieve a common goal or to complete a task in the most effective and efficient way. This concept is seen within the greater framework of a team, which is a group of interdependent individuals who work together towards a common goal. Basic requirements for effective _____ are an adequate team size, available resources for the team to make use of, and clearly defined roles within the team in order for everyone to have a clear purpose. _____ is present in any context where a group of people are working together to achieve a common goal. These contexts include an industrial organization, athletics, a school, and the healthcare system. In each of these settings, the level of _____ and interdependence can vary from low, to intermediate, to high, depending on the amount of communication, interaction, and collaboration present between team members.

Exam Probability: **High**

33. *Answer choices:*

(see index for correct answer)

- a. Teamwork
- b. Character
- c. empathy
- d. open system

Guidance: level 1

:: ::

_____ is a means of protection from financial loss. It is a form of risk management, primarily used to hedge against the risk of a contingent or uncertain loss

Exam Probability: **Low**

34. *Answer choices:*

(see index for correct answer)

- a. Insurance
- b. information systems assessment
- c. surface-level diversity
- d. Sarbanes-Oxley act of 2002

Guidance: level 1

:: Business law ::

The _____, first published in 1952, is one of a number of Uniform Acts that have been established as law with the goal of harmonizing the laws of sales and other commercial transactions across the United States of America through UCC adoption by all 50 states, the District of Columbia, and the Territories of the United States.

Exam Probability: **High**

35. *Answer choices:*

(see index for correct answer)

- a. Legal tender
- b. Managed service company
- c. Uniform Commercial Code
- d. Business valuation

Guidance: level 1

:: Marketing ::

_____ is the percentage of a market accounted for by a specific entity. In a survey of nearly 200 senior marketing managers, 67% responded that they found the revenue- "dollar _____ " metric very useful, while 61% found "unit _____ " very useful.

Exam Probability: **High**

36. *Answer choices:*

(see index for correct answer)

- a. Observatory of prices
- b. Email production
- c. Audience development
- d. Market share

Guidance: level 1

:: Accounting source documents ::

A _____ is a commercial document and first official offer issued by a buyer to a seller indicating types, quantities, and agreed prices for products or services. It is used to control the purchasing of products and services from external suppliers. _____ s can be an essential part of enterprise resource planning system orders.

Exam Probability: **Medium**

37. *Answer choices:*

(see index for correct answer)

- a. Banknote
- b. Invoice
- c. Parcel audit
- d. Remittance advice

Guidance: level 1

:: ::

Business is the activity of making one's living or making money by producing or buying and selling products . Simply put, it is "any activity or enterprise entered into for profit. It does not mean it is a company, a corporation, partnership, or have any such formal organization, but it can range from a street peddler to General Motors."

Exam Probability: **Medium**

38. *Answer choices:*

(see index for correct answer)

- a. cultural
- b. Firm
- c. interpersonal communication
- d. empathy

Guidance: level 1

:: Direct marketing ::

_____ is a form of advertising where organizations communicate directly to customers through a variety of media including cell phone text messaging, email, websites, online adverts, database marketing, fliers, catalog distribution, promotional letters, targeted television, newspapers, magazine advertisements, and outdoor advertising. Among practitioners, it is also known as direct response marketing.

Exam Probability: **Low**

39. *Answer choices:*

(see index for correct answer)

- a. Guthy-Renker
- b. Direct marketing
- c. Multi-level marketing
- d. Stream Energy

Guidance: level 1

:: Credit cards ::

A _____ is a payment card issued to users to enable the cardholder to pay a merchant for goods and services based on the cardholder's promise to the card issuer to pay them for the amounts plus the other agreed charges. The card issuer creates a revolving account and grants a line of credit to the cardholder, from which the cardholder can borrow money for payment to a merchant or as a cash advance.

Exam Probability: **High**

40. *Answer choices:*

(see index for correct answer)

- a. Smiley v. Citibank
- b. Credit card
- c. NexG PrePaid
- d. PayAnywhere

Guidance: level 1

:: Management ::

In business, a _____ is the attribute that allows an organization to outperform its competitors. A _____ may include access to natural resources, such as high-grade ores or a low-cost power source, highly skilled labor, geographic location, high entry barriers, and access to new technology.

Exam Probability: **Medium**

41. *Answer choices:*

(see index for correct answer)

- a. Narcissistic leadership
- b. Six phases of a big project
- c. Industrial market segmentation
- d. Competitive advantage

Guidance: level 1

:: Marketing ::

_____ comes from the Latin neg and otsia referring to businessmen who, unlike the patricians, had no leisure time in their industriousness; it held the meaning of business until the 17th century when it took on the diplomatic connotation as a dialogue between two or more people or parties intended to reach a beneficial outcome over one or more issues where a conflict exists with respect to at least one of these issues. Thus, _____ is a process of combining divergent positions into a joint agreement under a decision rule of unanimity.

Exam Probability: **High**

42. *Answer choices:*

(see index for correct answer)

- a. Cause-related loyalty marketing
- b. Negotiation
- c. Consumer-to-business
- d. Active adult retail

Guidance: level 1

Walter Elias Disney was an American entrepreneur, animator, voice actor and film producer. A pioneer of the American animation industry, he introduced several developments in the production of cartoons. As a film producer, Disney holds the record for most Academy Awards earned by an individual, having won 22 Oscars from 59 nominations. He was presented with two Golden Globe Special Achievement Awards and an Emmy Award, among other honors. Several of his films are included in the National Film Registry by the Library of Congress.

Exam Probability: **Low**

43. *Answer choices:*

(see index for correct answer)

- a. open system
- b. levels of analysis
- c. hierarchical
- d. Walt Disney

Guidance: level 1

:: ::

_____ is the social science that studies the production, distribution, and consumption of goods and services.

Exam Probability: **Medium**

44. *Answer choices:*

(see index for correct answer)

- a. co-culture
- b. process perspective
- c. Economics
- d. Character

Guidance: level 1

:: ::

In logic and philosophy, an _____ is a series of statements, called the premises or premisses, intended to determine the degree of truth of another statement, the conclusion. The logical form of an _____ in a natural language can be represented in a symbolic formal language, and independently of natural language formally defined " _____ s" can be made in math and computer science.

Exam Probability: **Low**

45. *Answer choices:*

(see index for correct answer)

- a. personal values
- b. hierarchical
- c. Argument
- d. interpersonal communication

Guidance: level 1

:: ::

A _____ manages, commands, directs, or regulates the behavior of other devices or systems using control loops. It can range from a single home heating controller using a thermostat controlling a domestic boiler to large Industrial _____ s which are used for controlling processes or machines.

Exam Probability: **High**

46. *Answer choices:*

(see index for correct answer)

- a. Character
- b. imperative
- c. Control system
- d. levels of analysis

Guidance: level 1

:: Commercial item transport and distribution ::

In a contract of carriage, the _____ is the entity who is financially responsible for the receipt of a shipment. Generally, but not always, the _____ is the same as the receiver.

Exam Probability: **Low**

47. *Answer choices:*

(see index for correct answer)

- a. Project cargo
- b. Point-to-point transit
- c. Zeppelin
- d. Consignee

Guidance: level 1

:: Industry ::

_____, also known as flow production or continuous production, is the production of large amounts of standardized products, including and especially on assembly lines. Together with job production and batch production, it is one of the three main production methods.

Exam Probability: **Low**

48. *Answer choices:*

(see index for correct answer)

- a. Private sector
- b. Sunrise industry
- c. Productivity improving technologies
- d. Mass production

Guidance: level 1

:: Retailing ::

A _____ or trolley, also known by a variety of other names, is a cart supplied by a shop, especially supermarkets, for use by customers inside the shop for transport of merchandise to the checkout counter during shopping. In many cases customers can then also use the cart to transport their purchased goods to their vehicles, but some carts are designed to prevent them from leaving the shop.

Exam Probability: **Low**

49. *Answer choices:*
(see index for correct answer)

- a. Window dresser
- b. Consignment
- c. Shopping concierge
- d. Shopping cart

Guidance: level 1

:: ::

An _____ is the production of goods or related services within an economy. The major source of revenue of a group or company is the indicator of its relevant _____. When a large group has multiple sources of revenue generation, it is considered to be working in different industries.
Manufacturing _____ became a key sector of production and labour in European and North American countries during the Industrial Revolution, upsetting previous mercantile and feudal economies. This came through many successive rapid advances in technology, such as the production of steel and coal.

Exam Probability: **Medium**

50. *Answer choices:*

(see index for correct answer)

- a. hierarchical
- b. surface-level diversity
- c. levels of analysis
- d. Industry

Guidance: level 1

:: Business terms ::

The _____ or reception is an area where visitors arrive and first encounter a staff at a place of business. _____ staff will deal with whatever question the visitor has and put them in contact with a relevant person at the company. Broadly speaking, the _____ includes roles that affect the revenues of the business. The term _____ is in contrast to the term back office which refers to a company's operations, personnel, accounting, payroll and financial departments which do not interact directly with customers.

Exam Probability: **Low**

51. *Answer choices:*

(see index for correct answer)

- a. Front office
- b. centralization
- c. year-to-date
- d. operating cost

Guidance: level 1

:: ::

_____ is a term frequently used in marketing. It is a measure of how products and services supplied by a company meet or surpass customer expectation. _____ is defined as "the number of customers, or percentage of total customers, whose reported experience with a firm, its products, or its services exceeds specified satisfaction goals."

Exam Probability: **Medium**

52. *Answer choices:*

(see index for correct answer)

- a. open system
- b. Customer satisfaction
- c. imperative
- d. interpersonal communication

Guidance: level 1

:: ::

A _____ is a person who trades in commodities produced by other people. Historically, a _____ is anyone who is involved in business or trade. _____ s have operated for as long as industry, commerce, and trade have existed. During the 16th-century, in Europe, two different terms for _____ s emerged: One term, meerseniers, described local traders such as bakers, grocers, etc.; while a new term, koopman (Dutch: koopman, described _____ s who operated on a global stage, importing and exporting goods over vast distances, and offering added-value services such as credit and finance.

Exam Probability: **Low**

53. *Answer choices:*

(see index for correct answer)

- a. imperative
- b. functional perspective
- c. process perspective
- d. cultural

Guidance: level 1

:: Real property law ::

A _____ is the grant of authority or rights, stating that the granter formally recognizes the prerogative of the recipient to exercise the rights specified. It is implicit that the granter retains superiority, and that the recipient admits a limited status within the relationship, and it is within that sense that _____ s were historically granted, and that sense is retained in modern usage of the term.

Exam Probability: **Low**

54. *Answer choices:*

(see index for correct answer)

- a. Land Registry
- b. Charter
- c. Land court
- d. Right to light

Guidance: level 1

:: Marketing ::

_____ or stock control can be broadly defined as "the activity of checking a shop's stock." However, a more focused definition takes into account the more science-based, methodical practice of not only verifying a business' inventory but also focusing on the many related facets of inventory management "within an organisation to meet the demand placed upon that business economically." Other facets of _____ include supply chain management, production control, financial flexibility, and customer satisfaction. At the root of _____, however, is the _____ problem, which involves determining when to order, how much to order, and the logistics of those decisions.

Exam Probability: **High**

55. *Answer choices:*

(see index for correct answer)

- a. All-commodity volume
- b. Inventory control
- c. Net idol
- d. Customer interaction tracker

Guidance: level 1

:: Business ethics ::

_____ is a type of harassment technique that relates to a sexual nature and the unwelcome or inappropriate promise of rewards in exchange for sexual favors. _____ includes a range of actions from mild transgressions to sexual abuse or assault. Harassment can occur in many different social settings such as the workplace, the home, school, churches, etc. Harassers or victims may be of any gender.

Exam Probability: **Low**

56. *Answer choices:*

(see index for correct answer)

- a. Institute for Business and Professional Ethics
- b. Integrity management
- c. Videntifier
- d. Symantec

Guidance: level 1

:: E-commerce ::

_____ Inc. was an electronic money corporation founded by David Chaum in 1989. _____ transactions were unique in that they were anonymous due to a number of cryptographic protocols developed by its founder. _____ declared bankruptcy in 1998, and subsequently sold its assets to eCash Technologies, another digital currency company, which was acquired by InfoSpace on Feb. 19, 2002.

Exam Probability: **Low**

57. *Answer choices:*

(see index for correct answer)

- a. Global Product Classification
- b. UsedSoft
- c. Ecash
- d. E-commerce in Southeast Asia

Guidance: level 1

:: Management accounting ::

_____ s are costs that change as the quantity of the good or service that a business produces changes. _____ s are the sum of marginal costs over all units produced. They can also be considered normal costs. Fixed costs and _____ s make up the two components of total cost. Direct costs are costs that can easily be associated with a particular cost object. However, not all _____ s are direct costs. For example, variable manufacturing overhead costs are _____ s that are indirect costs, not direct costs. _____ s are sometimes called unit-level costs as they vary with the number of units produced.

Exam Probability: **Medium**

58. *Answer choices:*

(see index for correct answer)

- a. Variable cost
- b. Invested capital
- c. Customer profitability
- d. Throughput accounting

Guidance: level 1

:: Materials ::

A _____, also known as a feedstock, unprocessed material, or primary commodity, is a basic material that is used to produce goods, finished products, energy, or intermediate materials which are feedstock for future finished products. As feedstock, the term connotes these materials are bottleneck assets and are highly important with regard to producing other products. An example of this is crude oil, which is a _____ and a feedstock used in the production of industrial chemicals, fuels, plastics, and pharmaceutical goods; lumber is a _____ used to produce a variety of products including all types of furniture. The term "_____" denotes materials in minimally processed or unprocessed in states; e.g., raw latex, crude oil, cotton, coal, raw biomass, iron ore, air, logs, or water i.e. "...any product of agriculture, forestry, fishing and any other mineral that is in its natural form or which has undergone the transformation required to prepare it for internationally marketing in substantial volumes."

Exam Probability: **Low**

59. *Answer choices:*
(see index for correct answer)

- a. Raw material

- b. Radiant barrier
- c. Exotic material
- d. Materials World

Guidance: level 1

Business ethics

Business ethics (also known as corporate ethics) is a form of applied ethics or professional ethics, that examines ethical principles and moral or ethical problems that can arise in a business environment. It applies to all aspects of business conduct and is relevant to the conduct of individuals and entire organizations. These ethics originate from individuals, organizational statements or from the legal system. These norms, values, ethical, and unethical practices are what is used to guide business. They help those businesses maintain a better connection with their stakeholders.

:: Minimum wage ::

The _____ are working people whose incomes fall below a given poverty line due to lack of work hours and/or low wages. Largely because they are earning such low wages, the _____ face numerous obstacles that make it difficult for many of them to find and keep a job, save up money, and maintain a sense of self-worth.

Exam Probability: **High**

1. *Answer choices:*

(see index for correct answer)

- a. Guaranteed minimum income
- b. National Anti-Sweating League
- c. Minimum wage in Taiwan
- d. Minimum Wage Fairness Act

Guidance: level 1

:: Professional ethics ::

In the mental health field, a _____ is a situation where multiple roles exist between a therapist, or other mental health practitioner, and a client. _____ s are also referred to as multiple relationships, and these two terms are used interchangeably in the research literature. The American Psychological Association Ethical Principles of Psychologists and Code of Conduct is a resource that outlines ethical standards and principles to which practitioners are expected to adhere. Standard 3.05 of the APA ethics code outlines the definition of multiple relationships. Dual or multiple relationships occur when.

Exam Probability: **High**

2. *Answer choices:*

(see index for correct answer)

- a. Continuous professional development
- b. ethical code
- c. professional conduct

Guidance: level 1

:: Writs ::

In common law, a writ of _____ is a writ whereby a private individual who assists a prosecution can receive all or part of any penalty imposed. Its name is an abbreviation of the Latin phrase _____ pro domino rege quam pro se ipso in hac parte sequitur, meaning "[he] who sues in this matter for the king as well as for himself."

Exam Probability: **Low**

3. *Answer choices:*

(see index for correct answer)

- a. Writ of assistance
- b. Writ of execution

Guidance: level 1

:: Corporate scandals ::

The _____ was a privately held international group of financial services companies controlled by Allen Stanford, until it was seized by United States authorities in early 2009. Headquartered in the Galleria Tower II in Uptown Houston, Texas, it had 50 offices in several countries, mainly in the Americas, included the Stanford International Bank, and said it managed US$8.5 billion of assets for more than 30,000 clients in 136 countries on six continents. On February 17, 2009, U.S. Federal agents placed the company into receivership due to charges of fraud. Ten days later, the U.S. Securities and Exchange Commission amended its complaint to accuse Stanford of turning the company into a "massive Ponzi scheme".

Exam Probability: **High**

4. *Answer choices:*

(see index for correct answer)

- a. Petters Group Worldwide
- b. Alexander Yakovlev
- c. PurchasePro
- d. AOL search data leak

Guidance: level 1

:: Human resource management ::

_____ encompasses values and behaviors that contribute to the unique social and psychological environment of a business. The _____ influences the way people interact, the context within which knowledge is created, the resistance they will have towards certain changes, and ultimately the way they share knowledge. _____ represents the collective values, beliefs and principles of organizational members and is a product of factors such as history, product, market, technology, strategy, type of employees, management style, and national culture; culture includes the organization's vision, values, norms, systems, symbols, language, assumptions, environment, location, beliefs and habits.

Exam Probability: **High**

5. *Answer choices:*

(see index for correct answer)

- a. Organizational culture
- b. IDS HR in Practice
- c. Job description management
- d. Mergers and acquisitions

Guidance: level 1

:: ::

The _____ Group is a global financial investment management and insurance company headquartered in Des Moines, Iowa.

Exam Probability: **Medium**

6. *Answer choices:*

(see index for correct answer)

- a. hierarchical perspective
- b. information systems assessment
- c. Sarbanes-Oxley act of 2002
- d. Principal Financial

Guidance: level 1

:: Corporations law ::

A normal _____ consists of various departments that contribute to the company's overall mission and goals. Common departments include Marketing, [Finance, [[Operations managementOperations, Human Resource, and IT. These five divisions represent the major departments within a publicly traded company, though there are often smaller departments within autonomous firms. There is typically a CEO, and Board of Directors composed of the directors of each department. There are also company presidents, vice presidents, and CFOs.There is a great diversity in corporate forms as enterprises may range from single company to multi-corporate conglomerate. The four main _____ s are Functional, Divisional, Geographic, and the Matrix.Realistically, most corporations tend to have a "hybrid" structure, which is a combination of different models with one dominant strategy.

Exam Probability: **Medium**

7. Answer choices:

(see index for correct answer)

- a. Directors register
- b. Director primacy
- c. Duty of loyalty
- d. Corporate structure

Guidance: level 1

:: ::

Sustainability is the process of people maintaining change in a balanced environment, in which the exploitation of resources, the direction of investments, the orientation of technological development and institutional change are all in harmony and enhance both current and future potential to meet human needs and aspirations. For many in the field, sustainability is defined through the following interconnected domains or pillars: environment, economic and social, which according to Fritjof Capra is based on the principles of Systems Thinking. Sub-domains of _____ development have been considered also: cultural, technological and political. While _____ development may be the organizing principle for sustainability for some, for others, the two terms are paradoxical . _____ development is the development that meets the needs of the present without compromising the ability of future generations to meet their own needs. Brundtland Report for the World Commission on Environment and Development introduced the term of _____ development.

Exam Probability: **Medium**

8. Answer choices:

(see index for correct answer)

- a. corporate values
- b. imperative
- c. Sustainable
- d. interpersonal communication

Guidance: level 1

:: Auditing ::

_____ refers to the independence of the internal auditor or of the external auditor from parties that may have a financial interest in the business being audited. Independence requires integrity and an objective approach to the audit process. The concept requires the auditor to carry out his or her work freely and in an objective manner.

Exam Probability: **Low**

9. *Answer choices:*
(see index for correct answer)

- a. Circulation Verification Council
- b. Auditor independence
- c. Detection risk
- d. Risk based internal audit

Guidance: level 1

:: Private equity ::

In finance, a high-yield bond is a bond that is rated below investment grade. These bonds have a higher risk of default or other adverse credit events, but typically pay higher yields than better quality bonds in order to make them attractive to investors.

Exam Probability: **Low**

10. *Answer choices:*

(see index for correct answer)

- a. Private equity in the 2000s
- b. Angel investor
- c. Pledge fund
- d. Junk bond

Guidance: level 1

:: Corporate governance ::

_____ refers to the practice of members of a corporate board of directors serving on the boards of multiple corporations. A person that sits on multiple boards is known as a multiple director. Two firms have a direct interlock if a director or executive of one firm is also a director of the other, and an indirect interlock if a director of each sits on the board of a third firm. This practice, although widespread and lawful, raises questions about the quality and independence of board decisions.

Exam Probability: **Medium**

11. *Answer choices:*
(see index for correct answer)

- a. Institute of Directors
- b. Audit committee
- c. Chief analytics officer
- d. Interlocking directorate

Guidance: level 1

:: Business ethics ::

The _____ are the names of two corporate codes of conduct, developed by the African-American preacher Rev. Leon Sullivan, promoting corporate social responsibility.

Exam Probability: **High**

12. *Answer choices:*

(see index for correct answer)

- a. International Association for Business and Society
- b. Sullivan principles
- c. Voluntary compliance
- d. Resource Conservation and Recovery Act

Guidance: level 1

:: Utilitarianism ::

_____ is a school of thought that argues that the pursuit of pleasure and intrinsic goods are the primary or most important goals of human life. A hedonist strives to maximize net pleasure. However upon finally gaining said pleasure, happiness may remain stationary.

Exam Probability: **High**

13. *Answer choices:*

(see index for correct answer)

- a. Hedonism
- b. Consequentialism
- c. Felicific calculus
- d. Paradox of hedonism

Guidance: level 1

:: Business ethics ::

_____ is a type of harassment technique that relates to a sexual nature and the unwelcome or inappropriate promise of rewards in exchange for sexual favors. _____ includes a range of actions from mild transgressions to sexual abuse or assault. Harassment can occur in many different social settings such as the workplace, the home, school, churches, etc. Harassers or victims may be of any gender.

Exam Probability: **Low**

14. *Answer choices:*

(see index for correct answer)

- a. Black Company
- b. Sexual harassment
- c. Integrity management
- d. Marketing ethics

Guidance: level 1

:: Hazard analysis ::

Broadly speaking, a _____ is the combined effort of 1. identifying and analyzing potential events that may negatively impact individuals, assets, and/or the environment ; and 2. making judgments "on the tolerability of the risk on the basis of a risk analysis" while considering influencing factors . Put in simpler terms, a _____ analyzes what can go wrong, how likely it is to happen, what the potential consequences are, and how tolerable the identified risk is. As part of this process, the resulting determination of risk may be expressed in a quantitative or qualitative fashion. The _____ is an inherent part of an overall risk management strategy, which attempts to, after a _____ , "introduce control measures to eliminate or reduce" any potential risk-related consequences.

Exam Probability: **Medium**

15. *Answer choices:*

(see index for correct answer)

- a. Risk assessment
- b. Hazardous Materials Identification System
- c. Hazard identification

Guidance: level 1

:: ::

_____ is the collection of mechanisms, processes and relations by which corporations are controlled and operated. Governance structures and principles identify the distribution of rights and responsibilities among different participants in the corporation and include the rules and procedures for making decisions in corporate affairs. _____ is necessary because of the possibility of conflicts of interests between stakeholders, primarily between shareholders and upper management or among shareholders.

Exam Probability: **High**

16. *Answer choices:*

(see index for correct answer)

- a. surface-level diversity
- b. Corporate governance
- c. open system
- d. Sarbanes-Oxley act of 2002

Guidance: level 1

:: Management ::

_____ or executive pay is composed of the financial compensation and other non-financial awards received by an executive from their firm for their service to the organization. It is typically a mixture of salary, bonuses, shares of or call options on the company stock, benefits, and perquisites, ideally configured to take into account government regulations, tax law, the desires of the organization and the executive, and rewards for performance.

Exam Probability: **Low**

17. *Answer choices:*

(see index for correct answer)

- a. Central administration
- b. Work breakdown structure
- c. Executive compensation
- d. Community-based management

Guidance: level 1

:: ::

MCI, Inc. was an American telecommunication corporation, currently a subsidiary of Verizon Communications, with its main office in Ashburn, Virginia. The corporation was formed originally as a result of the merger of _____ and MCI Communications corporations, and used the name MCI _____ , succeeded by _____ , before changing its name to the present version on April 12, 2003, as part of the corporation's ending of its bankruptcy status. The company traded on NASDAQ as WCOM and MCIP. The corporation was purchased by Verizon Communications with the deal finalizing on January 6, 2006, and is now identified as that company's Verizon Enterprise Solutions division with the local residential divisions being integrated slowly into local Verizon subsidiaries.

Exam Probability: **Medium**

18. *Answer choices:*

(see index for correct answer)

- a. cultural
- b. Sarbanes-Oxley act of 2002
- c. information systems assessment
- d. WorldCom

Guidance: level 1

:: United States federal trade legislation ::

The _____ of 1914 established the Federal Trade Commission. The Act, signed into law by Woodrow Wilson in 1914, outlaws unfair methods of competition and outlaws unfair acts or practices that affect commerce.

Exam Probability: **Medium**

19. *Answer choices:*

(see index for correct answer)

- a. Trade and Tariff Act of 1984
- b. Export Administration Act of 1979
- c. Trade Expansion Act
- d. Federal Trade Commission Act

Guidance: level 1

:: Labour law ::

An _____ is special or specified circumstances that partially or fully exempt a person or organization from performance of a legal obligation so as to avoid an unreasonable or disproportionate burden or obstacle.

Exam Probability: **Medium**

20. *Answer choices:*

(see index for correct answer)

- a. Involvement and Participation Association
- b. Undue hardship
- c. Occupational exposure limit
- d. International Association of Labour Law Journals

Guidance: level 1

:: Carbon finance ::

The _____ is an international treaty which extends the 1992 United Nations Framework Convention on Climate Change that commits state parties to reduce greenhouse gas emissions, based on the scientific consensus that global warming is occurring and it is extremely likely that human-made CO2 emissions have predominantly caused it. The _____ was adopted in Kyoto, Japan on 11 December 1997 and entered into force on 16 February 2005. There are currently 192 parties to the Protocol.

Exam Probability: **Low**

21. *Answer choices:*

(see index for correct answer)

- a. Carbon Trust
- b. Carbon retirement
- c. Regional Greenhouse Gas Initiative
- d. Climate Change Capital

Guidance: level 1

:: United States law ::

The ABA _____ , created by the American Bar Association , are a set of rules that prescribe baseline standards of legal ethics and professional responsibility for lawyers in the United States. They were promulgated by the ABA House of Delegates upon the recommendation of the Kutak Commission in 1983. The rules are merely recommendations, or models, and are not themselves binding. However, having a common set of Model Rules facilitates a common discourse on legal ethics, and simplifies professional responsibility training as well as the day-to-day application of such rules. As of 2015, 49 states and four territories have adopted the rules in whole or in part, of which the most recent to do so was the Commonwealth of the Northern Mariana Islands in March 2015. California is the only state that has not adopted the ABA Model Rules, while Puerto Rico is the only U.S. jurisdiction outside of confederation has not adopted them but instead has its own Código de Ética Profesional.

Exam Probability: **Medium**

22. *Answer choices:*

(see index for correct answer)

- a. Pro se
- b. Model Rules of Professional Conduct

Guidance: level 1

:: ::

The _____ to Fight AIDS, Tuberculosis and Malaria is an international financing organization that aims to "attract, leverage and invest additional resources to end the epidemics of HIV/AIDS, tuberculosis and malaria to support attainment of the Sustainable Development Goals established by the United Nations." A public-private partnership, the organization maintains its secretariat in Geneva, Switzerland. The organization began operations in January 2002. Microsoft founder Bill Gates was one of the first private foundations among many bilateral donors to provide seed money for the partnership.

Exam Probability: **Low**

23. *Answer choices:*

(see index for correct answer)

- a. levels of analysis
- b. Global Fund
- c. corporate values
- d. hierarchical perspective

Guidance: level 1

:: ::

The _____ is an institution of the European Union, responsible for proposing legislation, implementing decisions, upholding the EU treaties and managing the day-to-day business of the EU. Commissioners swear an oath at the European Court of Justice in Luxembourg City, pledging to respect the treaties and to be completely independent in carrying out their duties during their mandate. Unlike in the Council of the European Union, where members are directly and indirectly elected, and the European Parliament, where members are directly elected, the Commissioners are proposed by the Council of the European Union, on the basis of suggestions made by the national governments, and then appointed by the European Council after the approval of the European Parliament.

Exam Probability: **Low**

24. *Answer choices:*

(see index for correct answer)

- a. information systems assessment
- b. hierarchical
- c. European Commission
- d. empathy

Guidance: level 1

:: Anti-capitalism ::

_____ is a range of economic and social systems characterised by social ownership of the means of production and workers' self-management, as well as the political theories and movements associated with them. Social ownership can be public, collective or cooperative ownership, or citizen ownership of equity. There are many varieties of _____ and there is no single definition encapsulating all of them, with social ownership being the common element shared by its various forms.

Exam Probability: **Low**

25. *Answer choices:*

(see index for correct answer)

- a. Socialism
- b. Combahee River Collective
- c. Lesbian Nation
- d. Collectivist anarchism

Guidance: level 1

:: ::

The _____ of 1906 was the first of a series of significant consumer protection laws which was enacted by Congress in the 20th century and led to the creation of the Food and Drug Administration. Its main purpose was to ban foreign and interstate traffic in adulterated or mislabeled food and drug products, and it directed the U.S. Bureau of Chemistry to inspect products and refer offenders to prosecutors. It required that active ingredients be placed on the label of a drug's packaging and that drugs could not fall below purity levels established by the United States Pharmacopeia or the National Formulary. The Jungle by Upton Sinclair with its graphic and revolting descriptions of unsanitary conditions and unscrupulous practices rampant in the meatpacking industry, was an inspirational piece that kept the public's attention on the important issue of unhygienic meat processing plants that later led to food inspection legislation. Sinclair quipped, "I aimed at the public's heart and by accident I hit it in the stomach," as outraged readers demanded and got the pure food law.

Exam Probability: **Medium**

26. *Answer choices:*

(see index for correct answer)

- a. interpersonal communication
- b. Sarbanes-Oxley act of 2002
- c. corporate values
- d. empathy

Guidance: level 1

:: Corporate scandals ::

Exxon Mobil Corporation, doing business as _____ , is an American multinational oil and gas corporation headquartered in Irving, Texas. It is the largest direct descendant of John D. Rockefeller's Standard Oil Company, and was formed on November 30, 1999 by the merger of Exxon and Mobil . _____ 's primary brands are Exxon, Mobil, Esso, and _____ Chemical.

Exam Probability: **High**

27. *Answer choices:*

(see index for correct answer)

- a. Bre-X
- b. Adelphia Communications Corporation
- c. Central Energy Italian Gas Holding
- d. ExxonMobil

Guidance: level 1

:: Marketing ::

_____ is the marketing of products that are presumed to be environmentally safe. It incorporates a broad range of activities, including product modification, changes to the production process, sustainable packaging, as well as modifying advertising. Yet defining _____ is not a simple task where several meanings intersect and contradict each other; an example of this will be the existence of varying social, environmental and retail definitions attached to this term. Other similar terms used are environmental marketing and ecological marketing.

Exam Probability: **Medium**

28. *Answer choices:*

(see index for correct answer)

- a. Price
- b. Market segmentation index
- c. Notability
- d. Green marketing

Guidance: level 1

:: Renewable energy ::

A _____ is a fuel that is produced through contemporary biological processes, such as agriculture and anaerobic digestion, rather than a fuel produced by geological processes such as those involved in the formation of fossil fuels, such as coal and petroleum, from prehistoric biological matter. If the source biomatter can regrow quickly, the resulting fuel is said to be a form of renewable energy.

Exam Probability: **Medium**

29. *Answer choices:*

(see index for correct answer)

- a. GREEN Cell Shipping
- b. Thermal energy storage

- c. Electric aircraft
- d. Biofuel

Guidance: level 1

:: Market-based policy instruments ::

Cause marketing is defined as a type of corporate social responsibility, in which a company's promotional campaign has the dual purpose of increasing profitability while bettering society.

Exam Probability: **High**

30. *Answer choices:*

(see index for correct answer)

- a. The Other Invisible Hand
- b. Tree credits
- c. Cause-related marketing
- d. Cobra effect

Guidance: level 1

:: ::

In ecology, a _____ is the type of natural environment in which a particular species of organism lives. It is characterized by both physical and biological features. A species' _____ is those places where it can find food, shelter, protection and mates for reproduction.

Exam Probability: **High**

31. *Answer choices:*

(see index for correct answer)

- a. personal values
- b. co-culture
- c. hierarchical perspective
- d. Habitat

Guidance: level 1

:: ::

A _____ is a proceeding by a party or parties against another in the civil court of law. The archaic term "suit in law" is found in only a small number of laws still in effect today. The term " _____ " is used in reference to a civil action brought in a court of law in which a plaintiff, a party who claims to have incurred loss as a result of a defendant's actions, demands a legal or equitable remedy. The defendant is required to respond to the plaintiff's complaint. If the plaintiff is successful, judgment is in the plaintiff's favor, and a variety of court orders may be issued to enforce a right, award damages, or impose a temporary or permanent injunction to prevent an act or compel an act. A declaratory judgment may be issued to prevent future legal disputes.

Exam Probability: **High**

32. *Answer choices:*

(see index for correct answer)

- a. hierarchical
- b. Lawsuit
- c. empathy
- d. co-culture

Guidance: level 1

:: Corporate scandals ::

_____ was a bank based in the Caribbean, which operated from 1986 to 2009 when it went into receivership. It was an affiliate of the Stanford Financial Group and failed when the its parent was seized by United States authorities in early 2009 as part of the investigation into Allen Stanford.

Exam Probability: **High**

33. *Answer choices:*

(see index for correct answer)

- a. Tunku Abdul Majid
- b. Eurest Support Services
- c. Stanford International Bank
- d. Harris myCFO

Guidance: level 1

:: ::

A _____ is the ability to carry out a task with determined results often within a given amount of time, energy, or both. _____ s can often be divided into domain-general and domain-specific _____ s. For example, in the domain of work, some general _____ s would include time management, teamwork and leadership, self-motivation and others, whereas domain-specific _____ s would be used only for a certain job. _____ usually requires certain environmental stimuli and situations to assess the level of _____ being shown and used.

Exam Probability: **High**

34. *Answer choices:*

(see index for correct answer)

- a. cultural
- b. Skill
- c. similarity-attraction theory
- d. personal values

Guidance: level 1

:: Social responsibility ::

The United Nations Global Compact is a non-binding United Nations pact to encourage businesses worldwide to adopt sustainable and socially responsible policies, and to report on their implementation. The _____ is a principle-based framework for businesses, stating ten principles in the areas of human rights, labor, the environment and anti-corruption. Under the Global Compact, companies are brought together with UN agencies, labor groups and civil society. Cities can join the Global Compact through the Cities Programme.

Exam Probability: **Low**

35. *Answer choices:*

(see index for correct answer)

- a. Social impact

- b. Mallen Baker
- c. Creating shared value
- d. UN Global Compact

Guidance: level 1

:: Euthenics ::

_____ is an ethical framework and suggests that an entity, be it an organization or individual, has an obligation to act for the benefit of society at large. _____ is a duty every individual has to perform so as to maintain a balance between the economy and the ecosystems. A trade-off may exist between economic development, in the material sense, and the welfare of the society and environment, though this has been challenged by many reports over the past decade. _____ means sustaining the equilibrium between the two. It pertains not only to business organizations but also to everyone whose any action impacts the environment. This responsibility can be passive, by avoiding engaging in socially harmful acts, or active, by performing activities that directly advance social goals. _____ must be intergenerational since the actions of one generation have consequences on those following.

Exam Probability: **Low**

36. *Answer choices:*

(see index for correct answer)

- a. Minnie Cumnock Blodgett
- b. Family and consumer science
- c. Social responsibility

- d. Euthenics

Guidance: level 1

:: Industrial ecology ::

_____ is a strategy for reducing the amount of waste created and released into the environment, particularly by industrial facilities, agriculture, or consumers. Many large corporations view P2 as a method of improving the efficiency and profitability of production processes by technology advancements. Legislative bodies have enacted P2 measures, such as the _____ Act of 1990 and the Clean Air Act Amendments of 1990 by the United States Congress.

Exam Probability: **Low**

37. *Answer choices:*

(see index for correct answer)

- a. Journal of Industrial Ecology
- b. James J. Kay
- c. Life-cycle assessment
- d. Energetics

Guidance: level 1

:: Business law ::

A _____ is an arrangement where parties, known as partners, agree to cooperate to advance their mutual interests. The partners in a _____ may be individuals, businesses, interest-based organizations, schools, governments or combinations. Organizations may partner to increase the likelihood of each achieving their mission and to amplify their reach. A _____ may result in issuing and holding equity or may be only governed by a contract.

Exam Probability: **High**

38. *Answer choices:*

(see index for correct answer)

- a. Board of directors
- b. Business courts
- c. Forged endorsement
- d. Unfair competition

Guidance: level 1

:: Management ::

A _____ describes the rationale of how an organization creates, delivers, and captures value, in economic, social, cultural or other contexts. The process of _____ construction and modification is also called _____ innovation and forms a part of business strategy.

Exam Probability: **Low**

39. Answer choices:

(see index for correct answer)

- a. Millennium software
- b. Coworking
- c. Technology scouting
- d. Business model

Guidance: level 1

:: Globalization-related theories ::

_____ is an economic system based on the private ownership of the means of production and their operation for profit. Characteristics central to _____ include private property, capital accumulation, wage labor, voluntary exchange, a price system, and competitive markets. In a capitalist market economy, decision-making and investment are determined by every owner of wealth, property or production ability in financial and capital markets, whereas prices and the distribution of goods and services are mainly determined by competition in goods and services markets.

Exam Probability: **High**

40. Answer choices:

(see index for correct answer)

- a. Capitalism
- b. Economic Development

- c. post-industrial

Guidance: level 1

:: Advertising techniques ::

The _____ is a story from the Trojan War about the subterfuge that the Greeks used to enter the independent city of Troy and win the war. In the canonical version, after a fruitless 10-year siege, the Greeks constructed a huge wooden horse, and hid a select force of men inside including Odysseus. The Greeks pretended to sail away, and the Trojans pulled the horse into their city as a victory trophy. That night the Greek force crept out of the horse and opened the gates for the rest of the Greek army, which had sailed back under cover of night. The Greeks entered and destroyed the city of Troy, ending the war.

Exam Probability: **Low**

41. *Answer choices:*
(see index for correct answer)

- a. Testimonial
- b. Trojan horse
- c. Surrogate advertising
- d. Transpromotional

Guidance: level 1

:: ::

The _____, the Calvinist work ethic or the Puritan work ethic is a work ethic concept in theology, sociology, economics and history that emphasizes that hard work, discipline and frugality are a result of a person's subscription to the values espoused by the Protestant faith, particularly Calvinism. The phrase was initially coined in 1904–1905 by Max Weber in his book The Protestant Ethic and the Spirit of Capitalism.

Exam Probability: **High**

42. *Answer choices:*

(see index for correct answer)

- a. imperative
- b. Protestant work ethic
- c. hierarchical
- d. process perspective

Guidance: level 1

:: Majority–minority relations ::

It was established as axiomatic in anthropological research by Franz Boas in the first few decades of the 20th century and later popularized by his students. Boas first articulated the idea in 1887: "civilization is not something absolute, but ... is relative, and ... our ideas and conceptions are true only so far as our civilization goes". However, Boas did not coin the term.

Exam Probability: **Medium**

43. *Answer choices:*

(see index for correct answer)

- a. Cultural relativism
- b. positive discrimination
- c. Affirmative action

Guidance: level 1

:: ::

_____ is the means to see, hear, or become aware of something or someone through our fundamental senses. The term _____ derives from the Latin word perceptio, and is the organization, identification, and interpretation of sensory information in order to represent and understand the presented information, or the environment.

Exam Probability: **High**

44. *Answer choices:*

(see index for correct answer)

- a. hierarchical
- b. cultural
- c. interpersonal communication
- d. Perception

Guidance: level 1

:: United States federal defense and national security legislation ::

The USA _____ is an Act of the U.S. Congress that was signed into law by President George W. Bush on October 26, 2001. The title of the Act is a contrived three letter initialism preceding a seven letter acronym, which in combination stand for Uniting and Strengthening America by Providing Appropriate Tools Required to Intercept and Obstruct Terrorism Act of 2001. The acronym was created by a 23 year old Congressional staffer, Chris Kyle.

Exam Probability: **Low**

45. *Answer choices:*

(see index for correct answer)

- a. USA PATRIOT Act
- b. Patriot Act

Guidance: level 1

:: ::

The Catholic Church, also known as the Roman Catholic Church, is the largest Christian church, with approximately 1.3 billion baptised Catholics worldwide as of 2017. As the world's oldest continuously functioning international institution, it has played a prominent role in the history and development of Western civilisation. The church is headed by the Bishop of Rome, known as the pope. Its central administration, the Holy See, is in the Vatican City, an enclave within the city of Rome in Italy.

Exam Probability: **High**

46. *Answer choices:*

(see index for correct answer)

- a. corporate values
- b. imperative
- c. hierarchical perspective
- d. Catholicism

Guidance: level 1

:: Business ethics ::

A _____ is a person who exposes any kind of information or activity that is deemed illegal, unethical, or not correct within an organization that is either private or public. The information of alleged wrongdoing can be classified in many ways: violation of company policy/rules, law, regulation, or threat to public interest/national security, as well as fraud, and corruption. Those who become _____ s can choose to bring information or allegations to surface either internally or externally. Internally, a _____ can bring his/her accusations to the attention of other people within the accused organization such as an immediate supervisor. Externally, a _____ can bring allegations to light by contacting a third party outside of an accused organization such as the media, government, law enforcement, or those who are concerned. _____ s, however, take the risk of facing stiff reprisal and retaliation from those who are accused or alleged of wrongdoing.

Exam Probability: **High**

47. *Answer choices:*

(see index for correct answer)

- a. TG Soft
- b. Whistleblower
- c. Price discrimination
- d. Business and Professional Ethics Journal

Guidance: level 1

:: Majority–minority relations ::

_____, also known as reservation in India and Nepal, positive discrimination / action in the United Kingdom, and employment equity in Canada and South Africa, is the policy of promoting the education and employment of members of groups that are known to have previously suffered from discrimination. Historically and internationally, support for _____ has sought to achieve goals such as bridging inequalities in employment and pay, increasing access to education, promoting diversity, and redressing apparent past wrongs, harms, or hindrances.

Exam Probability: **Medium**

48. *Answer choices:*

(see index for correct answer)

- a. Affirmative action
- b. positive discrimination
- c. cultural Relativism

Guidance: level 1

:: ::

The _____ of 1973 serves as the enacting legislation to carry out the provisions outlined in The Convention on International Trade in Endangered Species of Wild Fauna and Flora. Designed to protect critically imperiled species from extinction as a "consequence of economic growth and development untempered by adequate concern and conservation", the ESA was signed into law by President Richard Nixon on December 28, 1973. The law requires federal agencies to consult with the Fish and Wildlife Service &/or the NOAA Fisheries Service to ensure their actions are not likely to jeopardize the continued existence of any listed species or result in the destruction or adverse modification of designated critical habitat of such species. The U.S. Supreme Court found that "the plain intent of Congress in enacting" the ESA "was to halt and reverse the trend toward species extinction, whatever the cost." The Act is administered by two federal agencies, the United States Fish and Wildlife Service and the National Marine Fisheries Service.

Exam Probability: **Low**

49. *Answer choices:*

(see index for correct answer)

- a. deep-level diversity
- b. hierarchical perspective
- c. Endangered Species Act
- d. levels of analysis

Guidance: level 1

:: Mortgage ::

In finance, _____ means making loans to people who may have difficulty maintaining the repayment schedule, sometimes reflecting setbacks, such as unemployment, divorce, medical emergencies, etc. Historically, subprime borrowers were defined as having FICO scores below 600, although "this has varied over time and circumstances."

Exam Probability: **Medium**

50. *Answer choices:*

(see index for correct answer)

- a. Mortgage arrangement fee
- b. Negative amortization
- c. Predatory mortgage securitization
- d. Subprime lending

Guidance: level 1

:: Anti-competitive behaviour ::

_____ is a secret cooperation or deceitful agreement in order to deceive others, although not necessarily illegal, as a conspiracy. A secret agreement between two or more parties to limit open competition by deceiving, misleading, or defrauding others of their legal rights, or to obtain an objective forbidden by law typically by defrauding or gaining an unfair market advantage is an example of _____ . It is an agreement among firms or individuals to divide a market, set prices, limit production or limit opportunities. It can involve "unions, wage fixing, kickbacks, or misrepresenting the independence of the relationship between the colluding parties". In legal terms, all acts effected by _____ are considered void.

Exam Probability: **Medium**

51. *Answer choices:*

(see index for correct answer)

- a. Dividing territories
- b. United States v. General Electric Co.
- c. Tying
- d. Fixed book price agreement

Guidance: level 1

:: Ethically disputed business practices ::

_____ is the trading of a public company's stock or other securities by individuals with access to nonpublic information about the company. In various countries, some kinds of trading based on insider information is illegal. This is because it is seen as unfair to other investors who do not have access to the information, as the investor with insider information could potentially make larger profits than a typical investor could make. The rules governing _____ are complex and vary significantly from country to country. The extent of enforcement also varies from one country to another. The definition of insider in one jurisdiction can be broad, and may cover not only insiders themselves but also any persons related to them, such as brokers, associates and even family members. A person who becomes aware of non-public information and trades on that basis may be guilty of a crime.

Exam Probability: **Low**

52. *Answer choices:*

(see index for correct answer)

- a. Insider trading
- b. Operation Red Spider
- c. Suicide bidding
- d. anti-competitive

Guidance: level 1

:: Parental leave ::

_____, or family leave, is an employee benefit available in almost all countries. The term "_____" may include maternity, paternity, and adoption leave; or may be used distinctively from "maternity leave" and "paternity leave" to describe separate family leave available to either parent to care for small children. In some countries and jurisdictions, "family leave" also includes leave provided to care for ill family members. Often, the minimum benefits and eligibility requirements are stipulated by law.

Exam Probability: **High**

53. *Answer choices:*

(see index for correct answer)

- a. Parental leave economics
- b. Additional Paternity Leave Regulations 2010
- c. Parental leave
- d. Motherhood penalty

Guidance: level 1

:: United Kingdom labour law ::

The _____ was a series of programs, public work projects, financial reforms, and regulations enacted by President Franklin D. Roosevelt in the United States between 1933 and 1936. It responded to needs for relief, reform, and recovery from the Great Depression. Major federal programs included the Civilian Conservation Corps, the Civil Works Administration, the Farm Security Administration, the National Industrial Recovery Act of 1933 and the Social Security Administration. They provided support for farmers, the unemployed, youth and the elderly. The _____ included new constraints and safeguards on the banking industry and efforts to re-inflate the economy after prices had fallen sharply. _____ programs included both laws passed by Congress as well as presidential executive orders during the first term of the presidency of Franklin D. Roosevelt.

Exam Probability: **High**

54. *Answer choices:*

(see index for correct answer)

- a. Paternity and Adoption Leave Regulations 2002
- b. Trade Boards Act 1918
- c. New Deal
- d. Eleventh and Final Report of the Royal Commissioners appointed to Inquire into the Organization and Rules of Trades Unions and Other Associations

Guidance: level 1

:: Confidence tricks ::

A _____ is a form of fraud that lures investors and pays profits to earlier investors with funds from more recent investors. The scheme leads victims to believe that profits are coming from product sales or other means, and they remain unaware that other investors are the source of funds. A _____ can maintain the illusion of a sustainable business as long as new investors contribute new funds, and as long as most of the investors do not demand full repayment and still believe in the non-existent assets they are purported to own.

Exam Probability: **Low**

55. *Answer choices:*

(see index for correct answer)

- a. Green goods scam
- b. Ponzi scheme
- c. Moving scam
- d. Fortune telling fraud

Guidance: level 1

:: ::

_____ is an eight-block-long street running roughly northwest to southeast from Broadway to South Street, at the East River, in the Financial District of Lower Manhattan in New York City. Over time, the term has become a metonym for the financial markets of the United States as a whole, the American financial services industry , or New York–based financial interests.

Exam Probability: **Low**

56. *Answer choices:*

(see index for correct answer)

- a. deep-level diversity
- b. levels of analysis
- c. open system
- d. similarity-attraction theory

Guidance: level 1

:: ::

_____ is a non-governmental environmental organization with offices in over 39 countries and an international coordinating body in Amsterdam, the Netherlands. _____ was founded in 1971 by Irving Stowe, and Dorothy Stowe, Canadian and US ex-pat environmental activists. _____ states its goal is to "ensure the ability of the Earth to nurture life in all its diversity" and focuses its campaigning on worldwide issues such as climate change, deforestation, overfishing, commercial whaling, genetic engineering, and anti-nuclear issues. It uses direct action, lobbying, research, and ecotage to achieve its goals. The global organization does not accept funding from governments, corporations, or political parties, relying on three million individual supporters and foundation grants. _____ has a general consultative status with the United Nations Economic and Social Council and is a founding member of the INGO Accountability Charter, an international non-governmental organization that intends to foster accountability and transparency of non-governmental organizations.

Exam Probability: **High**

57. *Answer choices:*

(see index for correct answer)

- a. Greenpeace
- b. functional perspective
- c. Character
- d. personal values

Guidance: level 1

:: ::

_____ generally refers to a focus on the needs or desires of one's self. A number of philosophical, psychological, and economic theories examine the role of _____ in motivating human action.

Exam Probability: **Low**

58. *Answer choices:*

(see index for correct answer)

- a. co-culture
- b. Sarbanes-Oxley act of 2002
- c. process perspective
- d. hierarchical perspective

Guidance: level 1

:: Data management ::

_____ is a form of intellectual property that grants the creator of an original creative work an exclusive legal right to determine whether and under what conditions this original work may be copied and used by others, usually for a limited term of years. The exclusive rights are not absolute but limited by limitations and exceptions to _____ law, including fair use. A major limitation on _____ on ideas is that _____ protects only the original expression of ideas, and not the underlying ideas themselves.

Exam Probability: **Medium**

59. *Answer choices:*

(see index for correct answer)

- a. Copyright
- b. DMAIC
- c. Asset Description Metadata Schema
- d. DAMA

Guidance: level 1

Accounting

Accounting or accountancy is the measurement, processing, and communication of financial information about economic entities such as businesses and corporations. The modern field was established by the Italian mathematician Luca Pacioli in 1494. Accounting, which has been called the "language of business", measures the results of an organization's economic activities and conveys this information to a variety of users, including investors, creditors, management, and regulators.

In the field of analysis of algorithms in computer science, the _____ is a method of amortized analysis based on accounting. The _____ often gives a more intuitive account of the amortized cost of an operation than either aggregate analysis or the potential method. Note, however, that this does not guarantee such analysis will be immediately obvious; often, choosing the correct parameters for the _____ requires as much knowledge of the problem and the complexity bounds one is attempting to prove as the other two methods.

Exam Probability: **High**

1. *Answer choices:*

(see index for correct answer)

- a. imperative
- b. surface-level diversity
- c. information systems assessment
- d. Accounting method

Guidance: level 1

:: Generally Accepted Accounting Principles ::

_____ is all a person's receipts and gains from all sources, before any deductions. The adjective "gross", as opposed to "net", generally qualifies a word referring to an amount, value, weight, number, or the like, specifying that necessary deductions have not been taken into account.

Exam Probability: **High**

2. *Answer choices:*

(see index for correct answer)

- a. Expense
- b. Matching principle
- c. Gross profit
- d. deferred revenue

Guidance: level 1

:: Management accounting ::

In finance, the _____ or net present worth applies to a series of cash flows occurring at different times. The present value of a cash flow depends on the interval of time between now and the cash flow. It also depends on the discount rate. NPV accounts for the time value of money. It provides a method for evaluating and comparing capital projects or financial products with cash flows spread over time, as in loans, investments, payouts from insurance contracts plus many other applications.

Exam Probability: **Low**

3. *Answer choices:*

(see index for correct answer)

- a. activity based costing

- b. Certified Management Accountant
- c. Net present value
- d. Process costing

Guidance: level 1

:: Generally Accepted Accounting Principles ::

In accounting, _____ is the income that a business have from its normal business activities, usually from the sale of goods and services to customers. _____ is also referred to as sales or turnover. Some companies receive _____ from interest, royalties, or other fees. _____ may refer to business income in general, or it may refer to the amount, in a monetary unit, earned during a period of time, as in "Last year, Company X had _____ of $42 million". Profits or net income generally imply total _____ minus total expenses in a given period. In accounting, in the balance statement it is a subsection of the Equity section and _____ increases equity, it is often referred to as the "top line" due to its position on the income statement at the very top. This is to be contrasted with the "bottom line" which denotes net income.

Exam Probability: **Medium**

4. *Answer choices:*

(see index for correct answer)

- a. Net income
- b. Cost principle
- c. Revenue

- d. Trial balance

Guidance: level 1

:: Management ::

_____ is a style of business management that focuses on identifying and handling cases that deviate from the norm, recommended as best practice by the project management method PRINCE2.

Exam Probability: **Low**

5. *Answer choices:*

(see index for correct answer)

- a. Management by exception
- b. Intelligent customer
- c. Earned schedule
- d. Allegiance

Guidance: level 1

:: International taxation ::

_____ is the levying of tax by two or more jurisdictions on the same declared income, asset, or financial transaction. Double liability is mitigated in a number of ways, for example.

Exam Probability: **Low**

6. *Answer choices:*

(see index for correct answer)

- a. Spahn tax
- b. Double taxation
- c. Tax equalization
- d. Advance pricing agreement

Guidance: level 1

:: ::

A _____ is an individual or institution that legally owns one or more shares of stock in a public or private corporation. _____ s may be referred to as members of a corporation. Legally, a person is not a _____ in a corporation until their name and other details are entered in the corporation's register of _____ s or members.

Exam Probability: **Low**

7. *Answer choices:*

(see index for correct answer)

- a. interpersonal communication
- b. information systems assessment
- c. Shareholder
- d. levels of analysis

Guidance: level 1

:: Inventory ::

_____ is the amount of inventory a company has in stock at the end of its fiscal year. It is closely related with _____ cost, which is the amount of money spent to get these goods in stock. It should be calculated at the lower of cost or market.

Exam Probability: **High**

8. *Answer choices:*

(see index for correct answer)

- a. Average cost method
- b. Ending inventory
- c. LIFO
- d. Specific identification

Guidance: level 1

:: Payment systems ::

A _____ is a bond of the redeemable transaction type which is worth a certain monetary value and which may be spent only for specific reasons or on specific goods. Examples include housing, travel, and food _____s. The term _____ is also a synonym for receipt and is often used to refer to receipts used as evidence of, for example, the declaration that a service has been performed or that an expenditure has been made. _____ is a tourist guide for using services with a guarantee of payment by the agency.

Exam Probability: **Low**

9. *Answer choices:*

(see index for correct answer)

- a. International Payments Framework
- b. Telegraphic transfer
- c. Voucher
- d. Betalingsservice

Guidance: level 1

:: Classification systems ::

_____ is the practice of comparing business processes and performance metrics to industry bests and best practices from other companies. Dimensions typically measured are quality, time and cost.

Exam Probability: **Low**

10. *Answer choices:*

(see index for correct answer)

- a. Benchmarking
- b. Bliss bibliographic classification
- c. Parataxonomy
- d. Classification of Types of Construction

Guidance: level 1

:: Stock market ::

A _____, securities exchange or bourse, is a facility where stock brokers and traders can buy and sell securities, such as shares of stock and bonds and other financial instruments. _____ s may also provide for facilities the issue and redemption of such securities and instruments and capital events including the payment of income and dividends. Securities traded on a _____ include stock issued by listed companies, unit trusts, derivatives, pooled investment products and bonds. _____ s often function as "continuous auction" markets with buyers and sellers consummating transactions via open outcry at a central location such as the floor of the exchange or by using an electronic trading platform.

Exam Probability: **High**

11. *Answer choices:*

(see index for correct answer)

- a. WeSeed
- b. Stop price
- c. Stock Exchange
- d. H share

Guidance: level 1

:: Generally Accepted Accounting Principles ::

_____ is, in accrual accounting, money received for goods or services which have not yet been delivered. According to the revenue recognition principle, it is recorded as a liability until delivery is made, at which time it is converted into revenue.

Exam Probability: **Low**

12. *Answer choices:*

(see index for correct answer)

- a. Deferred income
- b. Deprival value
- c. Revenue recognition

- d. Earnings before interest and taxes

Guidance: level 1

:: ::

_____ is the income that is gained by governments through taxation. Taxation is the primary source of income for a state. Revenue may be extracted from sources such as individuals, public enterprises, trade, royalties on natural resources and/or foreign aid. An inefficient collection of taxes is greater in countries characterized by poverty, a large agricultural sector and large amounts of foreign aid.

Exam Probability: **High**

13. *Answer choices:*
(see index for correct answer)

- a. corporate values
- b. empathy
- c. open system
- d. co-culture

Guidance: level 1

:: United States Generally Accepted Accounting Principles ::

In a companies' financial reporting, _____ "includes all changes in equity during a period except those resulting from investments by owners and distributions to owners". Because that use excludes the effects of changing ownership interest, an economic measure of _____ is necessary for financial analysis from the shareholders' point of view

Exam Probability: **High**

14. *Answer choices:*

(see index for correct answer)

- a. Single Audit
- b. Working Group on Financial Markets
- c. Cost segregation study
- d. Asset retirement obligation

Guidance: level 1

:: ::

_____ is the act of compensating someone for an out-of-pocket expense by giving them an amount of money equal to what was spent.

Exam Probability: **Low**

15. *Answer choices:*

(see index for correct answer)

- a. surface-level diversity
- b. hierarchical perspective
- c. Reimbursement
- d. interpersonal communication

Guidance: level 1

:: Financial ratios ::

In finance, the _____ , also known as the acid-test ratio is a type of liquidity ratio which measures the ability of a company to use its near cash or quick assets to extinguish or retire its current liabilities immediately. Quick assets include those current assets that presumably can be quickly converted to cash at close to their book values. It is the ratio between quickly available or liquid assets and current liabilities.

Exam Probability: **Low**

16. *Answer choices:*

(see index for correct answer)

- a. Beta
- b. Interest coverage ratio
- c. Quick ratio
- d. AlphaIC

Guidance: level 1

:: Economic globalization ::

_____ is an agreement in which one company hires another company to be responsible for a planned or existing activity that is or could be done internally, and sometimes involves transferring employees and assets from one firm to another.

Exam Probability: **Low**

17. *Answer choices:*

(see index for correct answer)

- a. reshoring
- b. global financial

Guidance: level 1

:: Banking ::

A _____ is a financial institution that accepts deposits from the public and creates credit. Lending activities can be performed either directly or indirectly through capital markets. Due to their importance in the financial stability of a country, _____ s are highly regulated in most countries. Most nations have institutionalized a system known as fractional reserve _____ ing under which _____ s hold liquid assets equal to only a portion of their current liabilities. In addition to other regulations intended to ensure liquidity, _____ s are generally subject to minimum capital requirements based on an international set of capital standards, known as the Basel Accords.

Exam Probability: **Low**

18. *Answer choices:*

(see index for correct answer)

- a. Mail banking
- b. Bank run
- c. Bank
- d. Deposit market share

Guidance: level 1

:: Personal taxes ::

A _____ is the completion of documentation that calculates an entity's income earned with the amount of tax payable to the government, government organisations or to potential taxpayers.

Exam Probability: **High**

19. *Answer choices:*

(see index for correct answer)

- a. Tax return
- b. Grantor retained annuity trust
- c. Pay-as-you-earn tax
- d. California Franchise Tax Board

Guidance: level 1

:: Financial statements ::

In financial accounting, a _____ or statement of financial position or statement of financial condition is a summary of the financial balances of an individual or organization, whether it be a sole proprietorship, a business partnership, a corporation, private limited company or other organization such as Government or not-for-profit entity. Assets, liabilities and ownership equity are listed as of a specific date, such as the end of its financial year. A _____ is often described as a "snapshot of a company's financial condition". Of the four basic financial statements, the _____ is the only statement which applies to a single point in time of a business' calendar year.

Exam Probability: **High**

20. *Answer choices:*

(see index for correct answer)

- a. Statement on Auditing Standards No. 55
- b. Statement on Auditing Standards No. 70: Service Organizations
- c. Balance sheet
- d. Financial report

Guidance: level 1

:: Management accounting ::

_____ is the process of reviewing and analyzing a company's financial statements to make better economic decisions to earn income in future. These statements include the income statement, balance sheet, statement of cash flows, notes to accounts and a statement of changes in equity . _____ is a method or process involving specific techniques for evaluating risks, performance, financial health, and future prospects of an organization.

Exam Probability: **High**

21. *Answer choices:*

(see index for correct answer)

- a. Financial statement analysis
- b. Dual overhead rate
- c. Direct material price variance
- d. Corporate travel management

Guidance: level 1

:: Accounting in the United States ::

_____ refers to a Memorandum of Understanding signed in September 2002 between the Financial Accounting Standards Board, the US standard setter, and the International Accounting Standards Board. The agreement is so called as it was reached in Norwalk.

Exam Probability: **Low**

22. *Answer choices:*

(see index for correct answer)

- a. Variable interest entity
- b. Accounting Today
- c. Governmental Accounting Standards Board
- d. Norwalk Agreement

Guidance: level 1

:: ::

A _____ is a fund into which a sum of money is added during an employee's employment years, and from which payments are drawn to support the person's retirement from work in the form of periodic payments. A _____ may be a "defined benefit plan" where a fixed sum is paid regularly to a person, or a "defined contribution plan" under which a fixed sum is invested and then becomes available at retirement age. _____ s should not be confused with severance pay; the former is usually paid in regular installments for life after retirement, while the latter is typically paid as a fixed amount after involuntary termination of employment prior to retirement.

Exam Probability: **Low**

23. *Answer choices:*

(see index for correct answer)

- a. Sarbanes-Oxley act of 2002
- b. Pension
- c. Character
- d. functional perspective

Guidance: level 1

:: United States Generally Accepted Accounting Principles ::

In the United States, a _____ is one of the five governmental fund types established by GAAP. It is classified as a restricted true endowment fund for governments and non-profit organizations. Put simply, a _____ may be used to generate and disburse money to those entitled to receive payments by qualification or agreement, as in the case of Alaska citizens or residents that satisfy the rules for payment from their _____ from State oil revenues. It was first introduced through GASB Statement 34. The name of the fund comes from the purpose of the fund: a sum of equity used to permanently generate payments to maintain some financial obligation. Also, a fund can only be classified as a _____ if the money is used to report the status of a restricted financial resource. The resource is restricted in the sense that only earnings from the resource are used and not the principal. For example, a fund can be classified as a _____ if it is being used to pay for accounting services for a perpetual endowment of a government-run cemetery or financial endowments towards a government-run library.

Exam Probability: **Medium**

24. *Answer choices:*

(see index for correct answer)

- a. GASB 45
- b. Single Audit
- c. GASB 34
- d. Permanent fund

Guidance: level 1

:: Accounting in the United States ::

Founded in 1887, the _____ is the national professional organization of Certified Public Accountants in the United States, with more than 418,000 members in 143 countries in business and industry, public practice, government, education, student affiliates and international associates. It sets ethical standards for the profession and U.S. auditing standards for audits of private companies, non-profit organizations, federal, state and local governments. It also develops and grades the Uniform CPA Examination. The AICPA maintains offices in New York City; Washington, DC; Durham, NC; and Ewing, NJ. The AICPA celebrated the 125th anniversary of its founding in 2012.

Exam Probability: **High**

25. *Answer choices:*

(see index for correct answer)

- a. Association of Certified Fraud Examiners
- b. Legal liability of certified public accountants
- c. Norwalk Agreement
- d. Trueblood Committee

Guidance: level 1

:: Generally Accepted Accounting Principles ::

_____ is the accounting classification of an account. It is part of double-entry book-keeping technique.

Exam Probability: **High**

26. *Answer choices:*

(see index for correct answer)

- a. AICPA Statements of Position
- b. Write-off
- c. Indian Accounting Standards
- d. Gross sales

Guidance: level 1

:: Stock market ::

A _____ , equity market or share market is the aggregation of buyers and sellers of stocks , which represent ownership claims on businesses; these may include securities listed on a public stock exchange, as well as stock that is only traded privately. Examples of the latter include shares of private companies which are sold to investors through equity crowdfunding platforms. Stock exchanges list shares of common equity as well as other security types, e.g. corporate bonds and convertible bonds.

Exam Probability: **High**

27. *Answer choices:*

(see index for correct answer)

- a. Big boy letter
- b. Automated trading system
- c. Slippage

- d. Green sheet

Guidance: level 1

:: Actuarial science ::

The _____ is the greater benefit of receiving money now rather than an identical sum later. It is founded on time preference.

Exam Probability: **Medium**

28. *Answer choices:*
(see index for correct answer)

- a. Late-life mortality deceleration
- b. Fictional actuaries
- c. Insurance cycle
- d. Time value of money

Guidance: level 1

:: Generally Accepted Accounting Principles ::

_____, also referred to as the bottom line, net income, or net earnings is a measure of the profitability of a venture after accounting for all costs and taxes. It is the actual profit, and includes the operating expenses that are excluded from gross profit.

Exam Probability: **Low**

29. *Answer choices:*

(see index for correct answer)

- a. Long-term liabilities
- b. Write-off
- c. Net profit
- d. Chinese accounting standards

Guidance: level 1

:: Notes (finance) ::

A _____, sometimes referred to as a note payable, is a legal instrument, in which one party promises in writing to pay a determinate sum of money to the other, either at a fixed or determinable future time or on demand of the payee, under specific terms.

Exam Probability: **Low**

30. *Answer choices:*

(see index for correct answer)

- a. Federal Reserve Note
- b. Principal protected note
- c. Demand Note
- d. Promissory note

Guidance: level 1

:: Management accounting ::

_____ is an accountancy practice, the aim of which is to provide an offset to the mark-to-market movement of the derivative in the profit and loss account. There are two types of hedge recognized. For a fair value hedge the offset is achieved either by marking-to-market an asset or a liability which offsets the P&L movement of the derivative. For a cash flow hedge some of the derivative volatility into a separate component of the entity's equity called the cash flow hedge reserve. Where a hedge relationship is effective, most of the mark-to-market derivative volatility will be offset in the profit and loss account. _____ entails much compliance - involving documenting the hedge relationship and both prospectively and retrospectively proving that the hedge relationship is effective.

Exam Probability: **Low**

31. *Answer choices:*
(see index for correct answer)

- a. Backflush accounting

- b. Net present value
- c. Notional profit
- d. Hedge accounting

Guidance: level 1

:: Management accounting ::

_____ are costs that are not directly accountable to a cost object. _____ may be either fixed or variable. _____ include administration, personnel and security costs. These are those costs which are not directly related to production. Some _____ may be overhead. But some overhead costs can be directly attributed to a project and are direct costs.

Exam Probability: **Low**

32. *Answer choices:*

(see index for correct answer)

- a. Indirect costs
- b. Net present value
- c. Customer profitability
- d. Corporate travel management

Guidance: level 1

:: Accounting terminology ::

_____ of something is, in finance, the adding together of interest or different investments over a period of time. It holds specific meanings in accounting, where it can refer to accounts on a balance sheet that represent liabilities and non-cash-based assets used in _____ -based accounting. These types of accounts include, among others, accounts payable, accounts receivable, goodwill, deferred tax liability and future interest expense.

Exam Probability: **Medium**

33. *Answer choices:*
(see index for correct answer)

- a. Chart of accounts
- b. Accrual
- c. Share premium
- d. Adjusting entries

Guidance: level 1

:: Accounting in the United States ::

The _____ is the source of generally accepted accounting principles used by state and local governments in the United States. As with most of the entities involved in creating GAAP in the United States, it is a private, non-governmental organization.

Exam Probability: **High**

34. *Answer choices:*

(see index for correct answer)

- a. Financial Accounting Foundation
- b. Positive assurance
- c. Variable interest entity
- d. National Association of State Boards of Accountancy

Guidance: level 1

:: Legal terms ::

_____ is a state of prolonged public dispute or debate, usually concerning a matter of conflicting opinion or point of view. The word was coined from the Latin controversia, as a composite of controversus – "turned in an opposite direction," from contra – "against" – and vertere – to turn, or versus , hence, "to turn against."

Exam Probability: **Low**

35. *Answer choices:*

(see index for correct answer)

- a. Antedated
- b. Legal benefit

- c. Prescription
- d. Controversy

Guidance: level 1

:: Generally Accepted Accounting Principles ::

Expenditure is an outflow of money to another person or group to pay for an item or service, or for a category of costs. For a tenant, rent is an _____ . For students or parents, tuition is an _____ . Buying food, clothing, furniture or an automobile is often referred to as an _____ . An _____ is a cost that is "paid" or "remitted", usually in exchange for something of value. Something that seems to cost a great deal is "expensive". "_____ s of the table" are _____ s of dining, refreshments, a feast, etc.

Exam Probability: **High**

36. *Answer choices:*

(see index for correct answer)

- a. Contributed capital
- b. Deferral
- c. Profit
- d. Expense

Guidance: level 1

:: Management accounting ::

In economics, _____ s, indirect costs or overheads are business expenses that are not dependent on the level of goods or services produced by the business. They tend to be time-related, such as interest or rents being paid per month, and are often referred to as overhead costs. This is in contrast to variable costs, which are volume-related and unknown at the beginning of the accounting year. For a simple example, such as a bakery, the monthly rent for the baking facilities, and the monthly payments for the security system and basic phone line are _____ s, as they do not change according to how much bread the bakery produces and sells. On the other hand, the wage costs of the bakery are variable, as the bakery will have to hire more workers if the production of bread increases. Economists reckon _____ as a entry barrier for new entrepreneurs.

Exam Probability: **Medium**

37. *Answer choices:*
(see index for correct answer)

- a. Fixed cost
- b. Invested capital
- c. Backflush accounting
- d. Management accounting in supply chains

Guidance: level 1

:: Business law ::

An _____ is a natural person, business, or corporation that provides goods or services to another entity under terms specified in a contract or within a verbal agreement. Unlike an employee, an _____ does not work regularly for an employer but works as and when required, during which time they may be subject to law of agency. _____s are usually paid on a freelance basis. Contractors often work through a limited company or franchise, which they themselves own, or may work through an umbrella company.

Exam Probability: **High**

38. *Answer choices:*

(see index for correct answer)

- a. Tacit relocation
- b. Independent contractor
- c. Wrongful trading
- d. Law of agency

Guidance: level 1

:: Finance ::

The _____ of a corporation is the accumulated net income of the corporation that is retained by the corporation at a particular point of time, such as at the end of the reporting period. At the end of that period, the net income at that point is transferred from the Profit and Loss Account to the _____ account. If the balance of the _____ account is negative it may be called accumulated losses, retained losses or accumulated deficit, or similar terminology.

Exam Probability: **Medium**

39. *Answer choices:*

(see index for correct answer)

- a. Retained earnings
- b. Separation property
- c. Remote deposit
- d. Multilateral trading facility

Guidance: level 1

:: Manufacturing ::

_____ costs are all manufacturing costs that are related to the cost object but cannot be traced to that cost object in an economically feasible way.

Exam Probability: **Medium**

40. *Answer choices:*

(see index for correct answer)

- a. Manufacturing resource planning
- b. Unhairing
- c. Priming
- d. Manufacturing overhead

Guidance: level 1

:: Banking ::

A _____ is a financial account maintained by a bank for a customer. A _____ can be a deposit account, a credit card account, a current account, or any other type of account offered by a financial institution, and represents the funds that a customer has entrusted to the financial institution and from which the customer can make withdrawals. Alternatively, accounts may be loan accounts in which case the customer owes money to the financial institution.

Exam Probability: **Low**

41. *Answer choices:*

(see index for correct answer)

- a. Bank account
- b. International Bank of Azerbaijan-Georgia
- c. Commercial finance advisor
- d. Daylight overdraft

Guidance: level 1

:: Fraud ::

In law, _____ is intentional deception to secure unfair or unlawful gain, or to deprive a victim of a legal right. _____ can violate civil law, a criminal law, or it may cause no loss of money, property or legal right but still be an element of another civil or criminal wrong. The purpose of _____ may be monetary gain or other benefits, for example by obtaining a passport, travel document, or driver's license, or mortgage _____, where the perpetrator may attempt to qualify for a mortgage by way of false statements.

Exam Probability: **Medium**

42. *Answer choices:*

(see index for correct answer)

- a. Lottery scam
- b. Cheat sheet
- c. Fraud Squad
- d. Money mule

Guidance: level 1

:: Insurance terms ::

A _____ in the broadest sense is a natural person or other legal entity who receives money or other benefits from a benefactor. For example, the _____ of a life insurance policy is the person who receives the payment of the amount of insurance after the death of the insured.

Exam Probability: **Low**

43. *Answer choices:*

(see index for correct answer)

- a. Omnibus clause
- b. Contingent commissions
- c. Co-insurance
- d. Aggression insurance

Guidance: level 1

:: Tax reform ::

_____ is the process of changing the way taxes are collected or managed by the government and is usually undertaken to improve tax administration or to provide economic or social benefits. _____ can include reducing the level of taxation of all people by the government, making the tax system more progressive or less progressive, or simplifying the tax system and making the system more understandable or more accountable.

Exam Probability: **Medium**

44. *Answer choices:*

(see index for correct answer)

- a. Joseph A. Pechman
- b. Tax shift

- c. Value-added tax
- d. Tax reform

Guidance: level 1

:: ::

An _____ is an asset that lacks physical substance. It is defined in opposition to physical assets such as machinery and buildings. An _____ is usually very hard to evaluate. Patents, copyrights, franchises, goodwill, trademarks, and trade names. The general interpretation also includes software and other intangible computer based assets are all examples of _____ s. _____ s generally—though not necessarily—suffer from typical market failures of non-rivalry and non-excludability.

Exam Probability: **High**

45. *Answer choices:*

(see index for correct answer)

- a. similarity-attraction theory
- b. functional perspective
- c. interpersonal communication
- d. cultural

Guidance: level 1

:: ::

Accounts _____ is a legally enforceable claim for payment held by a business for goods supplied and/or services rendered that customers/clients have ordered but not paid for. These are generally in the form of invoices raised by a business and delivered to the customer for payment within an agreed time frame. Accounts _____ is shown in a balance sheet as an asset. It is one of a series of accounting transactions dealing with the billing of a customer for goods and services that the customer has ordered. These may be distinguished from notes _____ , which are debts created through formal legal instruments called promissory notes.

Exam Probability: **High**

46. *Answer choices:*

(see index for correct answer)

- a. Receivable
- b. levels of analysis
- c. imperative
- d. cultural

Guidance: level 1

:: United States Generally Accepted Accounting Principles ::

A _____ is a set of U.S. government financial statements comprising the financial report of a state, municipal or other governmental entity that complies with the accounting requirements promulgated by the Governmental Accounting Standards Board . GASB provides standards for the content of a CAFR in its annually updated publication Codification of Governmental Accounting and Financial Reporting Standards. The U.S. Federal Government adheres to standards determined by the Federal Accounting Standards Advisory Board .

Exam Probability: **High**

47. *Answer choices:*

(see index for correct answer)

- a. Asset retirement obligation
- b. Comprehensive annual financial report
- c. GASB 34
- d. Accounting for leases in the United States

Guidance: level 1

:: Valuation (finance) ::

The _____ is one of three major groups of methodologies, called valuation approaches, used by appraisers. It is particularly common in commercial real estate appraisal and in business appraisal. The fundamental math is similar to the methods used for financial valuation, securities analysis, or bond pricing. However, there are some significant and important modifications when used in real estate or business valuation.

Exam Probability: **Medium**

48. *Answer choices:*

(see index for correct answer)

- a. Graham number
- b. Value date
- c. Turnaround stock
- d. Income approach

Guidance: level 1

:: Accounting in the United States ::

_____ were documents issued by the Committee on Accounting Procedure between 1938 and 1959 on various accounting problems. They were discontinued with the dissolution of the Committee in 1959 under a recommendation from the Special Committee on Research Program. In all, 17 bulletins were issued; however, the lack of binding authority over AICPA's membership reduced the influence of, and compliance with the content of the bulletins. The _____ have all been superseded by the Accounting Standards Codification .

Exam Probability: **Medium**

49. *Answer choices:*

(see index for correct answer)

- a. Variable interest entity

- b. Statements on Auditing Procedure
- c. Accounting Research Bulletins
- d. Norwalk Agreement

Guidance: level 1

:: Expense ::

An _____, operating expenditure, operational expense, operational expenditure or opex is an ongoing cost for running a product, business, or system. Its counterpart, a capital expenditure, is the cost of developing or providing non-consumable parts for the product or system. For example, the purchase of a photocopier involves capex, and the annual paper, toner, power and maintenance costs represents opex. For larger systems like businesses, opex may also include the cost of workers and facility expenses such as rent and utilities.

Exam Probability: **Medium**

50. *Answer choices:*
(see index for correct answer)

- a. Expense account
- b. Tax expense
- c. Operating expense
- d. Freight expense

Guidance: level 1

:: Management accounting ::

_____ is a professional business study of Accounts and management in which we learn importance of accounts in our management system.

Exam Probability: **Low**

51. *Answer choices:*
(see index for correct answer)

- a. Spend management
- b. Certified Management Accountant
- c. Accounting management
- d. Variance

Guidance: level 1

:: Inventory ::

In business and accounting/accountancy, _____ or continuous inventory describes systems of inventory where information on inventory quantity and availability is updated on a continuous basis as a function of doing business. Generally this is accomplished by connecting the inventory system with order entry and in retail the point of sale system. In this case, book inventory would be exactly the same as, or almost the same, as the real inventory.

Exam Probability: **High**

52. *Answer choices:*

(see index for correct answer)

- a. Average cost method
- b. Perpetual inventory
- c. Safety stock
- d. New old stock

Guidance: level 1

:: Real estate ::

An _____ is to, interest in, or legal liability on real property that does not prohibit passing title to the property but that may diminish its value. _____ s can be classified in several ways. They may be financial or non-financial. Alternatively, they may be divided into those that affect title or those that affect the use or physical condition of the encumbered property. _____ s include security interests, liens, servitudes, leases, restrictions, encroachments, and air and subsurface rights. Also, those considered as potentially making the title defeasible are _____ s, for example, charging orders, building orders and structure alteration. _____ : charge upon or claim against land arising out of private grant or a contract.

Exam Probability: **High**

53. *Answer choices:*

(see index for correct answer)

- a. Encumbrance
- b. Real estate license
- c. Estate liquidation
- d. Real Estate Weekly

Guidance: level 1

:: Information systems ::

An accounting as an information system is a system of collecting, storing and processing financial and accounting data that are used by decision makers. An _____ is generally a computer-based method for tracking accounting activity in conjunction with information technology resources. The resulting financial reports can be used internally by management or externally by other interested parties including investors, creditors and tax authorities.
_____ s are designed to support all accounting functions and activities including auditing, financial accounting & reporting, managerial/ management accounting and tax. The most widely adopted accounting information systems are auditing and financial reporting modules.

Exam Probability: **Low**

54. *Answer choices:*

(see index for correct answer)

- a. Self-service software
- b. Automated information system
- c. Modeling perspective
- d. Accounting information system

Guidance: level 1

:: ::

_____ is the field of accounting concerned with the summary, analysis and reporting of financial transactions related to a business. This involves the preparation of financial statements available for public use. Stockholders, suppliers, banks, employees, government agencies, business owners, and other stakeholders are examples of people interested in receiving such information for decision making purposes.

Exam Probability: **Medium**

55. *Answer choices:*

(see index for correct answer)

- a. empathy
- b. functional perspective
- c. levels of analysis
- d. imperative

Guidance: level 1

:: Television terminology ::

A nonprofit organization, also known as a non-business entity, _____ organization, or nonprofit institution, is dedicated to furthering a particular social cause or advocating for a shared point of view. In economic terms, it is an organization that uses its surplus of the revenues to further achieve its ultimate objective, rather than distributing its income to the organization's shareholders, leaders, or members. Nonprofits are tax exempt or charitable, meaning they do not pay income tax on the money that they receive for their organization. They can operate in religious, scientific, research, or educational settings.

Exam Probability: **Medium**

56. *Answer choices:*

(see index for correct answer)

- a. Satellite television
- b. distance learning
- c. Not-for-profit
- d. nonprofit

Guidance: level 1

:: International Financial Reporting Standards ::

_____, usually called IFRS, are standards issued by the IFRS Foundation and the International Accounting Standards Board to provide a common global language for business affairs so that company accounts are understandable and comparable across international boundaries. They are a consequence of growing international shareholding and trade and are particularly important for companies that have dealings in several countries. They are progressively replacing the many different national accounting standards. They are the rules to be followed by accountants to maintain books of accounts which are comparable, understandable, reliable and relevant as per the users internal or external. IFRS, with the exception of IAS 29 Financial Reporting in Hyperinflationary Economies and IFRIC 7 Applying the Restatement Approach under IAS 29, are authorized in terms of the historical cost paradigm. IAS 29 and IFRIC 7 are authorized in terms of the units of constant purchasing power paradigm.IAS 2 is related to inventories in this standard we talk about the stock its production process etcIFRS began as an attempt to harmonize accounting across the European Union but the value of harmonization quickly made the concept attractive around the world. However, it has been debated whether or not de facto harmonization has occurred. Standards that were issued by IASC are still within use today and go by the name International Accounting Standards , while standards issued by IASB are called IFRS. IAS were issued between 1973 and 2001 by the Board of the International Accounting Standards Committee . On 1 April 2001, the new International Accounting Standards Board took over from the IASC the responsibility for setting International Accounting Standards. During its first meeting the new Board adopted existing IAS and Standing Interpretations Committee standards . The IASB has continued to develop standards calling the new standards " _____ ".

Exam Probability: **High**

57. *Answer choices:*

(see index for correct answer)

- a. IAS 1
- b. IFRS 5
- c. IFRS 1

- d. International Financial Reporting Standards

Guidance: level 1

:: Accounting source documents ::

_____ is a letter sent by a customer to a supplier to inform the supplier that their invoice has been paid. If the customer is paying by cheque, the _____ often accompanies the cheque. The advice may consist of a literal letter or of a voucher attached to the side or top of the cheque.

Exam Probability: **High**

58. *Answer choices:*
(see index for correct answer)

- a. Remittance advice
- b. Credit memo
- c. Air waybill
- d. Purchase order

Guidance: level 1

:: ::

From an accounting perspective, _____ is crucial because _____ and _____ taxes considerably affect the net income of most companies and because they are subject to laws and regulations .

Exam Probability: **High**

59. *Answer choices:*

(see index for correct answer)

- a. Payroll
- b. hierarchical perspective
- c. information systems assessment
- d. similarity-attraction theory

Guidance: level 1

INDEX: Correct Answers

Foundations of Business

1. a: Project

2. c: Bias

3. d: Bankruptcy

4. a: Procurement

5. b: Performance

6. a: Analysis

7. : Explanation

8. b: Solution

9. a: Shareholders

10. d: Perception

11. : Corporate governance

12. b: Recession

13. b: Partnership

14. b: Trade agreement

15. b: Committee

16. a: Business plan

17. b: Affirmative action

18. : Preference

19. : Benchmarking

20. c: Capitalism

21. a: Brainstorming

22. c: Trademark

23. b: Dimension

24. b: Consumer Protection

25. c: SWOT analysis

26. : Bribery

27. c: Law

28. d: Negotiation

29. d: Loan

30. d: Availability

31. b: Cooperation

32. d: Property rights

33. a: Fixed cost

34. c: Mission statement

35. b: Subsidiary

36. : Small business

37. a: Training

38. a: Interview

39. c: Marketing mix

40. c: Credit card

41. c: Health

42. c: Exercise

43. d: Human resources

44. : Project management

45. d: Internal control

46. c: Logistics

47. a: Asset

48. a: Import

49. d: Buyer

50. d: American Express

51. b: Integrity

52. a: Size

53. a: Common stock

54. a: Limited liability

55. b: Raw material

56. b: Globalization

57. : Internal Revenue Service

58. b: Information

59. d: Innovation

Management

1. b: Skill

2. a: Decision tree

3. : Accounting

4. b: Restructuring

5. d: Creativity

6. d: Quality circle

7. b: Outsourcing

8. c: Customer

9. a: Learning organization

10. a: Dimension

11. : Change management

12. : Performance

13. c: Expert power

14. d: Total quality management

15. b: Purchasing

16. d: Leadership style

17. b: Interdependence

18. a: Training and development

19. d: Organizational performance

20. b: Organizational commitment

21. : Profit sharing

22. a: Offshoring

23. b: Performance appraisal

24. : Raw material

25. d: Income

26. b: Utility

27. a: Statistical process control

28. b: Resource management

29. b: Expatriate

30. b: Meeting

31. b: Explanation

32. d: Goal

33. b: Mass customization

34. : Officer

35. a: Layoff

36. c: Joint venture

37. a: Wage

38. c: Bargaining

39. : Span of control

40. d: Good

41. c: Entrepreneur

42. d: Product design

43. c: Virtual team

44. : Reason

45. a: Distance

46. c: Industry

47. c: Best practice

48. d: Ownership

49. b: Management process

50. d: Incentive

51. c: Knowledge management

52. c: Myers-Briggs type

53. : Policy

54. b: Goal setting

55. : Ratio

56. a: Industrial Revolution

57. d: Human resources

58. : Operations management

59. a: Initiative

Business law

1. c: Disclaimer

2. b: Offeree

3. c: Dividend

4. : Real property

5. c: Contract

6. c: Writ

7. c: White-collar crime

8. b: Federal Arbitration Act

9. b: Buyer

10. c: Preference

11. c: Trade

12. : Acceleration clause

13. a: Reasonable person

14. : Garnishment

15. b: Statute of limitations

16. a: Inventory

17. : Condition precedent

18. a: First Amendment

19. d: Tangible

20. c: Social responsibility

21. : Revenue

22. a: Statute of frauds

23. : Holder in due course

24. a: Advertising

25. b: Judicial review

26. a: Categorical imperative

27. a: Commerce Clause

28. d: Risk

29. c: Embezzlement

30. c: Voidable

31. : Utility

32. c: Disparagement

33. : Probate

34. d: Interest

35. d: Federal government

36. d: Incentive

37. : Trespass

38. a: Wire fraud

39. : Money laundering

40. b: Aid

41. a: Insider trading

42. : Apparent authority

43. d: Contract Clause

44. : Forgery

45. a: Security

46. : Consumer credit

47. b: Impossibility

48. a: Directed verdict

49. c: Undue influence

50. a: Plaintiff

51. : Private law

52. a: Damages

53. b: Scienter

54. : Subrogation

55. a: Mediation

56. b: Due diligence

57. c: Limited partnership

58. b: Broker

59. b: Copyright

Finance

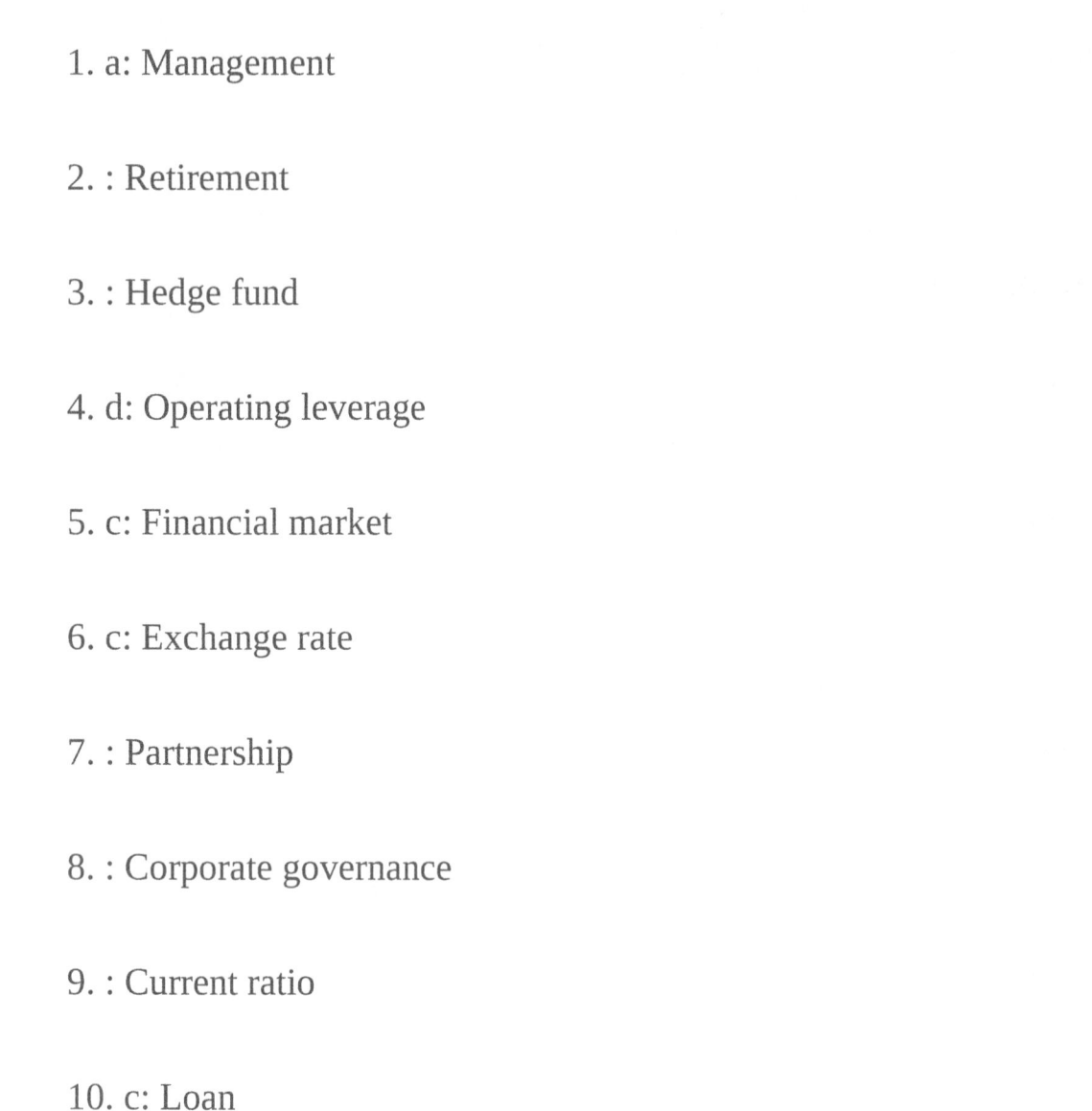

1. a: Management

2. : Retirement

3. : Hedge fund

4. d: Operating leverage

5. c: Financial market

6. c: Exchange rate

7. : Partnership

8. : Corporate governance

9. : Current ratio

10. c: Loan

11. c: Financial crisis

12. d: Trial balance

13. c: Amortization

14. a: Property

15. : Monetary policy

16. a: Capital market

17. a: General ledger

18. b: Shareholder

19. d: Saving

20. : Bank reconciliation

21. : Face

22. : Return on investment

23. d: Capital budgeting

24. : Capital asset pricing model

25. d: Investment

26. d: Historical cost

27. b: Fair value

28. b: Cash management

29. c: Financial risk

30. a: Net asset

31. : Financial Accounting Standards Board

32. : Credit risk

33. b: Sinking fund

34. d: Break-even

35. c: Bond market

36. : Revenue recognition

37. d: Buyer

38. c: Normal balance

39. c: Managerial accounting

40. b: Primary market

41. c: Average Cost

42. b: Capital expenditure

43. d: Accrual

44. a: International Financial Reporting Standards

45. : Worksheet

46. b: Tax rate

47. a: Rate risk

48. b: Fixed asset

49. a: Board of directors

50. b: Deferral

51. d: Inflation

52. a: Futures contract

53. a: Budget

54. : Municipal bond

55. d: Activity-based costing

56. d: Interest expense

57. b: Equity method

58. : Bank statement

59. c: Petty cash

Human resource management

1. d: Drug test

2. a: Executive compensation

3. d: Halo effect

4. b: Aptitude

5. c: Conformity

6. b: Executive search

7. d: Learning organization

8. : Grievance

9. a: Departmentalization

10. b: Asset

11. b: Labor force

12. a: Retraining

13. b: Human resources

14. a: Vesting

15. b: Pay grade

16. : Body language

17. : Service Employees International Union

18. b: Authoritarianism

19. a: Officer

20. a: Knowledge management

21. b: Reinforcement

22. d: Problem solving

23. b: Organizational learning

24. b: Restructuring

25. a: Internship

26. : Job enlargement

27. d: Scientific management

28. a: Wage curve

29. c: Foreign worker

30. c: Severance package

31. b: Aggression

32. : Occupational Information Network

33. a: Content validity

34. c: Training and development

35. b: Equal Employment Opportunity Commission

36. d: Total Quality Management

37. a: Work ethic

38. : Workplace bullying

39. a: Management

40. d: Partnership

41. : Love contract

42. b: Restricted stock

43. a: Kelly Services

44. a: Job evaluation

45. c: Predictive validity

46. c: Pregnancy discrimination

47. a: Ingratiation

48. c: 360-degree feedback

49. c: Executive officer

50. a: Bundy v. Jackson

51. b: Job security

52. b: Arbitration

53. b: Unemployment

54. a: Employment

55. b: Flexible spending account

56. : Rating scale

57. c: Goal setting

58. a: Payroll

59. : Kaizen

Information systems

1. a: Tacit knowledge

2. d: Service level agreement

3. : Acceptable use policy

4. d: Structured query language

5. : Government-to-government

6. : Data center

7. d: Spyware

8. : Data

9. : Google Maps

10. b: Query by Example

11. : Identity theft

12. : Packet switching

13. b: Botnet

14. a: Data analysis

15. d: Radio-frequency identification

16. c: Privacy policy

17. c: Backbone network

18. c: Transport Layer Security

19. b: Fraud

20. d: Competitive intelligence

21. : Carnivore

22. b: Drill down

23. : Semantic Web

24. c: Information security

25. d: Google Docs

26. c: Enterprise resource planning

27. a: Open source

28. d: Pop-up ad

29. a: Computer-aided manufacturing

30. a: Zynga

31. c: Asset

32. c: Subscription

33. : Consumer-to-consumer

34. b: Database management system

35. a: Information flow

36. b: Flash memory

37. a: Service level

38. c: Second Life

39. c: Mobile payment

40. a: Network management

41. b: Microprocessor

42. a: YouTube

43. a: Data visualization

44. : Code

45. b: Commercial off-the-shelf

46. d: Crowdsourcing

47. d: Disaster recovery

48. c: Avatar

49. b: Management information system

50. : Web server

51. a: Usability

52. d: Interaction

53. c: Phishing

54. : Information

55. c: Information technology

56. d: World Wide Web

57. : Information literacy

58. a: Fault tolerance

59. a: Facebook

Marketing

1. d: Advertising

2. a: Fixed cost

3. a: Market share

4. : Creativity

5. b: Market research

6. a: Testimonial

7. : Raw material

8. : Brand awareness

9. d: Infomercial

10. a: Focus group

11. a: Product development

12. : Customer service

13. c: Data warehouse

14. c: Presentation

15. a: Direct marketing

16. c: Retailing

17. b: Demand

18. b: Convenience

19. : Dimension

20. a: Economies of scale

21. c: Consideration

22. : Supply chain

23. b: Consumer behavior

24. c: Marketing mix

25. : Market development

26. : Customer

27. a: Sales

28. c: Organizational culture

29. : Publicity

30. d: Universal Product Code

31. b: Business marketing

32. c: Household

33. d: Customer satisfaction

34. a: Pricing strategies

35. : Preference

36. d: Resource

37. : Hearing

38. a: Inventory

39. c: Vendor

40. b: Performance

41. a: Competition

42. b: Competitive advantage

43. : Health

44. a: Security

45. a: Target audience

46. b: Consumer Protection

47. d: Stock

48. : Planning

49. : Budget

50. : Problem Solving

51. a: Services marketing

52. b: Patent

53. c: Trademark

54. d: Audit

55. b: Customer retention

56. b: Image

57. : Advertising agency

58. : Negotiation

59. : Commerce

Manufacturing

1. b: Heat exchanger

2. : Business process

3. : Economies of scope

4. c: Scientific management

5. c: Bullwhip effect

6. c: Quality Engineering

7. c: Information management

8. : Project team

9. d: Control chart

10. a: Transaction cost

11. c: Turbine

12. d: Electronic data interchange

13. : Production schedule

14. : Consensus

15. d: Supply chain network

16. d: Reverse auction

17. a: Natural resource

18. d: Downtime

19. : Ball

20. a: Original equipment manufacturer

21. d: Materials management

22. d: Resource management

23. a: Schedule

24. c: Average cost

25. a: Vendor

26. c: Total cost of ownership

27. : Supply chain

28. : Request for proposal

29. c: Prize

30. b: Purchase order

31. : Performance

32. d: Cost

33. c: Procurement

34. a: Process management

35. : Remanufacturing

36. b: Thomas Register

37. b: Waste

38. a: Minitab

39. c: Capacity planning

40. : Inspection

41. : Toshiba

42. a: PDCA

43. a: Gantt chart

44. b: Asset

45. : Perfect competition

46. a: Management process

47. b: Zero Defects

48. d: Material requirements planning

49. d: EFQM

50. c: Raw material

51. c: Sputnik

52. a: Credit

53. b: Kaizen

54. b: Sunk costs

55. c: Process engineering

56. d: Durability

57. b: Customer

58. d: Steel

59. b: Certification

Commerce

1. c: Standing

2. : Customer service

3. b: Minimum wage

4. b: Broker

5. c: Basket

6. b: Outsourcing

7. d: Cost structure

8. d: Game

9. b: Business-to-business

10. d: Confirmed

11. c: Buyer

12. b: Enabling

13. b: Vendor

14. : Disintermediation

15. b: GeoCities

16. d: Wage

17. b: Microsoft

18. : Deregulation

19. a: Trade show

20. b: Management team

21. a: Level of service

22. c: Compromise

23. b: Brand

24. c: Free market

25. b: Audit

26. c: Consortium

27. b: Collaborative filtering

28. : Value-added network

29. c: Liquidation

30. c: Management

31. : Americans with Disabilities Act

32. a: Revenue

33. a: Teamwork

34. a: Insurance

35. c: Uniform Commercial Code

36. d: Market share

37. : Purchase order

38. b: Firm

39. b: Direct marketing

40. b: Credit card

41. d: Competitive advantage

42. b: Negotiation

43. d: Walt Disney

44. c: Economics

45. c: Argument

46. c: Control system

47. d: Consignee

48. d: Mass production

49. d: Shopping cart

50. d: Industry

51. a: Front office

52. b: Customer satisfaction

53. : Merchant

54. b: Charter

55. b: Inventory control

56. : Sexual harassment

57. : DigiCash

58. a: Variable cost

59. a: Raw material

Business ethics

1. : Working poor

2. d: Dual relationship

3. c: Qui tam

4. : Stanford Financial Group

5. a: Organizational culture

6. d: Principal Financial

7. d: Corporate structure

8. c: Sustainable

9. b: Auditor independence

10. d: Junk bond

11. d: Interlocking directorate

12. b: Sullivan principles

13. a: Hedonism

14. b: Sexual harassment

15. a: Risk assessment

16. b: Corporate governance

17. c: Executive compensation

18. d: WorldCom

19. d: Federal Trade Commission Act

20. b: Undue hardship

21. : Kyoto Protocol

22. b: Model Rules of Professional Conduct

23. b: Global Fund

24. c: European Commission

25. a: Socialism

26. : Pure Food and Drug Act

27. d: ExxonMobil

28. d: Green marketing

29. d: Biofuel

30. c: Cause-related marketing

31. d: Habitat

32. b: Lawsuit

33. c: Stanford International Bank

34. b: Skill

35. d: UN Global Compact

36. c: Social responsibility

37. : Pollution Prevention

38. : Partnership

39. d: Business model

40. a: Capitalism

41. b: Trojan horse

42. b: Protestant work ethic

43. a: Cultural relativism

44. d: Perception

45. b: Patriot Act

46. d: Catholicism

47. b: Whistleblower

48. a: Affirmative action

49. c: Endangered Species Act

50. d: Subprime lending

51. : Collusion

52. a: Insider trading

53. c: Parental leave

54. c: New Deal

55. b: Ponzi scheme

56. : Wall Street

57. a: Greenpeace

58. : Self-interest

59. a: Copyright

Accounting

1. d: Accounting method

2. : Gross income

3. c: Net present value

4. c: Revenue

5. a: Management by exception

6. b: Double taxation

7. c: Shareholder

8. b: Ending inventory

9. c: Voucher

10. a: Benchmarking

11. c: Stock Exchange

12. a: Deferred income

13. : Tax revenue

14. : Comprehensive income

15. c: Reimbursement

16. c: Quick ratio

17. c: Outsourcing

18. c: Bank

19. a: Tax return

20. c: Balance sheet

21. a: Financial statement analysis

22. d: Norwalk Agreement

23. b: Pension

24. d: Permanent fund

25. : American Institute of Certified Public Accountants

26. : Normal balance

27. : Stock Market

28. d: Time value of money

29. c: Net profit

30. d: Promissory note

31. d: Hedge accounting

32. a: Indirect costs

33. b: Accrual

34. : Governmental Accounting Standards Board

35. d: Controversy

36. d: Expense

37. a: Fixed cost

38. b: Independent contractor

39. a: Retained earnings

40. d: Manufacturing overhead

41. a: Bank account

42. : Fraud

43. : Beneficiary

44. d: Tax reform

45. : Intangible asset

46. a: Receivable

47. b: Comprehensive annual financial report

48. d: Income approach

49. c: Accounting Research Bulletins

50. c: Operating expense

51. c: Accounting management

52. b: Perpetual inventory

53. a: Encumbrance

54. d: Accounting information system

55. : Financial accounting

56. c: Not-for-profit

57. d: International Financial Reporting Standards

58. a: Remittance advice

59. a: Payroll

CPSIA information can be obtained
at www.ICGtesting.com
Printed in the USA
LVHW011545301019
635718LV00004B/357/P